Praise for
Dr. Alexander Avila's *LoveTypes*

"*LoveTypes* offers a fun, easy-to-use system for finding the love of your life."
—Barbara De Angelis, Ph.D., bestselling author of *Are You the One For Me?*

"*LoveTypes* is a useful guide for singles who would like to know more about themselves and how to identify their soul mate. It is clearly written and well illustrated with concrete cases."
—Harville Hendrix, Ph.D., bestselling author of *Getting the Love You Want* and *Keeping the Love You Find*

"Alexander Avila has taken Carl Jung's work to the marketplace of dating and mating. Highly recommended for every man and woman who wants to balance their compatible and not their competitive energy."
—Dr. Pat Allen, bestselling author of *Getting to I Do*

"*LoveTypes* takes you way past the simplistic 'male-female' model of relationship psychology and introduces you to an in-depth model based on sound research. Alexander Avila has written a rare book that is both fun and practical."
—Gregory J.P. Godek, bestselling author of *1001 Ways to Be Romantic*

"*LoveTypes* is an absolute must-read for anyone who really wants to find Mr. or Ms. Right."
—Don Gabor, bestselling author of *How to Start a Conversation and Make Friends*

"*LoveTypes* is the most surefire way I have seen to find the person of your dreams, based on sound psychological principles that work!"
—Dr. Lorin Lidner, clinical psychologist and founder of Psych Psingles, the first singles group for mental health professionals

"I highly recommend *LoveTypes*. This brilliant work will lead you to know yourself and help you magnetize the love of your life."
—Renee Piane, TV/radio singles personality and the featured dating coach on the #1 Internet dating service

LoveTypes

DISCOVER YOUR
ROMANTIC STYLE
AND FIND YOUR
SOUL MATE

DR. ALEXANDER AVILA

Quill

An Imprint of HarperCollins*Publishers*

HarperCollins books may be purchased for educational, business, or sales promotional use. For information please write: Special Markets Department,
HarperCollins Publishers Inc., 10 East 53rd Street, New York, NY 10022.

First Avon Books edition published 1999.

Reprinted in Quill 2002.

Designed by Rhea Braunstein

Library of Congress Cataloging-in-Publication Data
Avila, Alexander.
Lovetypes : discover your romantic style and find your soul
mate / Alexander Avila.
p. cm.
Includes bibliographical references.
1. Typology (Psychology). 2. Love. 3. Man-woman relationships.
I. Title.
BF698.3.A85   1999   98-46457
155.2'64—dc21   CIP

ISBN 0-380-80014-4

04 05 06 RRD 10 9 8 7 6

Acknowledgments

To Dr. Carl Jung: Thanks for developing the system of personality typology.

To my family and friends: Antonio, Julie, Beatriz, Toshiko, Yasuko, Leroy, Andrew, Alex, Guy Amir, M.D., Derrick (Roberto), Majid, Robert, Little Carolina, and, of course, to my beloved mother, Eneida, whose spirit reigns in my mind: Thank you for all the support, kindness, and love you have shown me throughout the crafting of my deepest wishes, thoughts, and emotions on paper.

To my wonderful agents: Sheree Bykofsky and Janet Rosen. Thanks for your patience, support, and faith in me.

To my outstanding editor at Avon Books: Tia Maggini. Thanks for your belief in this project.

To my colleagues and mentors: Dr. Seymour Zelen, Dr. Arthur Kovacs, Jamie Johnson from CAPT, Beverly Pennichini, Jamie Forbes, Roy King, and Dr. Lorin Lidner: Thanks for your editorial advice, guidance, and encouragement. You are all professionals in the finest sense of the word.

Contents

Part One: Unmasking Yourself

1 The Dating Masquerade   3
2 First, Know Yourself   8
3 The Energizing Dimension   20
4 The Focusing Dimension   24
5 The Deciding Dimension   27
6 The Organizing Dimension   30
7 Unleashing the Power of Your True LoveType   34

Part Two: Unmasking Your Soul Mate

The Meaning Seekers   49
 8 The Idealistic Philosopher (INFP)   51
 9 The Mystic Writer (INFJ)   62
10 The Social Philosopher (ENFP)   71
11 The Growth Teacher (ENFJ)   80

The Knowledge Seekers   89
12 The Scholar (INTP)   91
13 The Expert (INTJ)   100
14 The Innovator (ENTP)   110
15 The General (ENTJ)   120

The Security Seekers 130

16 The Caretaker (ISFJ) 132
17 The Administrator (ISTJ) 141
18 The Dutiful Host (ESFJ) 150
19 The Traditionalist (ESTJ) 158

The Excitement Seekers 168

20 The Gentle Artist (ISFP) 170
21 The Craftsperson (ISTP) 179
22 The Performer (ESFP) 189
23 The Wheeler-Dealer (ESTP) 197

Part Three: Putting the LoveType System to Work for You

24 Going Where Your Ideal LoveType Is 211
25 Making a Great First Impression 216
26 LoveTyping Anyone, Anywhere 224
27 Making the Date with Your Future Soul Mate 239
28 Cutting-Edge LoveType Dating Strategies 245

APPENDIX A: The LoveType Quiz and the
Sixteen LoveTypes 260
APPENDIX B: The Main Characteristics
of the Sixteen LoveTypes 267
APPENDIX C: A Summary of Your Best
LoveType Match(es) 272
APPENDIX D: The Assumptive Personality Traits 277
APPENDIX E: Start Your Own LoveType
Singles Group 281
APPENDIX F: LoveType Singles Resource Directory 286

Notes on Sources 288
Suggested Reading 292

PART ONE

UNMASKING
YOURSELF

CHAPTER ONE

The Dating Masquerade

Imagine sneaking into a glitzy costume ball where single men and women primp and prance in the hopes of finding Mr. or Ms. Right. Concealing their real personalities behind psychological "masks," the partygoers position themselves to make the best impression possible. Who knows? The next person they meet could be their long-awaited soul mate, their future husband or wife.

As the band heats up, so do the masqueraders. Ricocheting off each other like billiard balls, they jump from one masked stranger to another in search of true romance. Finally it happens: love at first disguise. A masked man and a masked woman fall in love with the image each is presenting. Perfection, bliss, happiness.

But then the inevitable happens: The ball ends, the masks come off. Now the masqueraders discover what their mate's personality is *really* like and their hearts harden: "How could I have been so blind? We have nothing in common!" they wail as they find themselves trapped again, miserable victims of the . . .

Dating Masquerade

Located somewhere between never-married-land and divorcehood, the Dating Masquerade is not so much a place as a state of mind. The Dating Masquerade is where single men and women fall in love with an illusion of an ideal person, only to discover that the real man or woman is far different from the Prince Charming or Ms. Universe they envisioned.

Have you ever fallen in love with a man or woman who appeared to click with you on every possible level: psychologically, sexually, and spiritually? But then, once you got to know him or her better, you discovered that the person you shared your love and life with was truly, and almost unbelievably, incompatible with you. You were crushed to discover that your mate's most important values, goals, and desires were totally in conflict with yours. The end result: fights, tears, and ultimately a heart-wrenching breakup.

Have you resigned yourself to the fact that you will never find that special person who could be your soul mate? Perhaps you are disgusted with the dating scene; tired of pickup lines and dead-end relationships; and drowning under the anchors of rejection, frustration, and loneliness. Or maybe you are at the point where you believe that all the good men and women are either married or gay (assuming you are not).

If I'm describing you, then listen up. There is good news for you, really good news:

All the good ones are *not* taken.

Yes, there are plenty of available, attractive, and loving singles out there. The trick is sifting through the mass of masqueraders to discover that wonderful man or woman who will be compatible with you in a long-term relationship—that life partner who can make your heart happy and offer you the love and companionship you deserve.

You are about to learn one of the most powerful dating programs available today: the LoveType system. With this program at your disposal, you will have the power to "unmask" your soul mate—to see into the true personality of every person you meet and determine if he or she is really the one for you. With this unique "X-ray vision," you can bypass the social masks that men and women show each other and find out now—not months or years from now—if someone has the potential to be your true soul mate.

By using the LoveType method, you will learn which of the sixteen LoveTypes, or relationship styles, is best suited for you in a long-term relationship.

Is your best match the Idealistic Philosopher, the type of person who is passionate about relationships and discovering life's deepest meaning? Or is your chosen one the down-to-earth Administrator, a man or woman who lives in the here and now and prefers relationships that offer security and stability? Or perhaps your future mate is one of the other fourteen LoveTypes. You will know soon enough.

Once you have identified your best match, the Love-Type system will teach you how to meet that person with a relaxed, no-pressure approach. It doesn't matter if you are shy and have a difficult time talking with the opposite sex. The LoveType system will show you how to create the type of rapport that can ultimately lead you to a happy, long-term relationship.

The research-based LoveType approach is grounded in the work of experts in the fields of personality psychology and relationship compatibility. These include Dr. Carl Jung, Dr. Nancy Marioles, Dr. Ruth Sherman, Dr. Roger Ware, Dr. Marvin Rytting, and Isabel Myers and Katharine Briggs, the founders of the most popular personality test today—the Myers-Briggs Type Indicator®.

Using the theories and research of these experts as a foundation, I invented my own revolutionary dating program, which I call the LoveType system. In this system, you first discover your personal LoveType, or relationship style, by taking a short quiz. You then learn how to quickly determine your prospective mate's LoveType by asking a few simple questions (or by making a few basic observations) based on personality concepts such as Introversion and Extraversion.

By applying the LoveType system to your dating life, you will have a wealth of information at your disposal to answer these crucial questions:

1. What is my LoveType—my unique relationship style?
2. Which of the sixteen LoveTypes is most compatible with mine?
3. Which LoveType will satisfy my sexual needs?
4. Which LoveType will provide me with the long-term emotional and/or financial security I desire?
5. Where do I meet my ideal LoveType?
6. How do I make a great first impression on him or her?
7. How can I win the heart of my ideal LoveType?
8. What kind of long-term relationship can I expect with my perfect LoveType?
9. Is the person I'm talking to right now my ideal LoveType?

The beauty of the LoveType approach is that people won't even realize you are using a dating system. When you see someone you want to get closer to, you discreetly ask him or her four simple LoveType questions. For example, you can ask "Do you prefer a structured, scheduled lifestyle or a flexible, spontaneous one?"

With the information you glean, you can quickly ascertain this person's LoveType and discover his or her most deeply held values, interests, goals, and preferences. If the attractive stranger happens to be your compatible LoveType, you can use the dating and relationship secrets in Part Two to make him or her fall in love with you.

Over the last four years, more than one thousand students—men and women from all walks of life—have used my LoveType system to improve their dating success. Seventy percent of these students have reported a substantial increase in dates within six months of using the system. Moreover, 90% of the students reported a significant improvement in the *quality* of their dates; they were meeting more compatible people and having more fun than ever before.

And best of all, many individuals reported the ultimate success story: a happy marriage which they largely attributed to the knowledge and self-confidence they gained from using the LoveType program.

You, too, can begin to reap the benefits of applying the LoveType system in your dating life.

In Chapter Two you will take a brief quiz and discover your unique LoveType profile. Then, in Part Two, you will learn, based on decades of relationship research, which LoveType is best for you. You will also uncover the secrets of where to find your dream mate, and how to say and do the right things to capture his or her interest and love. Finally, in Part Three, you will develop your custom-tailored social program for breaking the ice and getting that first date with the love of your life.

It's time now to leave the dating masquerade and begin a new dance: a sizzling tango or romantic waltz with your ideal LoveType. With the LoveType system as your dating guide, you will come to a fantastic realization: *Your soul mate is waiting for you.*

Follow the steps outlined in the chapters to come, and you may soon be walking, arm in arm, with the man or woman who is compatible with your most important values and desires—that sweetheart who will make you happy for the rest of your life.

CHAPTER TWO

First, Know Yourself

Natasha, a petite thirty-nine-year-old office administrator, had horrendous luck when it came to picking Mr. Right.

Sometimes she thought she wanted a spontaneous, fun-loving guy who could jolt her out of her structured, schedule-focused rut. When she dated Pierre, a fast-living forty-six-year-old futures broker, everything was exciting at first: the champagne-drenched lovemaking in the limo, the trips to Cancún, the all-night salsa dance parties.

But eventually Natasha had to admit that she couldn't keep up with Pierre's dynamo social pace, nor could she stand the extravagant way he spent money that wasn't even his. He had been bankrupt twice, but he said it didn't matter; enjoying life was the key. Natasha shuddered at his irresponsibility.

Sometimes Natasha thought her best match might be a sensitive, Bohemian artist type who could balance her logical, no-nonsense personality. Trouble was, Natasha was turned off by guys who didn't take care of the practical aspects of life—like making money and taking care of their family.

The last artist Natasha dated had lived with her, rent-free, for ten months without so much as offering her gas money. She'd finally had to kick him out when he'd talked about *needing a couple of years of "free-space time" to craft his masterpiece. "Well, you're not getting any freeloading time from me!" were the last words she screamed at him.*

At thirty-nine, Natasha had never married, and it didn't look like she was getting any closer to her goal.

Have you ever dated someone you suspected was fundamentally incompatible with you, but you just couldn't help yourself? As the promise of a new relationship beckoned, you ignored the warning signals and made excuses for your mate's idiosyncrasies and annoying habits:

"So what if he scatters some of his clothes around his apartment? He's just a free-spirited and spontaneous bachelor; he'll get organized after we marry."

"So what if she's extremely quiet around my friends and family? She's the type of peaceful person who can soothe my nerves after a whirlwind of social engagements. I'm sure she'll open up and participate in my busy social life after we've been together awhile."

Of course, things only got worse once the honeymoon phase of the relationship ended. Once you were committed to this person—perhaps living together or married—you were forced to face the truth: Your messy darling didn't just scatter clothes around the house, he also disposed of beer cans, pizza boxes, and assorted piles of junk in every nook and cranny of your home.

And your quiet teddy bear wasn't just peace-loving: She was irredeemably antisocial. Her idea of a great house party was holing up in the bedroom with the VCR while the guests socialized in the backyard.

Now what? Now you finally realized what you should have known all along: You had no business being with a person who made your life unbearable, a stranger in disguise who was wholly incompatible with you from the very beginning.

THE BEGINNINGS OF THE LOVETYPE™ SYSTEM

In 1921 psychiatrist Carl Jung, a former disciple of Dr. Sigmund Freud, published his classic text on the psychological types. In his book, Jung laid out a theory of personality differences that, he believed, both determined and limited a person's judgment. He named these differences *Introversion/Extraversion, Intuition/ Sensation,* and *Thinking/Feeling,* and understood them to be inherited and relatively stable over a person's lifetime.

In the 1940s a mother/daughter team created a personality test based on Jung's theory of psychological types. Isabel Myers and Katharine Briggs named the test after themselves and called it the Myers-Briggs Type Indicator® (the MBTI®). Today the MBTI® is the most popular test for normal personality and is widely used in business, education, and the military.

In 1992 I devised the LoveType™ system based on the work of Dr. Jung and the Myers-Briggs team. The LoveTypes are sixteen distinct personality styles, each of which has unique characteristics and preferences when it comes to intimate relationships. By determining a person's LoveType, you can immediately access secrets about that person's relationship tendencies: whether this individual will be compatible with you, how to win his or her love, and what kind of relationship you can expect to have with him or her.

In 1993 I began studying relationship satisfaction among the LoveTypes, and I subsequently tested 378 heterosexual couples who were either newly dating (one week to three months), engaged, or married at least five years. I gave these subjects an instrument (called the LoveType quiz) that I had devised to measure their relationship style, or LoveType. In addition, I measured their relationship satisfaction.

The subjects were generally well educated (with a mean educational level of two years of college) and averaged thirty-two years of age. Married couples in the study had been married, on average, approximately eight years. Eighty-one percent of the people I surveyed were Caucasian, 14 percent Hispanic, 3 percent African-American, and 2 percent Asian.

One important finding was that, regardless of the stage of their relationship (newly dating, engaged, or married), couples tended to be more satisfied when they were similar on certain key personality dimensions. Throughout this book I will discuss these important results as I make recommendations on how to

find and develop a lasting relationship with your ideal
LoveType.

The Answer to Real Compatibility Lies Within You

The LoveType system is based on the simple premise
that people have distinct preferences when it comes to
dating, making love, and developing quality relationships. In the system there are sixteen unique relationship
styles, known as LoveTypes. Unless you know your own
LoveType, and the LoveType best suited for you, you will
be hard-pressed to find a mate who shares your vision of
what love and life should be like.

Sadly, there are many people like Natasha—bright, successful singles—who can't articulate their relationship
preferences, and who have no idea what type of mate
would be best for them in a long-term relationship. These
individuals have a lot of love to give but can end up
bitter, alone, and frustrated because they keep choosing
mates whose values and lifestyle preferences are diamet-
rically opposed to their own.

To avoid the "I'll take the first attractive person who
comes along" trap, you first need to unmask yourself.
You need to discover your one-of-a-kind LoveType or
"love fingerprint": the habits, values, and preferences
you have when you are in a relationship.

Once you have this information, you can begin to create the ultimate dating plan to meet the person who can
fulfill your deepest romantic dreams.

Unmask Yourself with the LoveType Quiz

In the LoveType quiz below, you will determine your
unique LoveType.

Take a few moments to answer the following questions. You may recognize yourself in both answers, but
choose the one that *best* fits you.

1. I tend to draw more energy from:
  E) other people.
  I) my own thoughts.

2. When I'm at a social gathering, I tend to have more energy:
  E) toward the end of the night, and once I get going, I may be the last person to leave.
  I) toward the early part of the night, and then I get tired and want to go home.

3. Which sounds more appealing?
  E) going with my date to a place where there are lots of people and social interaction, such as a nightclub or party.
  I) staying home and doing something special with my date—such as watching an entertaining video and eating my favorite take-out food.

4. When on a date, I'm usually:
  E) quite talkative throughout.
  I) more quiet and reserved until I feel comfortable.

5. In the past, I have tended to meet most of my dates:
  E) when I'm doing things in the outside world: at parties, nightclubs, work, recreational activities, chance meetings, or when friends introduce me to their friends.
  I) through private methods such as personal ads, video dating, or sometimes by personal introductions from close friends and family.

6. I tend to have:
  E) many acquaintances and many (or a few) close friends.
  I) a few close friends and/or a few acquaintances.

7. In the past, my loved ones and partners tended to say this about me:
 E) "Can't you be quiet and still for once?"
 I) "Can you come out of your shell, please?"

8. I tend to gather information more through:
 N) my imagination and expectation of what is possible.
 S) my realistic sense of the here and now.

9. I tend to trust:
 N) my leaps of intuition.
 S) my direct observation and hands-on experience.

10. When I'm in a relationship, I tend to believe:
 N) there is always room for improvement.
 S) "if it ain't broke, don't fix it."

11. When I'm comfortable with a date, I prefer talking about:
 N) the future, improving or creating things, and the possibilities of life; for example, I may talk about a new scientific discovery or a better way to express my feelings.
 S) practical, concrete, and "here and now" subjects; for example, I may talk about the fine points of wine tasting or the exciting trip I'm about to take.

12. I am the kind of person who:
 N) likes to see the big picture first.
 S) likes to grasp the details first.

13. I am the type of person who:
 N) prefers to live in my imagination instead of reality.
 S) prefers to dwell in reality instead of my imagination.

14. I usually:
    N) tend to fantasize a great deal about a date I'm about to go on.
    S) tend to fantasize sparingly and simply allow the date to turn out the way it's going to.

15. I tend to make decisions:
    F) first with my heart, then (perhaps) with my logic.
    T) first with my logic, then (perhaps) with my heart.

16. I tend to be better at noticing:
    F) when people need emotional support.
    T) when people are being illogical.

17. When breaking up with someone:
    F) I often let my feelings get in the way, and it's very hard for me to let go.
    T) although I can feel hurt, once I make up my mind, I am usually quite straightforward about putting my ex-partner out of my mind.

18. When dating someone, I tend to value:
    F) emotional compatibility: expressing affection and being sensitive to each other's needs.
    T) intellectual compatibility: communicating important ideas; discussing and debating matters objectively.

19. When I disagree with my partner:
    F) I do everything I can to avoid hurting his or her feelings, and I may not say anything if it will hurt too much.
    T) I usually speak up and set my mate straight because right is right.

20. People who know me tend to describe me as:
    F) warmhearted and sensitive.
    T) logical and straightforward.

21. I see most of my encounters with people as:
    F) being friendly and important in themselves.
    T) having a purpose.

22. If I had the time and money, and a friend invited me to an exotic location and gave me one day's notice, I would:
    J) have to check my schedule first.
    P) pack my bags without a second thought.

23. When on a first date, I:
    J) get upset if my date is late.
    P) don't worry about it since I'm usually late myself.

24. I prefer:
    J) to know, in advance, what's going to happen on my dates: where I'm going, who is going to be there, how long I will be there, how I should dress.
    P) to let the dates happen spontaneously without much (if any) advance planning.

25. I prefer a life that revolves around:
    J) schedules and organization.
    P) spontaneity and flexibility.

26. Which is more common?:
    J) I'm on time and everyone else is late.
    P) everyone else is on time, and I'm late.

27. I am the type of person who likes to:
    J) make up my mind and come to definite conclusions.

P) keep my options open and continue gathering information.

28. I am the type of person who:
J) likes to work on one thing at a time until completion.
P) enjoys working on several things at once.

Scoring

For each set of seven questions, add up your answers and put the numbers on the appropriate lines below. Then circle the higher number for each pair.

Your LoveType

E	I	N	S	F	T	J	P

The letters of each pair that had the higher numbers represent your four strongest preferences and, when combined, determine your LoveType. For example, you may be an ENFP (Social Philosopher), or ISTJ (Administrator), or any of the sixteen LoveTypes, depending on your four-letter combination.

IS YOUR PREFERENCE STRONG OR MODERATE?

If you scored a 4 on any of the preference letters, that indicates you are moderate on that preference. Scores of 5 or 6 indicate increasingly stronger preferences, while a 7 indicates a very strong preference.

For example, if you scored a 7 on E, you have a very strong preference for Extraversion. You like spending a lot of time with others, and you enjoy talking more than most people.

On the other hand, if you scored a 4 on E, you have a moderate preference for Extraversion. This means you are probably more outgoing and talkative than a typical Introvert (I), but more reserved and inner-focused than a strong Extravert (E).

This distinction will become important as you start to examine LoveType combinations in Part Two. Some LoveType matches work best when one of the partners is moderate on a preference, while in other pairings, the strength of the partners' preferences doesn't matter as much.

In the four spaces below, write down the four-letter LoveType you just received.

_____   _____   _____   _____

Continually refer to this four-letter LoveType as you read this book—it will be your signature for determining your romantic preferences, goals, and most compatible mate.

The Building Blocks of the LoveType System: Dimensions and Preferences

The letters of your LoveType refer to four main dimensions, or pillars, of your personality. They include the following:

I. **The Energizing dimension:** how you generate life energy
II. **The Focusing dimension:** what you pay attention to as you take in information about the world
III. **The Deciding dimension:** how you make decisions
IV. **The Organizing dimension:** how you organize and structure your life

Each of the four personality dimensions offers two options, also known as preferences. Preferences are your favorite ways of dealing with the things, people, and ideas that inhabit your world. These preferences are as follows:

I. **The Energizing dimension**
You prefer to get energy either through:
A. **Introversion (I):** by spending time alone with your own thoughts, OR
B. **Extraversion (E):** by socializing in the outside world.

II. **The Focusing dimension**
You prefer to experience the world either through:
A. **Intuition (N):** your imagination and ideas about the future, OR
B. **Sensing (S):** your five senses in the actual, present moment.

III. **The Deciding dimension**
You prefer to make decisions based on your:
A. **Feeling (F):** feelings and values, OR
B. **Thinking (T):** logic and impersonal analysis.

IV. **The Organizing dimension**
You prefer a lifestyle that is:
A. **Perceiving (P):** flexible, spontaneous, and unstructured, OR
B. **Judging (J):** structured, scheduled, and time-sensitive.

Remember: Preferences are either/or choices. That means you prefer to use one approach or style most of the time, while using the secondary choice the rest of the time.

You may love spending most of your time in a hurricane of social activities; therefore, you have a preference for getting your life energy from Extraversion (E). Although you may occasionally covet quiet time alone—Introversion (I)—your primary preference is for Extraversion because that is what you choose most of the time.

Consider an example. Assume that, after taking the

quiz, you received the four letters ESTJ as your Love-Type. This means your four main preferences are as follows:

1. **Extraversion (E):** You prefer to get energy by socializing in the outside world.
2. **Sensation (S):** You prefer to process information through your senses in the actual, present moment.
3. **Thinking (T):** You prefer to use logic to make decisions.
4. **Judging (J):** You prefer a structured lifestyle.

By knowing your four main preferences (as represented by the four letters in your LoveType), you will become aware of the pitfalls and advantages of dating someone who has a preference that is different from or similar to yours.

In the next four chapters, you will examine each letter of your LoveType as it relates to finding a compatible mate. Then, in Part Two, you will learn what your complete four-letter LoveType stands for and which of the sixteen LoveTypes is best for you.

Get ready now to examine each of your four favorite preferences as you develop the uncanny ability to choose the right mate for you. It's time to unmask yourself and find out who you really are.

CHAPTER THREE

The Energizing Dimension: Do You Get More Energy from Your Own Thoughts or by Spending Time with Other People?

When they were first introduced, Isaac, thirty-three, and Sarah, thirty-four, appeared to have a great deal in common. Both were divorced successful professionals—Isaac was a partner in his accounting firm, and Sarah was a TV producer with a hit series. Both loved children and family life, both had been raised in Orthodox Jewish families.

There was one problem. Sarah liked to talk and talk and talk, and Isaac valued silence more than anything. In fact, Isaac's favorite activities were staying home, reading, meditating, and listening to his collection of jazz CDs. Sarah, on the other hand, never missed a party or social event.

After six weeks of dating, Sarah and Isaac's relationship was deteriorating rapidly. Isaac kept leaving Sarah nasty notes that read: "I'm sick and tired of your friends. When will we spend some quality time together, alone, just you and I? Stop being such a social butterfly."

When Sarah confronted Isaac about the notes, he would remain quiet and infuriate her even more. The more Sarah pressured Isaac to talk, the more he clammed up and thought: "She really is so domineering!"

"You're a weak-minded nobody," Sarah would say in response to Isaac's silence. "Why don't you just tell me what

20

*you're thinking instead of leaving those cowardly notes? Why
don't you act like a man?"*

*Unfortunately, neither one understood the other. Their re-
lationship was headed for disaster, and all the promise of
their nice beginning seemed wasted.*

Do you get revved up when you are surrounded by
people, socializing, and doing things in the outside world?
If so, you are an Extravert, and you scored the letter **E**
on the LoveType quiz. You make up the majority of society (about 55 percent of the population).

Or are you the kind of person who treasures your own
company most of the time, and is rejuvenated when you
read, think, write, or meditate with silence as your only
companion? If so, you are an Introvert, and you received
the letter **I** on the LoveType quiz. As an Introvert, you
are part of a minority (about 45 percent of society).

If you are an Extravert, you like to express your
thoughts and feelings in a relationship. You want your
partner to give you constant feedback so you know how
the relationship is progressing.

On the other hand, if you are an Introvert, you believe
the most cherished moments in a relationship are spent
with your loved one in a quiet, intimate setting. In this
cozy cocoon you enjoy gazing into your partner's eyes
lovingly—speaking only when you have something meaningful to say.

When an Introvert is coupled with an Extravert (as in
the case of Sarah and Isaac), conflicts can easily arise.
For example, Extraverts frequently want to go out with,
or without, their mates and have fun with a lot of people.
Introverts, on the other hand, often like nothing better
than to spend quiet time with their loved one at home
or in a peaceful setting.

Of course, Introverts like to go out at times, and Extraverts like to stay in, but their natural tendencies are what
guide them most of the time.

In 1981 researcher Ruth Sherman—from the University

of Hawaii—shed light on the problems that can arise when Introverts get involved with Extraverts. In her study Sherman found that male Introvert/female Extravert pairings reported more problems than any other Introvert/Extravert combinations in the areas of sex, chores, friends, finances, and communication.

Sherman's findings may be explained, in part, by the way society shapes male-female roles in intimate relationships. Although society is gradually changing, men have traditionally been socialized to be the speakers and leaders in the community, while women have been trained to be more quiet and subservient.

Thus, Introvert men who have been raised this way may feel intimidated and overwhelmed by outspoken Extravert women. At the same time, an Extravert female may interpret her Introvert man's quiet nature as representing weakness and submissiveness, and she may lose respect for him as a result.

BEING AN INTROVERT DOESN'T MEAN YOU ARE SHY

Let's eliminate one popular misconception right now: If you are an Introvert, it doesn't mean you are shy.

As we have already defined it, Introversion is a preference for getting your energy—the life force that makes you get up and do things—primarily from your own thoughts and by spending time alone.

Shyness, on the other hand, is a state of anxiety in which a person is afraid of rejection, ridicule, or embarrassment. To prevent such a catastrophe, shy people tend to avoid others to protect themselves from being humiliated or rebuffed in social settings.

You may be a non-shy Introvert, someone who is very comfortable and confident with people, talking with them, being with them, and even entertaining them. But because your social energy is limited as an Introvert, you tend to become tired if you have to be around too many people for too long, talking too much and exerting too much of your energy. To rejuvenate yourself, you need to spend time alone—far away from energy-draining crowds.

If you are a shy person (whether you are Introvert or Extravert), you will benefit by reading Dr. Phillip Zimbardo's book, *Shyness: What It Is, What to Do About It,* available from Addison-Wesley Publishing (1977).

When Introverts and Extraverts
Get Tired of Each Other

As you begin to date someone new, always be aware of that person's social energy level, and his or her need (or lack thereof) to talk things out. In the beginning, being with Extraverts can be exhilarating. Similarly, when first dating Introverts, their calm, relaxing style can be a refreshing pause.

But as the novelty wears off, both Introverts and Extraverts need to be aware of the compromises they make and the benefits they gain when they are with someone who possesses a different social energy style. Sometimes it works out well, and sometimes it doesn't. Part Two will shed even more light on this Introvert-Extravert dilemma.

CHAPTER FOUR

The Focusing Dimension: Are Your Feet on the Ground or Is Your Head in the Clouds?

Farnaz, forty-two, met Amir, forty-five, at a party to celebrate the building of a new mosque in their city. He was a very handsome Iranian doctor, and she felt drawn to his dark good looks and gentle bearing. After twenty minutes of conversation, she agreed to go out with him the next day on a lunch date.

Disaster! She was bored from the moment she sat down with him; all Amir could talk about was his favorite basketball team. Barely pausing to take a breath, Amir spent the entire date reciting his favorite players' season and career numbers and elaborating on how each of them compared with the legends of the game.

Although Farnaz had a mild interest in sports, she was really attracted to psychological and spiritual topics. She wanted to talk about the things that made a difference in the world, but Amir only cared to talk about boring statistics and trivial matters. Oh, what a mistake she had made!

If you are a Sensor, you tallied the letter **S** on the LoveType quiz, and you make up about 70 percent of the population. You are the type of person who tends to have a realistic grasp of what a relationship is all about—

you focus on the details and practicalities of being with a particular person. You like to spend time with your partner talking about down-to-earth things, such as buying a new car, fixing up your house or apartment, going to a certain classy restaurant, or checking out the latest hot band or movie.

As a Sensor, you enjoy the sights, smells, and sounds of love. You can get turned on by a romantic setting with candlelight and music. But you can also quickly get turned off by odors, noises, or other distractions that prevent you from enjoying the sensual pleasures of the romantic experience.

On the other hand, if you are an Intuitive, and scored the letter **N** on the LoveType quiz, you represent about 30 percent of society. You are the type of person who places less importance on the real or immediate. You prefer to deal with relationships through your "sixth sense," "gut feeling," or "hunch." You treasure the possibilities of a relationship, the way a relationship could or should be. You enjoy talking with your partner about philosophy, psychology, science, and ideas that can influence events and change the world.

As an Intuitive, you like to use your imagination to indulge in romantic or sexual fantasies. Often, however, the reality of a romantic encounter may not live up to what you imagined. When this happens, you may feel disappointed, at least for a moment.

In 1992 Dr. Marvin Rytting and Dr. Roger Ware—two professors of psychology from Indiana University–Purdue University at Indianapolis—documented the importance of the Focusing dimension in relationships. In their study they asked men and women to describe their ideal mate. Rytting and Ware found that over 70 percent of the participants preferred mates who were equally matched with them on the Focusing dimension; that is, Intuitives preferred Intuitives and Sensors preferred Sensors.

Although there are exceptions, couples usually communicate better, and therefore have better relationships

and marriages, when they share the same Focusing preference. When they differ on this important dimension,
problems can quickly arise.

Once the honeymoon period is over, the philosophical,
"head in the clouds" Intuitive may think his practical,
realistic Sensor mate is a "stick in the mud." All she
wants to talk about are the details of living: balancing
the checkbook, saving for retirement, and fixing the
house. In a word, boring.

Meanwhile, the Sensor thinks the Intuitive talks too
much about "pie in the sky" scenarios, indulging himself
in fantasy conversations about building empires or changing the world. "Why don't you take out the garbage, for
once?" shrieks the Sensor.

In Part Two you will study LoveType combinations
that work. You will learn that some Sensor-Intuitive combinations can succeed if the couples are not too far apart
on the Focusing dimension. For example, someone who
has a moderate preference for Sensing can be successfully matched with someone who has a moderate preference for Intuition.

Overall, however, it's a good idea for couples to share
the same preference on the Focusing dimension because
this dimension largely determines how they communicate on a day-to-day basis. If two people have difficulty
understanding and appreciating each other's communication style, their relationship can sour in a hurry.

CHAPTER FIVE

The Deciding Dimension: Which Is Your Guide—Your Head or Your Heart?

John was a cuddler. He loved to be affectionate with his dates: Hugging, caressing, and handing out stuffed teddy bears were John's specialties. In fact, John was like a big teddy bear himself, with his ample belly, sensitive blue eyes, and fluffy beard.

When he answered Virginia's personal ad—in which she stated she was a romantic woman looking for a romantic man—he was excited. He thought he finally had a chance to meet a lady who valued a nontraditional guy like himself: a caring man who was gentle and open with his feelings.

Boy, was he disappointed when he picked her up for their date. From the moment he saw her, he felt the cool breeze of her personality. She didn't smile at all, didn't offer her hand, and appeared very distant during the date. All Virginia talked about was the computer system she was designing for her office, and how nobody there was smart enough to understand what she was doing.

After dinner, John took her home, convinced that Virginia didn't like him at all. As he was getting ready to say goodbye, she surprised him by saying: "I believe we may have a future together; we seem to be intellectually compatible. I'll call you when my schedule clears."

I'm not sure if we're intellectually compatible, thought John, but I know we're definitely not emotionally compatible. Staying home alone would be infinitely better than spending another evening with a distant, unemotional date like Virginia.

If you are a Thinker, you scored the letter **T** on the LoveType quiz. You are the type of person who prefers to think things through first—calculating all the angles and possibilities—and then, if necessary, allow your feelings and values to play a part in the decision.

But if you are a Feeler, and you received the letter **F** on the LoveType quiz, you lead with your heart. You base decisions on your values, feelings, and desire to build relationships—and then, if necessary, allow your logic to back up what you just decided.

In the preceding case, Virginia, a Thinker, valued intellectual compatibility when it came to choosing her mate. John, on the other hand, was a Feeler and yearned for an intimate, emotional bond with his partner. Unfortunately, neither person got what he or she wanted, and both went home unhappy.

WHY MORE WOMEN ARE FEELERS
AND MORE MEN ARE THINKERS

Thinkers and Feelers are divided fifty-fifty in society. However, of those 50 percent who are classified as Thinkers, approximately two thirds are men and one third are women. The situation is reversed for Feelers: about two thirds of the Feelers are women and one third are men. Traditional gender roles may explain the male/female differences along the Deciding dimension.

Although society is changing, women have traditionally been socialized to be more nurturing, expressive of their feelings, and invested in personal relationships. And men have been socialized to be more logical, analytical, and less relationship-focused.

As it stands today, more women are classified as Feelers, and more men are labeled Thinkers. However, as society continues to encourage and educate men to be more aware of their feelings, and women to be more analytical, this trend may change over time.

If you are a Feeler in a love relationship, you enjoy expressions of affection in any form. You cherish backrubs, caresses, and verbal tokens of affection: "I love you" is always welcomed. At the same time, you loathe manipulative behavior, aggressiveness, and insensitivity from your mate.

If you are a Thinker, you value competence, a keen sense of humor, stimulating conversation, respect, and individuality in your mate. You are turned off by too much emotional or physical clutching, and especially by excessive sentimentality, "the touchy-feely stuff" as you may call it.

Since most men are Thinkers and most women are Feelers, the female Feeler and male Thinker combination is quite common. In Part Two you will see recommendations for other pairings, such as male Feelers with female Feelers and male Thinkers with female Thinkers. These combinations can yield successful relationships, assuming the couples are compatible on the other preferences.

CHAPTER SIX

The Organizing Dimension: Do You Live by a Daily Planner or by the Seat of Your Pants?

Raul was already one hour late for his dinner date with Juanita.

As a Perceiver with a flexible and spontaneous personality style, he was always running late. It wasn't that he meant to be flaky or irresponsible; it was just that Raul always had one more thing to do: one more call to make, one more letter to write. He really loved his lifestyle, but he also realized others didn't always share his appreciation for it.

When he arrived at Juanita's house, she was already past mad. She was into rage, hate, and a few other emotional states too scary to mention.

"How could you be so late when I keep telling you how much it bothers me!" cried Juanita. "Now we're late for my company dinner, and I'm going to look like a fool. You don't love me!"

Juanita had been born on time. She was meticulous, organized, and always early, and being late was one of the worst sins she could imagine. She was the perfect role model of the Judger—the structured, organized, time-sensitive individual.

Ever since they started dating five months before, their lifestyle preferences had been clashing. Otherwise, they liked each other a lot, but this difference was tough.

"I'm sorry, mi amorcito (my love)," Raul said as he tried to charm his way out of trouble. "I just had to take Roberto's phone call; it was urgent. It will never happen again. I love you to death."

A bit mollified by Raul's sweet talk, Juanita decided she would forgive him, this time. She climbed into Raul's car, but as she sat down, she heard a nasty squish and experienced a horrible sensation as the remains of Raul's potato-salad lunch magnetized to her new black dress.

Instantly Juanita emitted a shriek heard around the neighborhood, and Raul cringed. Oh no, he forgot to clean up his car in the rush. Wait until she finds out about the broken fountain pen underneath the salad. This is going to be trouble, thought Raul.

Are you always on time, while everyone else is always late? Is your home or office painstakingly clean and organized, and people think you are the most organized person they know? If so, you are a Judger, and you received a letter **J** on your LoveType quiz. You are part of 60 percent of society.

Or are you the type of person who is usually late because you had one more thing to do? Do you hate schedules and savor a flexible and spontaneous lifestyle? Are you relaxed in your housekeeping and organization standards—preferring a fun, easygoing environment to one that is compulsively neat? If so, you are a Perceiver, and you received the letter **P** on your LoveType quiz. You make up about 40 percent of society.

The differences between Judgers and Perceivers are not always clear-cut.

You may be the type of Judger who allows your desire for organization to slide because other pressing matters demand your attention. Yet you would readily admit that being disorganized is one of your greatest nightmares.

Or you could be the type of Perceiver who seems fairly well organized in your work life, but when it comes to your personal life, you let everything fall where it may.

If you had to choose between living a free-flowing, un-structured lifestyle and one filled with schedules and structure, you would opt for the former every time.

If you are a Judger, you enjoy schedules in everything you do, including your love life. You like to plan ahead and arrange all the details of your romantic endeavors.

As a Judger, you also attach a great value to commit-ment in relationships. From the moment you start going out with someone, you are already trying to determine where the relationship is heading: Are marriage and chil-dren the end result, or merely fun dating? You want to know what to expect as soon as possible.

On the other hand, if you are a Perceiver, you hate schedules and time pressures, especially in your love life. When it comes to romance, you crave the mystery and suspense of not knowing what will happen next, the pos-sibility that anything can, and will, happen.

As a Perceiver, you have a tremendous need for fun, excitement, and variety in your relationships. At the same time, you may have a terrible time making up your mind and committing to a partner. Because you value spontaneity and flexibility, you tend to delay commit-ment as long as possible. You like to weigh your options in your current relationship—while staying open to the potential of other relationships—before you profess undy-ing love and sign on the bottom line.

"WHY ARE YOU ALWAYS LATE FOR OUR DATES?"

Time is a big issue when Judgers date Perceivers. The Judger is usually early, while the Perceiver is often late. One Perceiver was exactly twenty-four hours late for a date. His excuse? He told his furious Judger date that he got the time right, but the day wrong. If you are a Perceiver, you can believe this. If you are a Judger, you will say, "Hang him from the highest tree."

The LoveType System Respects Individual Differences

As you use the LoveType system and start dating people who have different personality preferences, remember this important point:

Different doesn't mean inferior.

One person can enjoy a relaxed, flexible lifestyle that doesn't insist on much organization or structure, while another person can thrive on orderliness and schedules. Neither approach is better than the other; each is a matter of personal preference.

Whatever you do, don't condemn either your own relationship style or anyone else's. By accepting your own built-in preferences, you are affirming your personal worth. Although your way of relating to others may be different and possibly uncommon, you are simply being who you are. And that is just fine.

By the same token, you should avoid attempting a renovation project on the people you date: Resist the temptation to mold your dating partners into the personalities you want them to be. First of all, they will probably not change twenty-five or more years worth of ingrained habits and preferences just to suit your fancy. And second, they will resent you for trying to make them over in your image.

You will be much happier—and enjoy higher-quality relationships—if you respect others' relationship preferences and allow them to express their unique personalities without undue criticism. If you can't accept a potential mate as he or she is, use the LoveType system to find someone who already possesses the personality type that best complements your individual style.

CHAPTER SEVEN

Unleashing the Power of Your True LoveType

You now know what each of the four letters of your Love-Type represents. You know what your four major love preferences are, and you are aware of some of the issues and problems that can arise when you are matched with a person who has different preferences.

This information alone has placed you at the head of the class. At least 90 percent of the singles population has no clue about their relationship preferences or what to expect when they are dating someone who may be their opposite. But there's more—much more.

The true power of the system comes from putting all four letters together and determining your unique Love-Type. In the chart below you will find your four-letter LoveType based on the quiz you took in Chapter Two.

Each LoveType is followed by a four-letter abbreviation that represents the four preferences of that LoveType, and a descriptive phrase to help you remember the LoveType. Here are the sixteen LoveTypes:

1. *The Idealistic Philosopher (INFP):* INTROVERTED INTUITIVE FEELING PERCEIVER: *"Love is the perfect place: quiet, peaceful and kind."*

2. *The Mystic Writer (INFJ)*: INTROVERTED INTU-ITIVE FEELING JUDGER: *"Love is in my mind, heart, and soul."*

3. *The Social Philosopher (ENFP)*: EXTRAVERTED IN-TUITIVE FEELING PERCEIVER: *"Love is mysterious, inspiring, and fun."*

4. *The Growth Teacher (ENFJ)*: EXTRAVERTED INTU-ITIVE FEELING JUDGER: *"Love is being consumed by my loved one."*

5. *The Scholar (INTP)*: INTROVERTED INTUITIVE THINKING PERCEIVER: *"Love is just another idea."*

6. *The Expert (INTJ)*: INTROVERTED INTUITIVE THINKING JUDGER: *"Love can be analyzed and perfected."*

7. *The Innovator (ENTP)*: EXTRAVERTED INTUITIVE THINKING PERCEIVER: *"I invent love in my mind first."*

8. *The General (ENTJ)*: EXTRAVERTED INTUITIVE THINKING JUDGER: *"Love is enhanced by power, influence, and achievement."*

9. *The Caretaker: (ISFJ)*: INTROVERTED SENSING FEELING JUDGER: *"Love is a goal worth sacrificing for."*

10. *The Administrator: (ISTJ)*: INTROVERTED SENSING THINKING JUDGER: *"Love is based on duty and responsibility."*

11. *The Dutiful Host (ESFJ)*: EXTRAVERTED SENSING FEELING JUDGER: *"Love is based on serving others."*

12. *The Traditionalist (ESTJ)*: EXTRAVERTED SENSING THINKING JUDGER: *"Love is grounded on the rock-solid values of family, tradition, and loyalty."*

13. *The Gentle Artist (ISFP)*: INTROVERTED SENSING FEELING PERCEIVER: *"Love is gentleness, nature, and devotion."*

14. *The Craftsperson (ISTP)*: INTROVERTED SENSING THINKING PERCEIVER: *"Love is action."*

15. *The Performer (ESFP)*: EXTRAVERTED SENSING

FEELING PERCEIVER: *"Love is savoring and reveling in the passions of now."*
16. *The Wheeler-Dealer (ESTP):* EXTRAVERTED SENSING THINKING PERCEIVER: *"Love should always be exciting and stimulating."*

From now on, I will refer to the sixteen LoveTypes by their names (Dutiful Host, for example), followed by their four-letter abbreviations, such as ESFJ (EXTRAVERTED SENSING FEELING JUDGER). For example, throughout the book you will see a reference to a Dutiful Host (ESFJ).

Take a moment now to look up your LoveType by flipping to its corresponding chapter (see Contents). Read the LoveType description on that page and return here when you are finished.

Did the profile seem to fit your personality? If the LoveType quiz indicated you were a Dutiful Host (ESFJ), did the description of a Dutiful Host generally coincide with what you know of your relationship style?

Or did you read another profile that seemed to be a much better match—one that was very appealing to you and appeared to describe your real tendencies?

If you found another LoveType that appeared to be a better fit, don't jump to conclusions—just yet.

First, the LoveType you received from the quiz may not seem 100 percent accurate even though it actually is. This could occur because there may be elements of your personality that you haven't yet recognized, traits that, although you are unconscious of them, are important aspects of your LoveType.

Also, a LoveType profile that appears to be a better match at first glance may not actually be your real Love-Type, but may instead be the LoveType of your ideal mate—the person most likely to be compatible with you in a long-term relationship.

Because you and your ideal LoveType probably have several important traits and preferences in common, you may mistakenly believe that your soul mate's profile is your own. Chances are, it is close to your personal Love-Type profile but also uniquely different.

If—after studying your LoveType profile—you are still not sure you have the right one, see the examples below.

WHAT IF YOU ARE STILL NOT SURE YOU HAVE CORRECTLY DETERMINED YOUR LOVETYPE?

There is always a slight chance you could have misidentified your LoveType because of factors (fatigue, emotional upset) that may have affected your results when you took the quiz. If you are not sure the LoveType you obtained from the quiz is correct, go back and check your scores. Determine which of the four dimensions (there may be more than one) had the closest scores between the two preferences of that dimension. Preference scores of 4 and 3 on the same dimension (like N and S below) are considered close.

For example, your scores may have been something like this:

6	1	4	3	5	2	0	7
E	I	N	S	F	T	J	P

When you initially scored the quiz, you discovered you were the Social Philosopher (ENFP). However, when you look at the closest scores, you find that you were N (Intuitive) only by a four-to-three count. Now write down the LoveType you would be if your closest scores were reversed (if S were 4, and N were 3).

6	1	3	4	5	2	0	7
E	I	N	S	F	T	J	P

Given these scores, you would now be the flamboyant, party-loving Performer (ESFP). Look up the ESFP description and compare it with the ENFP LoveType description you received earlier.

By reversing your closest scores as you have just done, you

can compare two (or more) LoveTypes that describe personality traits you may possess. Doing so will give you a better idea of which LoveType most accurately describes your true romantic style. At this point you may decide to stick with your earlier LoveType, or you may choose one that seems to fit better.

As you gain more experience with the LoveType system, your LoveType will become clearer to you, and you will see how your personality preferences affect every aspect of your life, including your romantic relationships.

Using the LoveType System to Find Your Soul Mate

In Part Two you will become acquainted with the Love-Types that leading experts in the field have determined are best for you.

In most cases you will have two or three ideal Love-Types to choose from. To make your reading easier, I will refer to "your ideal LoveType" throughout the book instead of using the cumbersome "ideal LoveType(s)."

When you start using the LoveType system, it's wise to date at least one person from each of your recommended LoveTypes. This way you may decide that you like one of your recommended LoveTypes better than the others, or you may come to the conclusion that you can be equally happy with any of the suggested choices.

As you become familiar with the sixteen LoveTypes, don't allow yourself to be overwhelmed by all the material. You don't have to learn everything at once. You can pick up one piece at a time, one LoveType at a time. Start by learning your own LoveType, move on to your best match(es), and finally, tackle the remaining types.

The LoveTemperaments: A Shortcut to the LoveTypes

To make the LoveType system even easier to learn, we have grouped the sixteen LoveTypes into four simple-to-remember groups known as LoveTemperaments. The term "LoveTemperament" refers to a set of relationship characteristics that identify a group of people.

Each LoveTemperament group is characterized by two personality preferences (letters) instead of the four preferences used when describing the LoveTypes.

For example, the Knowledge Seeker LoveTemperament Group consists of all the LoveTypes that include the two preferences Intuitive (N) and Thinking (T). The LoveTypes that fall within the NT group have certain elements in common. They value logic, stimulating debate, intelligence, competence, and continual growth in their relationships.

By knowing that someone has these two preferences (N and T), you immediately know crucial information about him or her, even though you don't know this person's complete LoveType.

Here are the four LoveTemperament groups and the personality traits common to each group:

The Meaning Seekers

This LoveTemperament group includes all LoveTypes that have N (Intuitive) and F (Feeling) in common.

The Meaning Seekers value intimacy, personal growth, the search for meaning, and the power of imagination in their relationships.

They consist of the following LoveTypes:

1. **IDEALISTIC PHILOSOPHER** (INFP): INTRO-VERTED INTUITIVE FEELING PERCEIVER
2. **MYSTIC WRITER** (INFJ): INTROVERTED INTU-ITIVE FEELING JUDGER
3. **SOCIAL PHILOSOPHER** (ENFP): EXTRAVERTED INTUITIVE FEELING PERCEIVER
4. **GROWTH TEACHER** (ENFJ): EXTRAVERTED IN-TUITIVE FEELING JUDGER

The Knowledge Seekers

This LoveTemperament group includes all LoveTypes that have N (Intuition) and T (Thinking) in common.

The Knowledge Seekers value logic, stimulating debate, intelligence, competence, and continual growth in their relationships.

They consist of the following LoveTypes:

1. **SCHOLAR** (INTP): INTROVERTED INTUITIVE THINKING PERCEIVER
2. **EXPERT** (INTJ): INTROVERTED INTUITIVE THINKING JUDGER
3. **INNOVATOR** (ENTP): EXTRAVERTED INTUITIVE THINKING PERCEIVER
4. **GENERAL** (ENTJ): EXTRAVERTED INTUITIVE THINKING JUDGER

The Security Seekers

This LoveTemperament group includes all LoveTypes that have S (Sensing) and J (Judging) in common.

The Security Seekers value tradition, loyalty, security, and structure in their relationships.

They consist of the following LoveTypes:

1. **CARETAKER** (ISFJ): INTROVERTED SENSING FEELING JUDGER
2. **ADMINISTRATOR** (ISTJ): INTROVERTED SENSING THINKING JUDGER
3. **DUTIFUL HOST** (ESFJ): EXTRAVERTED SENSING FEELING JUDGER
4. **TRADITIONALIST** (ESTJ): EXTRAVERTED SENSING THINKING JUDGER

The Excitement Seekers

This LoveTemperament group includes all LoveTypes that have S (Sensing) and P (Perceiving) in common.

The Excitement Seekers value fun, excitement, adventure, and spontaneity in their relationships.

They consist of the following LoveTypes:

1. **GENTLE ARTIST:** (I_S_F_P): INTROVERTED SENSING FEELING PERCEIVER
2. **CRAFTSPERSON** (I_S_T_P): INTROVERTED SENSING THINKING PERCEIVER
3. **PERFORMER** (E_S_F_P): EXTRAVERTED SENSING FEELING PERCEIVER
4. **THE WHEELER-DEALER** (E_S_T_P): EXTRAVERTED SENSING THINKING PERCEIVER

Because four categories are easier to learn than sixteen, you may want to start by learning the four Love-Temperaments first. Then you can fill in the gaps of your knowledge by adding the specific LoveTypes that fall within each LoveTemperament.

Knowing the LoveTemperament groups can also come in handy when you forget some of the LoveType questions or when you are too nervous to do a complete job LoveTyping that irresistible stranger.

When Kendra, a thirty-one-year-old police officer, started learning the LoveType system, she would always forget one or two of the four standard LoveType questions. One night at a singles event, she met Al—a thirty-seven-year-old paramedic—and offered to LoveType him. Al readily agreed, but there was a small problem: Kendra couldn't recall all the LoveType questions.

"Are you a . . ." she began nervously. "Are you more imaginative or practical?" she finally blurted out.

"Practical."

*"If you had a choice, would you prefer a structured, sched-
uled lifestyle or a flexible, spontaneous one?"*

"A spontaneous one."

At this point Kendra was so mesmerized by Al's clear blue
eyes that she couldn't think of another question. But she re-
called the LoveTemperament groupings. Al belonged in the
SP (Sensing Perceivers—Excitement Seekers) group because
he said he was practical (Sensing—S) and spontaneous (Perceiving—P).

*"You are one of the Excitement Seekers—the kind of guy
who yearns for fun, excitement, adventure, and spontaneity
in your relationships."*

"Yes, that's amazing."

Kendra thought it was amazing that she could think
straight while talking with such a heartthrob. Fortunately,
she recovered enough to invite Al for coffee, and their relationship developed nicely.

Throughout the rest of the book, we will be referring
to the four LoveTemperament groups and the sixteen
LoveTypes that fall within each group. It's a good idea
to learn the LoveTemperament groups as soon as possible so you can begin to dazzle others with your uncanny
knowledge of their relationship preferences.

Take a Grain of Salt with Your LoveType Meal

As you start to reap the benefits of the LoveType system,
keep the following points in mind:

1. Some people can modify their LoveType over time.

Dr. Carl Jung believed that people inherited their dominant personality preferences and kept them, largely un-
changed, throughout their lives. Jung also believed (and
other researchers agree) that an individual could, through
intensive work, change his or her less developed traits.

The development of preferences is analogous to a left-handed person learning how to write with his or her right hand. Although this person's natural preference (and best skill) is still writing with the left hand, he or she can become much better at writing with the right.

When he was twenty, Joe was a natural Introvert. He had rarely dated in high school and college and accepted his role as a smart loner. In his late twenties, Joe made a concerted effort to change his social style; he took acting and stand-up comedy classes, joined a local Toastmasters (public speaking) group, and shifted to a career in sales.

Although Joe still considered himself to be an Introvert (and scored as a moderate Introvert on the LoveType quiz), he was now a much more socially active person and better able to tap into his Extraverted qualities.

Some of us, like Joe, strive for balance by enhancing the less preferred sides of our personality as we get older. Even though we still rely primarily on our strongest preferences (as Joe did with Introversion), we can gradually strengthen the less well developed aspects of our personality.

2. Most people have a combination of personality preferences.

It's true that most people are a blend when it comes to the personality preferences. For example, very few people, if any, are 100 percent Feelers or 100 percent Thinkers. Some of us are 90 percent/10 percent in the Feeling/Thinking dimension, while others are fifty-fifty. It is simply a matter of degree.

Margarita, a thirty-five-year-old actuary, prefers dating freewheeling, spontaneous men. Recently she has been dating two men, Nelson and Buck, both of whom scored as Perceivers (spontaneous) on the LoveType quiz. Despite their similarity on the Perceiving preference, however, the men are quite different.

Although Buck will do fun and unplanned things, he also likes to schedule dates in advance. Nelson, on the other hand, is a complete free spirit; he is likely to show up at her house anytime, day or night, and whisk her off for a spontaneous rendezvous.

After reexamining their profiles, Margarita realized what the difference was: Buck had only scored a 4 for Perceiving on the LoveType quiz, while Nelson had scored a perfect 7 on Perceiving. They were both Perceivers, but at entirely different levels.

You can take a cue from Margarita's experience and pay close attention to the strength of the preferences when you evaluate a person's LoveType. As mentioned in Chapter Two, scores of 5 and 6 on the LoveType quiz indicate a moderately strong preference on a dimension, while a score of 7 indicates a very strong preference. At the other end of the spectrum, a score of 4 indicates someone who is on the borderline of that preference; that is, he or she does not strongly prefer this factor.

3. The LoveType system can enhance your romance if used properly.

Some people may argue that the LoveType system takes the romance out of a new relationship; once you know everything about a person, you have taken all the mystery out of the romance.

Nonsense. The mystery is the fun part; it is still alive when you use the LoveType system. There will still be a great deal you don't know about your new acquaintance—what his or her hobbies are, what kind of family background he or she came from, what his or her religious beliefs are. You have simply learned enough to do a preliminary screening and answer the question: Is this individual's personality type likely to be compatible with mine in a long-term relationship?

You still need to decide if someone is attractive enough for you, if the other aspects of the physical and mental chemistry are just right. The LoveType approach simply gives you a great head start so you can determine a potential relationship's foundation at the very beginning and then fill in the important elements as you go along.

Okay, enough preliminaries. It is time to explore your personal LoveType in detail and meet your ideal LoveType.

The next sixteen chapters are divided into four parts based on the four LoveTemperament groups. Find the chapter that corresponds to the LoveTemperament group and the specific LoveType you are interested in knowing more about.

Each chapter is further divided into two sections.

The first section is titled: **If You Are a** (your particular LoveType). Here you will find an information-packed description of the romantic and relationship characteristics of your LoveType. You will also learn who your best LoveType match is based on the research of trailblazers in the fields of Jungian typology and compatible relationships.

Once you know who your recommended LoveType is, you can turn to the appropriate chapter and peruse the section titled: **If Your Ideal LoveType Is** (whatever that LoveType is). Here you will be exposed to the nitty-gritty of the LoveType dating system: the never-before-revealed secrets of how to attract, date, and win the love of your perfect LoveType.

Good luck and happy LoveTyping to you.

PART TWO

UNMASKING YOUR SOUL MATE

THE MEANING SEEKERS

Idealistic Philosopher
(INFP: INTROVERTED INTUITIVE FEELING PERCEIVER)

Mystic Writer
(INFJ: INTROVERTED INTUITIVE FEELING JUDGER)

Social Philosopher
(ENFP: EXTRAVERTED INTUITIVE FEELING PERCEIVER)

Growth Teacher
(ENFJ: EXTRAVERTED INTUITIVE FEELING JUDGER)

If any LoveTypes could lay claim to the title of "eternal romantics," it would be the LoveTemperament group we are about to meet: the Meaning Seekers—those whose two middle preferences are Intuitive Feeling, NF.

The Meaning Seekers consist of the four LoveTypes who value intimacy, personal growth, the search for meaning, and the power of imagination in their relationships.

You Take But You Give As Well

As one of the Meaning Seekers, you give your partner an abundance of love, but you expect a lot in return. For those who don't know you well, you may come across as picky or demanding. "Not true," you say. You simply hold high expectations of what a true love relationship should be like. You believe you and your soul mate should offer each other everything: body, mind, and soul.

You are more than willing to make up for your stringent expectations and requirements by being the most emotionally affirming, supportive, and inspiring partner imaginable. If you find the right person, you will constantly test the boundaries to see how much love, passion, devotion, and meaning you can bring to your soulful relationship.

In the next four chapters, we will meet you and your compatriots in love as you search for that elusive blend of meaning, passion, and personal growth that symbolizes your quest for love.

CHAPTER EIGHT

The Idealistic Philosopher

(INFP): INTROVERTED INTUITIVE FEELING PERCEIVER

If You Are an Idealistic Philosopher

Imagine a deep lush valley, caressed by flowers and trees that eternally blossom, inhabited by animals that serve as gentle companions and by people who spend their days loving, creating, and selflessly serving humanity. This is the world of the rare (only about 3 percent of the population) Idealistic Philosopher: the person who is forever striving to live in a perfect world where love and harmony abound.

When You Are in Love

As an Idealistic Philosopher, you believe that love requires a profound emotional and spiritual connection. You may also believe that, to attain this desired state, you will have to endure a great deal of pain and sacrifice. Yet all the suffering will be worth it once you find your perfect love. When that blessed day comes, you will be a complete person, as you and your partner will work together to make the world a better place.

In the beginning of a relationship, you tend to idealize your mate as the greatest person in the world; you'd easily give up your life for him or her. Later, when reality intrudes, you may find yourself disappointed as you realize that no real human being can match the fantastic images of love and romance you created in your imagination. Fortunately, despite your disillusionment, you somehow recover and begin to accept the flaws of your partner, ever so slowly, while still wishing you could change him or her into the perfect image you had when you first fell in love.

Your Best LoveTypes

Research shows that a male Idealistic Philosopher is the LoveType most likely to marry his mirror image: the female Idealistic Philosopher.

Moreover, research indicates that Idealistic Philosophers—whether male or female—tend to be happiest marrying their own LoveType. Idealistic Philosophers who marry each other report the fewest conflicts in communication, finances, child rearing, and chores than any other LoveType combination in which one partner is an Idealistic Philosopher.

If You Are a Female Idealistic Philosopher

You can be happy with your Idealistic Philosopher counterpart, and you can also do well with the Mystic Writer (INFJ), Growth Teacher (ENFJ), or Social Philosopher (ENFP). Because the Growth Teacher and Social Philosopher have Extraverted natures, either one can bring out your social side and help balance your natural inward focus.

If You Are a Male Idealistic Philosopher

Your best bets are the female Idealistic Philosopher or the female Mystic Writer (INFJ). The female Mystic Writer is a wise, reflective lady who can offer you the structure you need to be successful. One caveat: Make sure she isn't very strong on the Judging (J) Preference;

otherwise, she may be too critical of your spontaneous ways.

If Your Ideal Mate Is the Idealistic Philosopher

Where can you meet an Idealistic Philosopher?

Idealistic Philosophers love writing, psychology, the arts, and relationships, and are drawn to activities that involve a crusade or mission. You can bump into them at bookstores, especially in sections related to the preceding topics. If you want to meet literary-minded Idealistic Philosophers, try Single Booklovers—a correspondence club where you can write to singles who enjoy quality books. Also, check out adult education courses, poetry readings, and book signings.

You can also find Idealistic Philosophers at the theater, art galleries, and museums—often walking slowly, by themselves, lost in their thoughts.

Because of their consuming desire to improve the world, Idealistic Philosophers often work behind the scenes for political and charitable causes. Good groups for meeting them, depending on your background and interests, include the following: Red Cross, American Cancer Society, American Heart Association, Greenpeace, Save the Whales, NAACP, Republican and Democratic parties, and the Peace Corps.

Meeting your Idealistic Philosopher is easy once you know where to look. For example, Roxanne, a civil rights attorney, explains how she met David, the love of her life:

"Bars, bars, bars," recited Idealistic Philosopher Roxanne. "Those were the only places I knew to meet men. That was where I met my ex-husband, a disaster worse than Hurricane Andrew. At thirty-three, I was sick of bars and the men I met in them, but I couldn't think of where else to look."

Fortunately, Roxanne took a hiatus from her bar romps

long enough to attend a LoveType seminar and learn that her ideal LoveType—the Idealistic Philosopher—was attracted to the arts.

Remembering her youthful passion for poetry, Roxanne decided to join a poetry reading group and make friends with like-minded individuals. After a few weeks of poetry readings, she met her perfect match in David, a thirty-four-year-old musician and fellow Idealistic Philosopher.

"He had a great butt and curly red hair—wow, he had so much hair!" recalls Roxanne. "But he was so shy. I sat next to him for three weeks, and he barely said hello to me.

"Finally, one day after the group, I asked him if he knew anything about the sixteen LoveTypes. It turned out he was a psychology major in college, and he knew about Dr. Jung's theory of personality types.

"Pretty soon we were exchanging ideas about the things I cared about most—religion and spirituality—and we connected as if we had known each other a long time. I'm thrilled I have finally met my soul mate."

How do you get a date with an Idealistic Philosopher?

According to my research, Idealistic Philosophers tend to be among the most insecure of the LoveTypes. Although they are often talented in many areas—languages, art, music, psychology—they usually do not give themselves credit for their accomplishments. Because Idealistic Philosophers tend to have a fearful outlook on life, it's important to be especially gentle and sensitive when talking with them.

On the positive side, Idealistic Philosophers respond exceptionally well to conversation about psychological, philosophical, or arts-related topics that appeal to their search for connection, meaning, and creative expression. If you can tap into an Idealistic Philosopher's valued interests, you can segue into setting up a date with him or her.

For example, at an art class, strike up a conversation with your cute Idealistic Philosopher classmate. Talk about your favorite artists, then invite your new friend to join you at a local art gallery where you can view some of the works you just discussed.

Or, at a book fair, chat with the Idealistic Philosopher standing next to you. Enthusiastically talk about one of your favorite authors—the one you know is giving a local book signing next week. Now tell your new acquaintance where and when the signing will be, and chances are, he or she will join you there.

What kind of videos would an Idealistic Philosopher enjoy on a date?

If you decide to have a quiet night watching home videos, you can't miss with these:

- *Alice Doesn't Live Here Anymore* (1974). Ellen Burstyn won an Academy Award for playing an Idealistic Philosopher character in the story of a single parent who goes on the road in hope of reclaiming her childhood happiness.
- *Phenomenon* (1996). In this touching, romantic drama, John Travolta is the simple country man who is transformed into a genius when he sees a mysterious light coming from the sky. Creative, gentle, loving, and ultimately redeeming, Travolta's character embodies many of the qualities Idealistic Philosophers hold dear.
- *Gandhi* (1982). This stirring epic chronicles the life of the esteemed Indian spiritual and political leader Mahatma Gandhi, the epitome of an Idealistic Philosopher. Timeless acting by Academy Award winner Ben Kingsley makes Ghandi come alive as one of the most inspiring figures of the twentieth century.
- *Dead Poets Society* (1989). This coming-of-age classic perfectly symbolizes the search for meaning that Idealistic Philosophers pursue. Robin Williams is an English teacher who urges his students to extract the essence from life—to *carpe diem,* seize the day, through the magic and mystery of poetry.

How do you win the love of an Idealistic Philosopher?

You can woo your Idealistic Philosopher with stimulating philosophical discussions in quiet, relaxed settings. Perhaps a stroll along the beach, poetry book in hand, might do the trick. Or you might take him or her to a cozy Asian restaurant (Idealistic Philosophers are fascinated by different cultures), capping off the evening with an art-house movie or philosophical play.

Remember: An Idealistic Philosopher is typically a quiet and gentle person who enjoys close companionship and sharing meaningful ideas. Although your Idealistic Philosopher may hesitate to reveal personal information at first, once he or she warms up to you, this soft-spoken soul can be a very stimulating conversationalist.

Hot Love Tip Number One:
Avoid conflict on your dates.

If you are the kind of person who likes to debate controversial topics, wait until you have established a strong rapport with your Idealistic Philosopher before you become argumentative. Because of the Idealistic Philosopher's intense yearning for harmony, he or she will go to great lengths to avoid conflict. If you bring disharmony into the relationship too soon, the Idealistic Philosopher might become intimidated and may not want to go out with you again.

Hot Love Tip Number Two:
Always be aware of your Idealistic Philosopher's social energy level, especially if you are an Extravert and you tend to talk more than the average person.

Too much talk and social activity can tire the Idealistic Philosopher. Be respectful of his or her need for privacy and quiet time, and your partner will reward you with gratitude and affection.

Consider how Jerome, a thirty-four-year-old high school teacher, used Hot Love Tips Number One and Two to make a splendid impression on his lady-to-be, Latisha.

Latisha was everything Jerome wanted in a lady. She had a delicious cocoa brown complexion, a no-nonsense personality, and a master's degree in clinical psychology. Best of all, she was his perfect LoveType—the Idealistic Philosopher.

One problem: She had an ex-boyfriend who was trying to win her back, a successful investment banker who could afford to wine and dine her like a princess.

Fortunately, Jerome had his own secret weapon: the Love-Type system. After a mutual friend introduced them, Jerome worked hard to appeal to Latisha's Idealistic Philosopher sensibilities. He talked about the things she loved most—philosophy, psychology, and literature—while carefully avoiding any topics that could result in arguments or conflicts.

Best of all, from Latisha's point of view, Jerome respected her need for quiet time. When they started going out, Jerome would consistently ask her: "Are you tired? Are there too many people for you? Would you like to go to a quieter place?"

Although some women would be annoyed by such questions, Latisha took them as a sign that Jerome really understood and cared for her. Soon her ex-boyfriend was history, and Latisha began planning her new life with Jerome—as his devoted wife.

Hot Love Tip Number Three:
Be wary of violating your Idealistic Philosopher's most deeply held values, whatever they may be.

Idealistic Philosophers can be as soft and tender as a marshmallow, *until* they feel you have violated one of their cherished values. When that happens, an Idealistic Philosopher can respond with a toughness and ferocity you would never have expected from such an easygoing person.

Because Idealistic Philosophers tend to keep their emotions inside, you may not even realize you have violated their important values. By the time you understand what has happened, it may already be too late: Your Idealistic Philosopher's pent-up feelings explode, and he or she does something to irrevocably damage the relationship.

Observe what happened to Kirsten, a thirty-nine-year-old English professor, when she unknowingly violated the values of her Idealistic Philosopher boyfriend, Robert, a fifty-year-old licensed clinical social worker.

"It was our third date, and I already knew Robert was the one for me," said Kirsten. "He was the most gentle and caring guy I had ever met. Handsome, with a salt-and-pepper beard and ripped body, he was more than enough man to keep me smiling.

"But then our first blowup happened, and it almost finished us. We were waiting in line at the movie theater to see a romantic film (one I had been dying to see) when Robert suddenly exploded with a fiery temper I had never observed before. In front of a crowd, he began shouting: 'I can't believe how domineering you're being! I'm leaving!'

"To my astonishment, he walked out, and I didn't hear from him for three days. I would have given up on him after the terrible scene he made at the theater, except that I remembered the importance of an Idealistic Philosopher's values.

"I decided to give Robert one chance to explain what was going on with him. I went to his house and asked him what had made him so mad.

"Robert said, 'You didn't ask me what movie I wanted to see. My last wife took advantage of my easygoing nature and

never respected my desires. I did want to see that movie, but I needed you to ask me what I wanted, just to show me that you respected my opinion.'

"Wow. That was a close call; our relationship could have been destroyed at the very beginning over a silly misunderstanding and because I forgot to examine my Idealistic Philosopher's deeply held values.

"After six weeks of couples therapy, we're communicating much better. It may seem weird, but I'm glad this happened early in our relationship, and I was able to learn how important it is to be extrasensitive to my Idealistic Philosopher's values."

To avoid the type of misunderstanding that Kirsten and Robert fell into, pay careful attention to your Idealistic Philosopher's mood changes. If he or she unexpectedly becomes silent, cold, or argumentative on a date, ask why.

If your Idealistic Philosopher accuses you of attacking his or her values, provide reassurance by saying, "I really respect and appreciate your values and feelings; I care about you and the things you believe in."

When you take this approach, your Idealistic Philosopher will quickly forget the real or imagined slight and will go back to being a loving and flexible mate. Your partner will love you all the more because he or she believes you are one of the few truly understanding and loving people in the world.

What kind of sexual relationship can you expect with an Idealistic Philosopher?

Idealistic Philosophers are hopeless romantics. Before they become sexually involved with you, they need to feel loved, treasured, and adored. They must feel that they share a soulful communion with you, an intimate connection that is authentic, passionate, and meaningful.

This doesn't mean that Idealistic Philosophers are

prudes, or that they must wait until marriage before they want sex. It just means that, before giving you their body and soul, they must feel an emotional alliance that meets their idealistic expectation of what true love should be.

Once Idealistic Philosophers feel that cherished bond, they can be very gentle, caring, and passionate lovers— thinking of you constantly as they write letters and poems to express their deepest sexual and romantic feelings.

When it comes to lovemaking, Idealistic Philosophers tend to be somewhat shy in the beginning. Although they have a great deal of love and passion to give, they need to be gently coaxed until they feel free to express themselves.

Hot Sex Tip:
Appeal to your Idealistic Philosopher's highly developed sense of imagination.

Before making love to your partner, perhaps as much as two hours in advance, ask him or her to imagine a beautiful and exciting scenario in which the two of you are making love.

With this imaginary warm-up, your Idealistic Philosopher will be more than ready to express his or her built-up passion when the real moment arrives. Now, instead of engaging a tame cub, you will find yourself happily grappling with a roaring lion or lioness, giving and receiving more pleasure than you ever thought possible.

What kind of long-term relationship can you expect with an Idealistic Philosopher?

Idealistic Philosophers, compared to the other Love-Types, tend to marry late in life and may never marry at all. Because they often have an idealistic view of how true love should be, Idealistic Philosophers can have a difficult time fulfilling their expectations in the real world.

One female Idealistic Philosopher was a virgin at twenty-nine and said that if she couldn't find the soul mate she was looking for, she would rather join a convent. Her family didn't understand her and called her "God's bride." But deep inside her heart, this caring Idealistic Philosopher yearned to have a perfect romantic relationship with a man: a union that would transform her, emotionally and spiritually.

On the positive side, Idealistic Philosophers (both males and females) are highly rated in the area of marital satisfaction; their spouses are usually quite content with them. When Idealistic Philosophers finally decide to marry, they can make excellent spouses and lifelong mates because of their sweet, giving, and easygoing nature.

If you can win the heart of an Idealistic Philosopher, this loving humanitarian will help you realize that two loving partners, working together, can indeed make a positive and life-transforming impact on the world.

Chapter Nine

The Mystic Writer

(INFJ): INTROVERTED INTUITIVE FEELING JUDGER

If You Are a Mystic Writer

The written word is sacred to you because through it, you can understand and express the mysteries of life. When you are not writing, you are exercising another of your supreme talents—the gift of listening—to comfort and aid those who come to you for advice and guidance.

When You Are in Love

When it comes to affairs of the heart, you prefer to express yourself with your pen: poetry, journal writing, and tender notes left on the bathroom mirror are your favorite methods of communicating your love and devotion.

As a Mystic Writer (only about 2 percent of the population), you tend to devote most of your time and energy to your mate. In fact, you can be quite content having your partner as your sole source of quality companionship—as your best and only friend.

Unfortunately, this near obsession with one individual as your sole source of emotional support could cause you grief. You may decide to avoid your loved ones and spend all your time with your partner, only to find out later, perhaps much later, that he or she is absolutely wrong for you. In the meantime, you prolong a bad relationship by deluding yourself—with your highly developed sense of imagination—into believing he or she is the right one.

Your Best LoveTypes
If You Are a Female Mystic Writer

You have a wider range of quality mating choices than your male counterpart. You can thrive with the male Mystic Writer, Scholar (INTP), or Idealistic Philosopher (INFP).

You even get along well with the Wheeler-Dealer (ESTP), the type of gent who will offer you a no-holds-barred, electrifying relationship.

If You Are a Male Mystic Writer

As an Introverted male, you usually have stress-free relationships with Introverted females; therefore, either the Mystic Writer or the Idealistic Philosopher (INFP) can be a good fit for you. The Idealistic Philosopher can be an excellent mate if you want a spontaneous partner to help balance your structured lifestyle.

If Your Ideal Mate Is the Mystic Writer

Where can you meet a Mystic Writer?

Mystic Writers are the most reclusive of the Meaning Seeker LoveTypes. You may have a hard time unearthing them because they often enjoy kicking back at home: reading, writing, thinking, praying, meditating, or listening to music.

Excellent places to meet Mystic Writers include churches, synagogues, or other religious institutions. Although any of the LoveTypes may be involved in religious or spiritual activities, Mystic Writers are especially known for their spiritual (although not necessarily religious in the traditional sense) nature.

Look for Mystic Writers working behind the scenes for the common good of a religious or humanitarian group. They can also be found at self-improvement/spiritual exploration workshops (yoga and transcendental meditation are favorites), retreats, and expos.

Like Idealistic Philosophers, Mystic Writers also enjoy museums, art galleries, and the theater. An excellent place to meet them is at a museum cafeteria, where you can catch them holed up with a book and a sandwich.

Since Mystic Writers love books so much, you can often meet them in religious or New Age bookstores, as well as in public libraries. You can also become acquainted with them by mail through Single Booklovers, an organization that publishes a monthly newsletter to help single booklovers correspond with and meet each other throughout the United States.

Raised in a conservative Bible Belt family, June, a twenty-five-year-old copy editor, was not the type to aggressively approach men or go to nightclubs and be outrageously flirtatious. But she did love to read.

So when June learned that her ideal LoveType—the Mystic Writer—was passionate about books and reading, she made an extra effort to spend more time at her local library and chat with the cute library clerks.

For the past several weeks she had her eye on Steven, a thirty-year-old library science graduate student. After a few snatches of conversation with him, June learned he was a Mystic Writer; she knew there was sure something mystic about his cute wavy hair and killer smile.

One day June brought a book about Hindu philosophy and asked Steven if the library had any more. Steve showed her the books on the topic and invited her to join him for a library lecture series on Eastern mysticism, starting that very week!

Although the lecture was not as interesting as they had

expected, they ended up having a fantastic time afterward—munching on sushi and talking till dawn. They are dating regularly now and are romancing each other at book speed: slow and steady.

How do you get a date with a Mystic Writer?

Because Mystic Writers may not be too communicative when you first meet them, you will probably have to take the initiative and start a conversation. Because they are usually fascinated by psychology, mysticism, and philosophy, these subjects are great places to start. If you know anything about astrology, now is the right time to mention it. Many Mystic Writers are acquainted with astrology and the transcendental aspects of life, including prophetic dreams. Once you spend time with a Mystic Writer, you might say something such as: "After speaking to you, I wonder if you are a . . ." (Say Capricorn or anything else that comes to mind.)

Take a guess. If you are wrong, don't worry about it. You don't have to be an astrological guru to win points with the Mystic Writer. Your Mystic Writer probably knows enough to fill in the gaps of the conversation, and he or she will appreciate your curiosity about metaphysical matters.

Once you have whetted your Mystic Writer's appetite about the supernatural, he or she will keep the conversation going. Before you know it, you may be on your way with your Mystic Writer to a lecture on psychic phenomena, astrology, or psychology.

Hot Dating Tip:
Cater to your Mystic Writer's love of reading.

Since most Mystic Writers are book aficionados, offer to lend your Mystic Writer something from your shelves,

especially something in the area of psychology or relationships. Now that you have to meet your Mystic Writer
somewhere to hand over the book, it might as well be
over dinner. Guess what. You are now on your first date.

What kind of videos would a Mystic Writer enjoy on a date?

Try these Mystic Writer pleasers:

- *Ghost* (1990). A murdered man, now a ghost, joins
  forces with a psychic to save his sweetheart from the
  men behind his murder. This heartwarming, romantic tale of a couple whose love survives death is sure
  to bring a lump to your Mystic Writer's throat.
- *The French Lieutenant's Woman* (1981). In this film,
  the action alternates between a contemporary extra-
  marital affair and a tragic Victorian romance. Mystic
  Writers will identify with Meryl Streep's passionate,
  Oscar-nominated performance as Sarah.
- *Defending Your Life* (1991). In this humorous yet
  touching story of life after death (where you can eat
  all you want and never get fat), Mystic Writers will
  receive their daily helping of mysticism—wrapped in
  a tender, yet never sugary-sweet, coating.
- *Fearless* (1993). Alternately sad, inspiring, and in-
  sightful, this is a hauntingly beautiful film that exam-
  ines how two survivors of a plane crash cope with
  their near-death experience and discover what it
  means to be alive.

How do you win the love of a Mystic Writer?

If you sense that your Mystic Writer is a strong Introvert, you might schedule dates that cater to his or her
need for solitude. Try quiet nights at home, with dinner
ordered in, soft music, and one of his or her favorite
videos.

Or if you feel your Mystic Writer is more outgoing,
you can suggest poetry readings or talks on metaphysical,

psychological, or philosophical topics. Afterward you can take your Mystic Writer to relaxed, intimate dinners, followed by long romantic walks.

~~~~~~~~~~~~~~~~~~~~~~~~~~~

Hot Love Tip:
Offer your Mystic Writer structured dates.

~~~~~~~~~~~~~~~~~~~~~~~~~~~

Because Mystic Writers value structure, a wise strategy is to give them an outline and schedule of what you are going to do on your dates. Mystic Writers are Intuitive, so they will take your plan and fantasize about all the pleasure they are going to have. In this way your Mystic Writer receives pleasure twice: once when he or she visualizes the date, and again when he or she actually goes out with you.

When they started going out, Fernando would fax Carmen, a Mystic Writer, a detailed itinerary of their dates—right down to the precise moment he would give her flowers and a kiss. At first Fernando felt silly doing this, but he knew how much Mystic Writers value schedules and structure.

Much to his surprise, the strategy worked: Carmen became increasingly tender and affectionate as the dates progressed. She would spend her spare time gleefully poring over the schedules and imagining how she would feel when her Prince Charming came for her.

Now, after seven months of dating, it doesn't matter where they go or what they do; they always end up having fun, and their relationship is getting better all the time.

What kind of sexual relationship can you expect with a Mystic Writer?

Mystic Writers are especially tender lovers who appreciate caresses, hugs, and loving gestures from their mates. They are also similar to Idealistic Philosophers in that they want to feel they are in a special, meaningful relationship before they make love: Loveless, soulless sex is not very appealing to the Mystic Writer.

Like most Meaning Seekers, Mystic Writers are sexually aroused by their imagination and their fantasies of what a sexual encounter with their loved one will be like. Their tendency toward modesty and shyness, however, may preclude them from fully expressing their volcanic passion.

~~~~~~~~~~~~~~~~~~~~~~~~~~

Hot Sex Tip:
Have your Mystic Writer concoct a sexy story.

~~~~~~~~~~~~~~~~~~~~~~~~~~

To access your lover's vivid and sensual imagination, encourage him or her to utilize the Mystic Writer's favorite medium: writing.

Tell your Mystic Writer that you would like him or her to create a sexy tale for you—to write down the most exciting and erotic scenario he or she can imagine. For example, your Mystic Writer may pen a story in which a Viking warrior ravishes his lady love on board a mighty ship.

Next have your Mystic Writer recite the tale to you (or volunteer to read it if he or she is too embarrassed). When your Mystic Writer's sexy scenarios spring forth, you will find yourselves becoming aroused. Soon the two of you will be making love with ever-increasing abandon.

What kind of long-term relationship can you expect with a Mystic Writer?

Among the Meaning Seeker LoveTypes, Mystic Writers tend to have the longest marriages: Once a Mystic Writer makes a marriage vow to you, he or she will likely stay a lifetime.

Mystic Writers are also perhaps the most privately passionate of the LoveTypes. Even though a Mystic Writer may not always communicate his or her profound feelings for you, rest assured, they are there.

One caveat: Because Mystic Writers love so deeply, they may appear to be possessive and jealous (and indeed they may be), but they don't see it that way. Instead, Mystic Writers would fervently insist that their strong emotional reactions stem from their belief that true love must be shared honestly and without reservation—soul to soul.

It's Love: Mystic Writer Style

Greg and Hillary were so much alike. Both were Mystic Writers, graduate students working on their advanced degrees in psychology, and lonely singles eager to find their soul mate. They had been observing each other for weeks now, ever since Hillary moved into the apartment complex where Greg lived. Hillary especially liked Greg's sensitive brown eyes, and Greg was bewitched by Hillary's smile and sweet presence.

One hitch: Both were too shy to make the first move. In fact, they would never have connected if Greg had not placed a personal ad in the local paper. When Hillary saw the personals section, she immediately responded to the ad, which read:

Introspective [Introvert], imaginative [Intuitive], sensitive [Feeler] twenty-nine-year-old graduate student in psychology with disciplined lifestyle [Judger] seeks woman, twenty-five to thirty-five, with similar personality traits for a soulful relationship.

After Greg and Hillary met—and realized how much they had in common, and still had been afraid to meet each other—they shared a memorable laugh.

Fortunately Greg and Hillary had been able to connect and were now developing a lasting relationship. But it almost didn't happen; Greg was considering moving to a new city and only placed the ad at the last minute.

Motto: Don't wait until you are the ultimate expert on the LoveType system before you approach that attractive person you have been dying to meet. Just learn the basics, practice a bit, and move forward confidently.

CHAPTER TEN

The Social Philosopher

(ENFP): EXTRAVERTED INTUITIVE FEELING PERCEIVER

If You Are a Social Philosopher

You believe life is abundant, love is plentiful, and creativity is always within your grasp. If God combined the bouncing energy of a cocker spaniel with the enthusiasm of a couple on their honeymoon, God would still be only halfway to duplicating your insatiable zest for life.

When You Are in Love

"Puppy love" is a good term for describing your take on romance: fun, frisky, playful, cuddly, and young at heart. No matter what your age or how many times your heart has been broken, you are an eternal optimist when it comes to love.

You are not someone who proceeds cautiously when you meet someone you find attractive. You are likely to fall passionately in love—or at least lust—quickly, spontaneously, and with total abandon. Holding something back for later is a concept you can't quite grasp, especially when it comes to the joy of creating a new and exciting relationship.

Yes, COMMITMENT can scare you. That one word

71

may explain why you are still single at thirty, forty, fifty, or beyond. But you love, absolutely love, the concept of intimacy, sharing, and relationships. If only you could find that special one, you would be set for life.

Of course, things don't always work out the way you planned. Your former lover was ridiculously possessive—constantly checking up on you at the gym to make sure you weren't cheating on her; your ex-boyfriend's *real* idea of fun turned out to be staying home with beer and basketball.

But never mind. You are always ready for one more sip of the "love cocktail." Who knows? This time you may get lucky and find someone equally eager to share your joys and adventures while allowing you to be yourself: an enthusiastic, extravagant, intelligent, and imaginative lover of life.

Your Best LoveTypes
If You Are a Female Social Philosopher

You will have a good relationship with the Growth Teacher (ENFJ) or your mirror image, the Social Philosopher. The Social Philosopher can be your perfect companion and lover—the type of person who can bring unlimited fun and creativity to your relationship.

If you choose the Growth Teacher, make sure he is not too strong on the Judging preference. If you pick an intense Judger, he may try to stifle your natural creative spontaneity.

If You Are a Male Social Philosopher

You are compatible with the female Social Philosopher or Idealistic Philosopher (INFP). Both are caring, romantic women who will complement your spontaneous, fun-loving personality.

If Your Ideal LoveType Is the Social Philosopher

Where can you meet a Social Philosopher?

Social Philosophers enjoy stimulating conversation and interesting people, and, like the Idealistic Philosopher and Mystic Writer, favor activities that revolve around psychology, philosophy, the arts, and helping others.

Unlike Idealistic Philosophers and Mystic Writers, Social Philosophers seize every opportunity for social contact. They love the spotlight and are known to be excellent teachers and public speakers.

Social Philosophers also routinely attend art gallery openings, wine tastings, fund-raisers, concerts, lectures, and plays. They may also be members of The Single Gourmet—a dining club for singles with sophisticated tastes.

In addition, Social Philosophers can be found at dance classes, pet shows, journalism clubs (many Social Philosophers are closet journalists), cultural festivals, and community events. They are also highly represented at human potential seminars like the Silva Method and psychology organizations such as the American Psychological Association (APA).

One of your best bets is to meet the socially conscious Social Philosopher at charitable or political organizations (they are often involved in leadership) such as Greenpeace, American Foundation for AIDS Research (AMFAR), Leukemia Society, Humane Society, Republican, Democratic, and Independent parties, American Cancer Society, and Big Brothers/Big Sisters of America.

Want to meet a Social Philosopher? Simple. Just go where the political, psychological, and philosophical action happens to be, and you will find your Social Philosopher deep in the mix.

In the last statewide elections Emily volunteered to work for the Democratic party and met Oscar, a Social Philosopher and Mexican-American who loved America and U.S. politics.

Impossibly gorgeous and intelligent, Oscar also loved salsa dancing, Latin cooking, and, before long, Emily.

Gabbing a mile a minute about everything from world peace to capital punishment, Emily and Oscar were soon planning to vote Democrat in a family sense: as husband and wife.

How do you get a date with a Social Philosopher?

Although Social Philosophers may be surrounded by a group of friends, don't worry: They are always open to meeting another interesting person. Their Extraverted and Perceiving (flexible) nature encourages them to initiate and easily respond to conversation about their most deeply held values, beliefs, and preferences. All you have to do is ask a Social Philosopher questions about his or her myriad interests revolving around human potential, the arts, making a difference in the world, and so forth.

Once your Social Philosopher starts talking, you may not be able to get him or her to stop. But that's okay; that means the Social Philosopher is having a great time and is being stimulated by your conversation. Now make a date by offering to join your Social Philosopher at one of his or her favorite activities—those he or she has just spent the last hour talking about.

What kind of videos would a Social Philosopher enjoy on a date?

On slower nights (with a Social Philosopher this may happen only rarely), try the following:

- *White Palace* (1990). This example of a relationship between a young male Administrator (ISTJ) executive and an older Social Philosopher (ENFP) waitress will appeal to a Social Philosopher's optimistic belief that anything is possible when two people fall in love.
- *The Lion King* (1994). Join your Idealistic Philosopher on an animated jungle journey into the life of Simba the lion cub (and future Lion King) in this beautifully

made coming-of-age fable. Much more than a children's film, this contains witty lines for adults, gorgeous music, and an inspirational message.

- *Thelma and Louise* (1991). Two female buddies hit the road in this tragic, and often humorous, look at gender politics and the suppression of women. Guaranteed to spark interesting philosophical discussions about the role of men and women in society.
- *Stand and Deliver* (1988). Question: What would you get if you combined a classroom of underachieving barrio hard cases with a masterful Chicano teacher who would not quit until his students learned calculus? Answer: This satisfying, uplifting film that appeals to the Social Philosopher's desire to encourage and motivate others.

How do you win the love of a Social Philosopher?

Share in your Social Philosopher's splendid curiosity and unquenchable zeal for life and join him or her on fun, active dates, such as:

- Mystery dinner theater. Invite your Social Philosopher to this entertaining dinner show where you can enjoy a meal while watching the waiters and waitresses (who are also actors) play out a murder mystery.
- Dancing. Go country line dancing, take up salsa dancing, or head to a night club. Be sure to kick up your heels with your Social Philosopher and a group of friends—the more the better.
- Kite flying at a park or beach. Bring a carafe of red wine and a slim volume of poetry, and get romantic under the stars.

Hot Love Tip:
Use your imagination to design unique dates.

The way to a Social Philosopher's heart is through his or her imagination. If you make a concerted effort to create novel and playful dating experiences for your Social Philosopher, you can expect, in return, the tremendous charm, enthusiasm, and sheer love of life that he or she is famous for.

Douglas let his imagination run wild when he wanted to impress his lovely date Shannon, a Social Philosopher and artist. After several weeks of the movie-and-dinner routine, Douglas felt it was time for something different—and much more exciting.

First Douglas arranged for one of Shannon's friends to dress up like a butler and transport Shannon to a romantic hideaway. As the butler escorted Shannon to the car, he handed her a scroll with these words:

"My darling, this servant will take you to a clandestine sea rendezvous. Prepare yourself for adventure.

Love, Douglas."

When Shannon arrived at her favorite beach, one of Douglas's friends gave her another note and a rose, and instructed her to follow the clues in the notes to come, as she made her way to her waiting love.

At the end of her journey, Shannon found Douglas lying on the beach, decked out in a bathing suit and bow tie, and surrounded by a feast of wine, shrimp, lobster, and assorted delicacies.

Deeply touched by his creativity and romantic spirit, Shannon shed happy tears. Until night fell, they wined and dined like aristocrats and made love like long-lost lovers. It was the most romantic experience of their lives.

What kind of sexual relationship can you expect with a Social Philosopher?

Like other Meaning Seekers, Social Philosophers want their relationship to have significance beyond the mere pleasure of sexual release; a spiritual or psychological connection is also important.

Although Social Philosophers may take their time nurturing this sense of attachment and meaning, they can easily become sexually involved with someone in a short period of time if they entertain the right feeling or hunch about that person.

Once they are in the mood for love, Social Philosophers enjoy role-playing and highly verbal sex: calling out their lover's name (real or make-believe) and stretching their imagination to the limit.

Want to make love to a Social Philosopher? Go ahead. Put on that nurse's uniform or cowboy outfit and allow your wildest fantasies to come true. It isn't just the sex that matters; it's the playfulness and creativity you bring to the bedroom that turn your Social Philosopher on.

Can't think of anything imaginative to do? Just think of the example that follows, and you may be able to come up with a few sexy twists of your own.

Normally a bit shy and reserved, Patricia, a thirty-seven-year-old author, wanted to enjoy some creative lovemaking with her Social Philosopher boyfriend, William, on his fortieth birthday. Knowing William was working late at his one-man law firm, she decided to surprise him in a way that would make him feel tingly for weeks.

She arrived at his office dressed in a maid's uniform with nothing underneath. In her right hand she toted exotic Asian massage oils.

As she gingerly knocked on his office door, she announced in a mock European accent: "I've come to do the windows and anything else you desire, sir."

After overcoming his initial surprise, William began to do his own office cleaning with Patricia as his eager accomplice. Their passionate lovemaking left them both feeling sated, happy, and even more deeply in love.

What kind of long-term relationship can you expect with a Social Philosopher?

Men consistently rate the female Social Philosopher as one of their top two (another top choice is the Dutiful

Hostess—ESFJ) ideal mates. This finding may be explained by the theory that the female Social Philosopher embodies a man's vision of his consummate companion, a woman who is witty, sensitive, intelligent, and imaginative; in many ways, his emotional and spiritual equal.

The male Social Philosopher is also a popular choice among females. His one flaw is that he may fall prey to the "over the rainbow, there may be someone better" chase. Some male Social Philosophers may feel compelled to pursue their impossible dream—a larger-than-life mythical woman who embodies the best of everything: beauty, brains, personality, and soul.

Of course, the nomadic Social Philosopher male will rarely find his ideal woman and may spend much of his life hopping from one relationship to another. His quest, unlike that of some other male LoveTypes, is not based on a desire to seduce women simply to gain "notches" on his bedpost. Instead, his search is built on a need to find the right woman—a complete lady who will help make him whole and who will satisfy his craving for meaning and connection.

Although wandering eyes can be a problem, the majority of Social Philosopher males are usually able to invest their imagination and love in one woman, as long as she matches his energy and enthusiasm for life.

Both male and female Social Philosophers, although often happy once they are in a long-term relationship, may find it difficult to commit to one person. According to my research, Social Philosophers are among the top three LoveTypes most reluctant to commit to marriage— next to the Wheeler-Dealer (ESTP) and the Performer (ESFP). Because Social Philosophers have a strong desire to be flexible and keep their options open, they may be hesitant to marry a person "forever and ever."

Despite the potential obstacles, you can develop a lasting, loving relationship with a Social Philosopher if you are able to understand and appreciate his or her eternal Alice in Wonderland mind-set, wonderful zest for life, insatiable curiosity, intense need to affirm others and be affirmed by them, and—above all—his or her need to be free and flexible. If you can give your Social Philosopher the leeway he or she needs, this playful and imaginative person can be a delightful and near-perfect partner for the long haul.

CHAPTER ELEVEN

The Growth Teacher

(ENFJ): EXTRAVERTED INTUITIVE FEELING JUDGER

If You Are a Growth Teacher

There is usually one thing on your mind: relationships. Your ability to create and sustain meaningful and loving relationships is an integral part of your happiness, or lack thereof. Whether you are dealing with people on a business, friendship, family, or romantic level, you place a great value on developing quality relationships and making sure they are always improving.

When You Are in Love

As an Extraverted Feeler, you absolutely love to communicate with your mate—verbally expressing feelings of affection and tenderness and discovering what your partner really values.

You also tend to have a consuming desire to spend time with your soul mate; you can barely stand it when he or she is away. Although you probably have many friends, you want to include your mate in your social life as much as possible.

The danger: Your 100 percent emotional investment in your loved one may leave you feeling overextended—

lacking the energy to take care of your own needs because you are so busy taking care of your lover's.

You may also have a tendency to take things too personally and feel hurt when your partner says something that sounds critical but really isn't. For example, you might become upset if your partner merely tells you that you look nice. You take it as a sarcastic jab because your lover has ignored you for the last fifteen minutes, and you think he or she is trying to patronize you with a mean comment about your looks. Now the argument really begins.

In the beginning of a romance, however, your lover can do no wrong. Although you are perceptive in many areas, when it comes to romance, you may fall in love with an ideal image of how a relationship should be, even though the real thing may not come close to your fantasy.

As the relationship progresses, you will begin to expect the same type of faithfulness and unwavering love and support that you freely give. If you believe your mate is not offering you an equal measure of attention and support, you will let him or her know in a very direct and sometimes not-too-pleasant manner.

Your Best LoveTypes
If You Are a Female Growth Teacher

You will have a loving relationship with either a male Growth Teacher or your exact opposite, the male Craftsperson (ISTP)—the ultimate man of adventure. With him by your side, you will enjoy real-life thrills (kayaking, rock climbing, motorcycle riding, or bungee jumping for starters), and you will participate in life more fully than ever before.

If You Are a Male Growth Teacher

You get along with the female Growth Teacher, Social Philosopher (ENFP), or Idealistic Philosopher (INFP).

You can also succeed with your exact opposite, the

Craftsperson (ISTP). The Craftsperson's hands-on, practical nature will keep you in tune to the realities of life. And her relaxed, easygoing personality will help soothe you when you become frantic with the "people problems" you tend to take too personally.

Paula, a hardworking forty-nine-year-old corporate trainer and Growth Teacher, was sick of the men she had been dating after her husband died: high-powered corporate types who were even more frantic and high-strung than she was.

After being introduced to the LoveType approach by her sister, she decided to change her dating plan.

"When I started studying the LoveType system, I realized that what I really needed was my exact opposite: the Craftsperson (ISTP). I wanted a man who wouldn't compete with me all the time, who could help me unwind, and who would show me the carefree and spontaneous side of life.

"I met my honey when my car broke down and I had to take it to the shop. Using the LoveType approach, I struck up a conversation with the cute, curly-haired service manager named Rex. After asking him a few questions, I knew he was my ideal Craftsperson. He was so fun and lighthearted; I was instantly attracted to him.

"When he asked me out motorcycle riding, I surprised myself by saying yes, and I'm glad I did. I had a marvelous time, and we're living together now. It's been two years, and our relationship is improving day by day."

If Your Ideal LoveType Is the Growth Teacher

Where can you meet a Growth Teacher?

You can find the Growth Teacher in leadership positions in business, teaching, and government. They have terrific social skills and are easy to approach.

Try some of these venues for finding your Growth Teacher:

- Political action committees
- Church leadership
- The Single Gourmet: a social dining club for singles
- Book superstores
- Public TV pledge drives
- Charity committees and local activist groups
- Self-improvement seminars and retreats
- Toastmasters, National Speakers Association, and other speaking clubs

Delia, an actress, met her Growth Teacher boyfriend, Andrew, at her local Toastmasters organization. A speaking club where members give speeches and are critiqued by other members, Toastmasters seemed like the perfect place to meet the type of people-focused leader she was looking for.

When Delia first saw Andrew—a Growth Teacher and corporate trainer for a Fortune 500 corporation—she was immediately mesmerized by his sparkling blue eyes, wavy brown hair, and sturdy six-foot-three-inch frame. And his booming manly voice sent shivers down her spine.

After observing Andrew at several meetings, Delia complimented him on his speaking ability. Conversation came naturally to them, and they soon shifted to the topics of love and relationships. Realizing how comfortable they were with each other, Delia and Andrew opted to continue their discussion over coffee at a nearby restaurant.

Six weeks later Delia and Andrew were still talking, only now it was about building a marriage and life together.

Just remember: You can meet Growth Teachers anywhere people are gathered for an important purpose, whether it's to initiate social change, improve work performance, or enrich the quality of life. Go where the intellectual action and human growth potential is, and you will find the Growth Teacher.

How do you get a date with a Growth Teacher?

Let him or her teach you something. Growth Teachers have opinions and knowledge about a multitude of subjects. They may be experts on the arts, religion, politics, current affairs, psychology, or business. Ask a Growth Teacher about any of these, and wait for his or her store of information to pour forth.

Hot Dating Tip: Use the Closure Technique.

〰〰〰〰〰〰〰〰〰〰〰

Once you find your Growth Teacher's hot button—the topic he or she is most interested in—say something like this:

"I have something important I want to tell you about . . . (the topic that intrigues him or her), but I don't have time now. Here's my card; give me a call, and we'll set up a time to talk."

Because Growth Teachers hate to leave things open-ended, they will want to seek closure of the conversation. They will be eager to meet with you again, soon, to find out what you promised to tell them. You can satisfy the Growth Teacher's need for completion, and your need to know him or her better, by offering to meet at a specific time to wrap up your discussion, perhaps over a bite to eat. Get ready: You have your first date.

Nathan, a thirty-year-old office manager, successfully used the closure technique to get close to his wife-to-be, Ivanna, a beautiful twenty-nine-year-old organizational psychologist.

"Ivanna was doing a workshop on employee relations at my company, but I couldn't concentrate on what she was saying. All I could think about was her purring exotic voice, hypnotic blue eyes, and lustrous blond hair. As she spoke about her personal struggles in corporate America, I recognized the traits of my ideal LoveType, the Growth Teacher. I knew I had to meet her.

"After her presentation I mustered up all my courage and

told her about the work I was doing with stress management. She was intrigued by what I told her, but I didn't give her too much information. I wanted to stimulate her Growth Teacher's need for closure by letting her know I was available for questions—at a later time.

"She called two days later, and we met for coffee. We started talking about business, but we soon switched gears and began talking about each other.

"After spending time with her, I not only confirmed my initial assumption that she was a Growth Teacher, but I also discovered that we were similar in many ways. We were both recently divorced, we loved children, and we were sincere professionals whose mission in life was to teach people how to grow, both personally and professionally.

"Our coffee meetings stretched into lunches, dinners, nights out, and finally into love. We're happily married now, and we have two beautiful boys: Aaron, one, and James, three."

What kind of videos would a Growth Teacher enjoy on a date?

The rich and complex characters in these films will appeal to the Growth Teacher's fascination with human relationships:

- *Fatal Attraction* (1987). Growth Teachers will be fascinated (and terrified) by Glenn Close's role as the professional woman who becomes obsessed with a married man and leaves a trail of mayhem and death.
- *Rain Man* (1988). This is a touching road story about the relationship between a man and his idiot savant brother. Dustin Hoffman will grab, and never let go, of your emotions in this beautifully made film that earned him a Best Actor Oscar.
- *Don Juan DeMarco* (1995). Your Growth Teacher will adore this modern Don Juan's romantic take on life and his fervent belief that love is everything. Won-

derful acting by Marlon Brando and Johnny Depp make this a must-see.

- *Citizen Kane* (1941). This Orson Welles film is widely considered to be one of the best movies of all time. Growth Teachers will empathize with the meaningful yet tragic life of Charles Foster Kane, the crusading newspaper tycoon who got everything he wanted but lost everything he loved.

How do you win the love of a Growth Teacher?

Don't make your Growth Teacher jealous. It's true that some Growth Teachers tend to be possessive and jealous, although the more emotionally developed they are, the less jealous they will be. To prevent problems, avoid being overly attentive to or conscious of other attractive people when you are on a date with a Growth Teacher.

Although confident in many areas, Growth Teachers can be insecure when it comes to romantic relationships. They want constant reassurance—as much by your words as by your actions—that you care about them. Give Growth Teachers the attention and verbal affection they crave, and they will reward you with their generous warmth and capacity for making you feel as if you are the most loved person in the world.

Hot Love Tip:
Be on time when you have a date with a Growth Teacher.

As Judgers (J), they demand punctuality and want you to follow through on the schedule you have committed to. Growth Teachers will let you know, in sometimes biting terms, when you have violated their expectations of what it means to be on time.

Assuming you are on time (now you know better), you

will impress a Growth Teacher by accompanying him or her to plays, concerts, psychology seminars, political debates, and any other form of mentally stimulating entertainment.

You will earn your Growth Teacher's affections by showing respect and support for his or her strongly held opinions, beliefs, and preferences. Always remember that your Growth Teacher must see in you the type of total devotion, and yes, even worship, that he or she offers you, unconditionally, for all time.

What kind of sexual relationship can you expect with a Growth Teacher?

Growth Teachers are fond of talking in bed. They like to shower their lover with verbal affection: "Lovey," "babycakes," and "honeypea" are common terms of endearment that flow from the romantic Growth Teacher's lips during lovemaking.

Like other Intuitives, the Growth Teacher's imagination of what sex will be like often carries them away, and they may end up enjoying their fantasy more than the actual sexual experience.

Hot Sex Tip:
Give your communication-loving Growth Teacher a sex-fantasy assignment.

Tell your Growth Teacher that you want to hear one of his or her favorite sexual fantasies, and that you will reciprocate by sharing one of yours.

By doing this, you will appeal to your Growth Teacher's love of imagination and his or her intense desire to share intimate thoughts and feelings. Rest assured: By the end of the night, you and your Growth Teacher will be enacting the fantasies you just discussed, while coming up with a half dozen more.

One final point: Although Growth Teachers are usually sensitive toward their partners, they have a tendency to speak up when they are not satisfied in bed. When this happens, Growth Teachers are not being critical; they are simply communicating openly with their partners so they can create the foundation for a mutually satisfying sex life.

What kind of long-term relationship can you expect with a Growth Teacher?

Growth Teachers love intensely and are not shy about telling their soul mate how they feel. Consequently, Growth Teachers are comfortable expressing hurt and anger if they feel their relationship has been threatened by the words or deeds of their partner.

Moreover, because of their emotional reactivity, Growth Teachers can take conflict and rejection—real or perceived—very personally. As a result, they may be profoundly hurt and can carry a grudge for a long time.

On the positive side, Growth Teachers believe in marriage and make loving and devoted spouses. They are also charismatic, fun to be with, and perfectly able to inspire their soul mate to peaks of love and happiness.

When you meet the right Growth Teacher, you will feel like a gold lover at Fort Knox. You will bask in the glorious feeling of being with someone who can favor you with the type of love, support, and attention you have been hoping for all your life.

THE KNOWLEDGE SEEKERS

The Scholar
(INTP): INTROVERTED INTUITIVE THINKING PERCEIVER

The Expert
(INTJ): INTROVERTED INTUITIVE THINKING JUDGER

The Innovator
(ENTP): EXTRAVERTED INTUITIVE THINKING PERCEIVER

The General
(ENTJ): EXTRAVERTED INTUITIVE THINKING JUDGER

To have power or not to have power; that is definitely the question that burns on your mind. If you are a Knowledge Seeker—those whose two middle preferences are Intuitive Thinking, NT—being powerless is one of the worst things that can happen to you. Of course, the power you crave doesn't have to be over others; it can be power over yourself or nature. As long as you are able to exert influence by understanding someone or something, you will be happy.

The Knowledge Seekers are the four LoveTypes who value logic, stimulating debate, intelligence, competence, and continual growth in their relationships.

Be Skeptical. That's Okay. We Have the Hard Data.

As one of the Knowledge Seekers, you may be skeptical of the LoveType system and the comments made about your group. Rest assured, years of research have confirmed what you will read about the Knowledge Seekers. Moreover, at the end of the book you will find a list of suggested readings to help you explore the validity and research base of the entire LoveType system.

Take your time as you evaluate the LoveType approach. As a Knowledge Seeker, you want to check all the facts thoroughly and then come to your own well thought out conclusions about the validity of the program. I'm confident you will be pleased with what you discover about Jungian typology and the LoveType method, and you will be convinced that your search for scientific truth and integrity has yielded fruit.

CHAPTER TWELVE

The Scholar

(INTP): INTROVERTED INTUITIVE THINKING PERCEIVER

If You Are a Scholar

Information is your lifeblood. Without you to research it, analyze it, and store it, the world would be a much more ignorant place. You possess an uncanny ability to mold raw data into original and complex theories that explain how and why things happen. To you, life is a never-ending series of theories that can, and must, be either proven or disproven.

When You Are in Love

As a Scholar, you are likely to be a puzzle to many of your dates. With your incisive and theoretical mind, you can run intellectual circles around almost anyone.

One woman who dated a Scholar had this to say:

"He just loved to argue. About everything, anything. One night I made a simple request, and before I knew it, he had me all twisted up in my own words—thoroughly proving that I was being illogical. And that was just because I wanted to see a romantic movie, and he wanted to see a sci-fi flick. Dammit."

As a Scholar, you have no patience for intellectual fools. Your soul mate must be witty, intelligent, and able to keep up with your excited, accelerated profusion of ideas, plans, and analysis. Looks count, but a person's brain power is a crucial consideration when you are selecting a life partner.

Although you may allow your emotions to get out of control for a short while when you first fall for someone, you are quickly able to shift gears and start thinking logically again. You are able to move rapidly from asking, "How do I love thee, let me count the ways" at the start of the relationship, to "In what ways does this person meet my criteria, my logical blueprint for what my ideal mate should be like?" No matter how nice or attractive a potential mate may be, he or she must satisfy your logical requirements before you consider giving away your heart.

Your Best LoveTypes

Despite the rarity of Scholars (only about 3 percent of the population), they have a strong tendency to attract each other. My research, however, indicates that happiness is elusive for Scholar couples because they bring the same weaknesses to a relationship. These potential problem areas include a lack of awareness of the emotional nuances of the relationship and a preference for working problems out through their imagination rather than talking things out with their partner in a realistic manner.

Therefore, better pairings for Scholars are as follows:

If You Are a Female Scholar

Your preferred LoveType is the Expert (INTJ), General (ENTJ), or Innovator (ENTP).

If you are paired with a General, you and your partner will enjoy a relationship based on competition and innovation. When your mate is the Expert or Innovator, you will partake of intellectual conversation and debate as you share your mate's fascinating plans for designing a better world.

If You Are a Male Scholar

Your ideal match is the female Mystic Writer (INFJ). She will intrigue you with her philosophical bent, while helping you get in touch with the soft, feeling side of your personality.

Caveat: As a male Scholar, you tend to have difficulties when evaluating relationships and making emotional decisions. Consequently, you may be carried away by a woman who appears to be flamboyantly emotional, such as the Performer (ESFP) or the Social Philosopher (ENFP). Although these women may seem irresistibly attractive and exciting in the beginning, they may drive you crazy in a long-term relationship with what you perceive to be their flaky and irresponsible nature.

If Your Ideal Mate Is the Scholar

Where can you meet a Scholar?

To find a Scholar, make sure to spend time at the places and activities where intellectual and highly educated men and women with good taste are likely to congregate.

Try the following:

- Wine tastings and wine connoisseur clubs
- Classical music and jazz concerts
- Art shows and auctions
- The Single Gourmet (a gourmet dining club for singles)
- Music societies and clubs
- Ballroom dance classes
- Chess clubs
- Science (and science fiction) clubs such as Star Trek (and Star Wars): The Official Fan Club and conven-

tions such as the Star Trek Convention (and Star Wars Convention)
- Computer fairs
- Advanced-degree singles clubs
- Single Booklovers: a correspondence club for literature-loving singles
- Engineering departments of local colleges
- Computer clubs

If you really want to make headway in meeting your Scholar, you can log on to one of their favorite playgrounds: the Internet.

At first Doris, a twenty-five-year-old linguist, was skeptical of meeting her ideal mate on a computer. But after speaking with two friends who had met their Scholar fiancés on-line (while chatting on the Internet), she decided to give it a try.

First she searched for a chat room (an electronic clubhouse where people converse by typing messages on their computer screens) in her on-line service that catered to intellectuals. She finally found her ideal on-line home in the chat room titled "University Professors Looking for Love."

On her third visit, Doris met her ideal mate, Vincent, screen name "Ivy League," a Scholar and thirty-three-year-old chemistry professor at an Ivy League school. He was brilliant (with a 165 IQ), funny, and surprisingly down-to-earth. And based on the picture he sent her by e-mail (electronic mail) and their subsequent meeting, she was pleased to discover that he was her favorite physical type: tall and broad-shouldered with sandy blond hair.

When Vincent finally traveled cross-country and met Doris after eight months of romantic e-mail and steamy lovemaking in their private chat rooms, they didn't waste any time. Vincent had a ring in his hand, and they married three days later.

How do you get a date with a Scholar?

Get him or her talking about theoretical and scholarly topics. If you are an expert in a particular field, talk about it.

Scholars respect people who are competent in any area they don't know much about. As you converse with a Scholar, don't worry if he or she asks you countless questions that may seem unrelated to the topic at hand. As Perceivers (P), Scholars love to explore many different avenues and options; their curiosity is endless.

Hot Dating Tip:
Use the Intellectual Puzzle Approach.

Because Scholars are excited by intellectual challenges, an excellent strategy is to grab their attention by asking them to help you solve a puzzle, riddle, brain teaser, or math problem.

After dating a string of incompatible men for six years, Rachel, a never-married twenty-eight-year-old graduate student, applied the Intellectual Puzzle Approach to arouse the romantic interest of her Scholar honey.

When she first met him, Rachel was stumped. Ben, a twenty-seven-year-old electrical engineer, was the smartest guy in her computer class and also the cutest, with his surfer-blond looks and all-American smile.

But he was also one of the shyest guys she had ever seen; Rachel knew it would take a miracle for him to approach her for a date. Their class was ending soon, and Rachel was becoming impatient to make a connection with her dream man.

Knowing he was a Scholar based on her observations, Rachel decided to appeal to Ben's intellect with the Intellectual Puzzle Approach. On the last day of class, she sat next to Ben and fiddled with a Rubik's Cube.

During breaks, she fiddled and fumbled with the cubes in growing frustration and disgust. "This is driving me crazy," she muttered loud enough for Ben to hear. At first Ben didn't even look at her, but as she grew increasingly exasperated, he started to pay attention.

Finally he timidly glanced at her and mumbled: "Can I give it a shot?"

Breathing a sigh of relief, Rachel replied: "Oh, could you help me? I've been trying to figure this out for weeks."

After class, Ben helped her solve the puzzle and later joined her for lunch. Rachel and Ben are now engaged, and the only puzzle left to solve is how many people to invite to their wedding.

What kind of videos would a Scholar enjoy on a date?

Here are some videos that will titillate your Scholar's mind:

- *The Maltese Falcon* (1941). The Scholar will enjoy the mazelike story line, snappy dialogue, and intriguing cast of characters in this classic Humphrey Bogart film about the adventures of private eye Sam Spade.
- *Dangerous Liaisons* (1988). Glenn Close and John Malkovich star as cunning French aristocrats in pre-revolutionary France who scheme to corrupt the affections of men and women for their own pleasure and gain. The intricate plot and accurate period detail will delight and intrigue Scholars.
- *Vertigo* (1958). In this Hitchcock masterpiece, James Stewart leads the viewer into the mind of a man whose obsession with a woman leads to mystery.
- *Star Trek* (all seven films: 1979 through 1994) and the original TV series (1966 through 1969). So what if Scholars have seen the "Star Trek" series a hundred times? To the Scholar, there is nothing better than watching the intergalactic adventures of the starship *Enterprise* and its crew as they battle the forces of evil and discover the secrets of the universe.

How do you win the love of a Scholar?

Take the Scholar to a science museum, or a talk on astrophysics or any other topic that appeals to your Scholar's thirst for knowledge and quest to understand how the world works.

As Introverts (I), Scholars enjoy spending time either alone with you or in a small group of close friends. They enjoy probing intellectual discussion, so this is an excellent time to bedazzle them with your knowledge.

~~~~~~~~~~~~~~~~~~~~~~~~~~~

Hot Love Tip:
Stimulate your Scholar's quest for new ideas, theories, and systems.

~~~~~~~~~~~~~~~~~~~~~~~~~~~

Find books on a topic (one you are interested in) that your Scholar knows little about. Read to him or her, or have him or her read to you. Then discuss and debate the material you just read. Challenge your Scholar to come up with a unique twist or alternative approach to deal with the issue you have been discussing.

You might ask your Scholar if he or she knows of a better method than using Jungian typology for classifying people into relationship types. Once you pose this issue, your Scholar will eagerly jump into the conversation and advance his or her ideas. In this way, you and your Scholar will bond in a manner that can only occur through shared intellectual discussion and debate.

Although this approach to romance may seem mechanical and unemotional to some LoveTypes, it is what attracts and excites the brainy Scholar. If you can intellectually challenge, provoke, and stimulate the Scholar in this way, you will decisively win his or her affections.

What kind of sexual relationship can you expect with a Scholar?

You may need to invest a significant amount of time and energy before you feel sexually comfortable with a

Scholar. Because Scholars are not particularly skilled at expressing their emotions, they may appear to be somewhat cold in bed.

Scholars aren't unloving, however. They just have a different way of sharing intimacy: through their pursuit of knowledge and quest for understanding the intricate and esoteric aspects of everything in life, including sex.

~~~~~~~~~~~~~~~~~~~~~~~~~~~~~~~~~~

Hot Sex Tip:
Use stimulating intellectual discourse as part of your foreplay.

~~~~~~~~~~~~~~~~~~~~~~~~~~~~~~~~~~

The key to arousing a Scholar's passion is to first spark his or her intellect. Your Scholar needs to have an intellectual connection with you and believe you are a worthy participant in his or her never-ending search for truth and understanding.

Before making love, introduce a theoretical and/or controversial topic that your Scholar enjoys discussing. Build the discussion up to a peak just before you decide to get amorous. Remember: The deeper you can dig into a Scholar's mind, the more sexual vitality he or she will offer you in return.

What kind of long-term relationship can you expect with a Scholar?

Scholars can offer an intellectual thirst, an optimistic vision of the future, and an easygoing, flexible presence in a committed relationship.

On the other hand, being involved in a long-term relationship with a Scholar poses definite challenges. Here are important research findings that attest to this:

- Female Scholars are the least happily married women among the sixteen LoveTypes.

- Women who marry Scholars, regardless of their own LoveType, are often unhappy with their marriages.
- Male Scholars, among the sixteen LoveTypes, are the most oblivious (that is, the least aware) of the emotional aspects of their relationships. Consequently, a male Scholar may think his relationship is going great, while his partner is miserable and wants out.
- Regardless of gender, Scholars tend to have the shortest marriages.

The trouble seems to stem from the fact that Scholars rely primarily on their inner vision of what a relationship should be like, while often ignoring the realities of the situation (hence the high degree of obliviousness among male Scholars).

To compound the problem, a substantial number of Scholars are not in tune with their Feeling side and are not aware of the emotional needs of their partners. Also, because of their Introverted nature, Scholars may not be attuned to social graces and can make blunders that embarrass, and even humiliate, their more socially aware partners.

Now for the good news: Scholars can become adaptable and quality mates as long as they work to overcome their areas of weakness, and focus on using their personality strengths—their powerful imagination and flexible nature—to enhance their relationships. When they do this, Scholars can enjoy successful, growth-filled relationships and marriages that last a lifetime.

CHAPTER THIRTEEN

The Expert

(INTJ): INTROVERTED INTUITIVE THINKING JUDGER

If You Are an Expert

You are the most independent and strong-willed (some might say stubborn) of all the LoveTypes. Once you make up your mind to do something—whether it's starting or ending a relationship, or anything in between— you will do what you want to do. And God help anyone who tries to dissuade you.

When You Are in Love

You, Ms. or Mr. Expert (only 2 percent of society), are a deep thinker who is always analyzing your relationships and asking the question: Does this person fit my detailed design of what an ideal mate should be like? Often the answer is no because your capacity for creating the blueprint for this "perfect mate" often exceeds your ability to find him or her in the real world.

Competence and intelligence are two of the most important qualities you look for in a mate: You admire someone who is well educated and successful in his or her chosen field. Although you prefer someone whose intellect is as sharp as yours, you may fall in love with someone who is not your intellectual equal. When this happens, you may always have that nagging doubt in the back of your mind: "Is this person smart enough for me?"

Your Best LoveTypes
If You Are a Female Expert

You already know you are not the typical, traditional woman. If, at an early age, you concluded that marriage was not for you, you won't marry no matter how attractive or desirable a man appears to be.

Or if you decide that you will marry at a specific age— say thirty, forty, or fifty—you will reject any suitor who enters your life before your designated time. You don't care if Prince Charming himself arrives at your door with wedding ring and roses galore. If he's not on schedule, forget it.

As a female Expert, you make your own decisions independent of any pressures from your family, friends, or society, and you will rarely change your mind once you have come to a carefully thought out, logical conclusion.

Your optimum match tends to be an equally independent and strong-willed man who can appreciate your individualistic, nonconformist streak. Either the Expert or the Traditionalist (ESTJ) will do.

The Traditionalist is an interesting choice. Because he is a strong, masculine type of male, you will be attracted to his power and competence. He is the cowboy, the man who takes charge. But watch out if he is a strong Sensor. If so, his conventional nature may override his other qualities, and he may try to mold you into his ideal traditional wife while ignoring your true personality. Beware of this potential flaw in his nature.

If You Are a Male Expert

You are compatibly matched with the female Expert or Scholar (INTP).

The Scholar can be an excellent choice for you. Her

facile mind will engage you intellectually, while her flexible and carefree nature will prevent you from taking yourself too seriously. You will learn how to relax and enjoy stimulating conversation when you spend time with the Scholar.

How Katherine Lassoed Her Cowboy

When Katherine, an Expert and thirty-four-year-old chemist, was introduced to Donald by a mutual friend, she was instantly attracted to him. But she also had serious reservations: Could she be happy with a macho traditional guy like Donald? Here are both sides of their romance:

Katherine: "When I became acquainted with Donald, I thought, wow, he's cute, but he can't possibly be my type. He was thirty-six and a Traditionalist (ESTJ), a high-powered corporate raider and rancher who had old-school views when it came to women and relationships."

Donald: "And when I met Katherine, I saw a terrifically attractive woman behind her horn-rimmed glasses and nervous laugh. A real bona fide intellectual like my mother. I was captivated by her charms."

Katherine: "I had never really gone out with a man like Donald before; I thought those macho types were all bluster and no character. And I was worried that I had much more education than Donald. But after hearing about successful Expert/Traditionalist combinations, I decided to give Donald a chance (he was cute), so I asked him out for coffee."

Donald: "I said yes, provided I pay. After all, a man should be a gentleman."

Katherine: "And a gentleman, he was. We had a wonderful time, and when he escorted me to my car, I leaned on his strong shoulders. Later that week, he introduced me to his charming southern family, and I felt right at home. We started dating seriously after that."

Donald: "In an old-fashioned courtship."

Katherine: "Yep, he's my cowboy, all right."

Donald: "I sure am."

Postscript: As strong-willed Thinkers, Donald and Katherine occasionally get into heated verbal battles, but they always make up afterward. Overall, their relationship is strong and getting better all the time.

If Your Ideal Mate Is the Expert

Where can you meet an Expert?

Here are some popular Expert hangouts:

- The Single Gourmet: a club for singles who enjoy fine dining
- Law school libraries and cafeterias
- The science department of local colleges
- Museum exhibitions
- Chess clubs and tournaments
- Wine tastings
- Jazz and classical music concerts
- Computer stores and fairs
- Exotic or antique car shows
- Single Booklovers: a correspondence club for singles who love books
- Star Trek and Star Wars Conventions
- Used-book stores (they like to save money)
- Graduate school test preparation centers (experts are always going for advanced degrees)
- History clubs

And anywhere competence, knowledge, education, and intellect are highly valued.

How do you get a date with an Expert?

You don't have to be a technological wizard to do well with an Expert. Experts respect competence and expertise, often even more than they esteem credentials or degrees. If you can show an Expert that you are genuinely knowledgeable in an area—and can withstand his or her rigorous challenges to your credibility—you will win over the Expert and earn a date with this brilliant intellect.

~~~~~~~~~~~~~~~~~~~~~~~~

Hot Dating Tip:
Spark your Expert's intellectual competitiveness.

~~~~~~~~~~~~~~~~~~~~~~~~

Experts are very competitive and hate to lose, but respect people who demonstrate competence and can beat them. If you do beat the Expert at his or her own game (chess is a favorite)—or at least trigger his or her intellectual competitiveness—you will have a friend, and maybe a mate, for life.

Alice, a twenty-seven-year-old C.P.A., successfully used her knowledge of chess to intrigue and attract Kurt, a cute twenty-eight-year-old Expert history professor. After exchanging a few pleasantries with Kurt over the course of several weeks at their local chess club, Alice decided to make her move.

During an evening session of the club, she sauntered over to where Kurt, an 1800 level player, was playing a speed chess match with a 1700 level player. She stood about two feet to Kurt's right and silently shook her head every time Kurt made a move.

At first Kurt didn't pay attention to Alice, but eventually he caught a whiff of her perfume and started noticing her head-shaking movements. In the middle of the match, with Kurt already up two pawns and a knight, she exhaled a deep breath, shook her head, and walked away. Of course, she did this only when Kurt had glanced over at her as he had been doing periodically throughout the match.

Kurt immediately interrupted his chess game and went

over to her: "Excuse me, Alice, is something wrong? I mean,
with my play, in your eyes?"

"No, of course not; you're a skilled player. Not everyone
can open as strong as Fischer."

"What do you mean? Was there something wrong with
my opening?"

"I'd love to explain, but I'm late for an appointment. If you
like, we can talk later."

"When?" queried Kurt. He fancied himself an excellent
chess player and couldn't stand to be second-guessed.

"Call me tomorrow; here's my card."

Two days later, they met for coffee. When Kurt asked her
what he'd done wrong in the opening, she said, "Nothing.
But the kind of opening I was expecting from you was, 'Hello,
I'd like to get to know you.' "

Kurt blushed and so did Alice, but there was definitely
chemistry there. They both laughed at her ruse, and Kurt
admitted he had been attracted to her for some time but had
been too shy to approach her. The time went by quickly as
they discovered how much they liked each other.

Two years later Alice took Kurt's last name and became
Mrs. Johnson. Today Alice and Kurt play chess all the time
as husband and wife, and Alice often opens with Fischer just
to keep Kurt guessing.

What kind of videos would an Expert enjoy on a date?

Experts enjoy mentally stimulating and competently
made films such as the following:

- *The Usual Suspects* (1995). A multilayered, puzzlelike
  heist movie that plays like a grand master's chess
  match. Who is the real villain, who's being set up?
  This brilliantly crafted ensemble film will keep your
  Expert thinking to the very end, and even beyond.
- *Total Recall* (1990). With dazzling special effects and
  a twisting, disorienting plot, this sci-fi film about a
  man who can't trust anything, including his own

memory, is perfect for the analytical and skeptical Expert.

- *Quiz Show* (1994). Experts will enjoy this film based on the real-life quiz-show scandals of 1959. This well-made movie takes the viewer into the world of a college professor who, seduced by fame and money, is a willing participant in a rigged quiz show in which the winner always knows the answers beforehand.
- *Searching for Bobby Fischer* (1993). Experts will love this true story about a seven-year-old chess prodigy and his instructor's relentless drive to make him into the next Bobby Fischer.

How do you win the love of an Expert?

Plan dates that tap into your Expert's knowledge of law, science, business, politics, or anything else he or she considers an area of expertise. Remember: Experts strive for mastery in everything, including their hobbies and pastimes. If you can encourage your Expert to display his or her knowledge and competence on a date, this intellectual connoisseur will begin to see you in a favorable light.

If, for example, your Expert knows about law (many Experts are fascinated by jurisprudence), watch Court TV together and ask him or her to explain the proceedings. Or, for a change of pace, accompany your Expert to a live trial—the more complex the better. As you snuggle next to your honey, he or she will enlighten you on the fine points of the RICO Act in white-collar fraud trials or the meticulous gathering of DNA evidence in capital murder cases.

Hot Love Tip:
Add spice to your date with a rousing debate.

Experts love to debate, and respect those who can keep up with them. For a stimulating date with your Expert, try the following:

Begin the evening with a spirited debate about some esoteric point as you enjoy haute cuisine at a five-star restaurant—one with a superbly competent chef, of course. Then follow it up by watching an intelligent, highly rated movie, and cap the night off by arguing the merits of the film and the quality of the acting. Whatever you do, keep your Expert thinking and debating; he or she will love you for it.

What kind of sexual relationship can you expect with an Expert?

Like Scholars, Experts may not be especially affectionate in bed: Sugary words and excessive cuddling are not their style.

At the same time, Experts, because of their straightforward Judging tendencies, may appear to be critical if they believe their sexual needs aren't being met. When Experts speak out about their sexual dissatisfaction, however, they don't intend to hurt their partner's feelings. Rather, their goal is to set the record straight so they can engineer a better sexual experience the next time around.

On the positive side, Experts are typically the most faithful of the Knowledge Seekers. They are not likely to sleep around and are often the most sexually prudent of all the LoveTypes. Female Experts especially do not have many sexual partners in their lives, and both sexes typically find the concept of casual sex to be intellectually distasteful.

Hot Sex Tip:
Win over your Expert's intellect first, then his or her libido.

To do well sexually with the Expert, satisfy his or her craving for information and knowledge. Let him or her know you have studied the important sex treatises by Masters and Johnson as well as the Kamasutra. (If you haven't read them yet, now is a good time to do so.)

Discuss your Expert's favorite sexual positions; find out why he or she likes them. Experts may initially appear reserved and intellectual, but once they are in a relationship with you, they may surprise you with their curiosity and knowledge of sexual technique and expression.

Once you have discussed your technical expertise with your Expert mate, this deeply analytical person will begin to respect your competence in sexual matters and will place his or her trust in you. At this point your Expert can begin to relax more and start to enjoy the delights of lovemaking.

What kind of long-term relationship can you expect with an Expert?

Next to the Scholar, the Expert is the LoveType who has the most trouble finding and keeping a mate. The same weaknesses inherent in a Scholar are often present in an Expert: relying too much on imagination instead of viewing relationships realistically, being oblivious to the emotional aspects of a relationship, and lacking interest in the social graces.

On the positive side, the Experts' Judging nature gives them the ability to implement changes in their relationships and to monitor the progress they are making. Because of their desire to improve themselves, Experts can always be counted on to work on their relationships— whether by reading books, participating in individual or couples therapy, or attending relationship-enhancement workshops.

Experts are also usually excellent providers for their families: Their novel way of thinking about life and their ability to implement changes in the world often bring them career and financial rewards. Their thirst for knowledge often places them among the most highly educated of the LoveTypes, with many M.B.A.s, Ph.D.s, J.D.s, and M.D.s among their ranks.

If your Expert partner can develop some of the same skills the Scholar needs (heightened sensitivity to his or her partner's emotional concerns, increased attention to the subtleties of social interaction, and a heightened awareness of the realities of the relationship), he or she will become a steady, loyal partner who can always be counted on to find new and stimulating ways of improving the relationship.

CHAPTER FOURTEEN

The Innovator

(ENTP): EXTRAVERTED INTUITIVE THINKING PERCEIVER

If You Are an Innovator

You are the inventor, the risk taker, and the developer of new ideas and schemes that can either plummet you into bankruptcy or catapult you to riches and glory. Dozens of ideas ricochet in your head at any given moment, and you can talk circles around anyone you know. You are the epitome of creativity.

When You Are in Love

Falling in love may take a while for you because of your selective nature: You are the type of person who may pass by several "quality candidates" until you feel you have found the ideal mate. As a result, you may be single for far longer than your friends and family expected you to be.

When you are in a relationship, your cleverness and nimble tongue can both help and hinder you.

On the plus side, you are able to use your charming, talkative ways to calm your partner down when he or she is mad. You are especially skilled at helping your mate see the logical side of things, especially when the logic happens to be on your side.

On the minus side, sometimes you are so smooth at talking your way out of conflicts with your lover that you don't take the time or make the effort to work on the problem areas in your relationship. Instead of facing the real issues, you skirt them with your verbal fluency and facile mind. But the price you pay later—in broken hearts, divorce, and wasted expectations—is all too real.

Since you can easily maintain intellectual distance from the people you date, partners with a stronger Feeling side may label you as "cold," even though you are simply acting according to your natural style—close, but not too close.

Even when you find the right person, you still want to maintain your sense of uniqueness and personal space. As a result, you need a partner who will leave you alone when you desire it—a partner who has his or her own sense of self-confidence and autonomy and doesn't need to be around you twenty-four/seven.

Your Best LoveTypes
If You Are a Female Innovator

Your ideal LoveType is the General (ENTJ). The General's confident, independent nature is just what you need to maintain the flexibility and independence you crave. You will have a creative partnership with this high-achieving type of man, a union in which both of you can share your substantial intellectual resources to build a successful life together.

If You Are a Male Innovator

You will take a liking to the female Scholar (INTP) or the Wheeler-Dealer (ESTP).

The Wheeler-Dealer is an exciting choice that can definitely pay off: You will have someone who may actually be more excited about your ideas than you are; a master promoter who is a virtuoso at helping you sell your brilliant creations to the highest bidder. No matter what happens, you are in for nonstop action with the Wheeler-Dealer.

If Your Ideal Mate Is the Innovator

Where can you meet an Innovator?

Innovators are the most eclectic of the Knowledge Seekers; their spontaneous and inquisitive nature takes them almost everywhere. They are especially delighted by social events that trigger their imaginative and logical minds. You can find them at the following locales:

- Science-related organizations
- Speaking organizations such as Toastmasters and the National Speakers Association: Innovators love to talk about everything and anything
- Literature appreciation clubs where members can verbally critique the works of great and not-so-great authors
- Trade shows
- Linguistic societies
- Inventor clubs: Innovators are always inventing things
- Entrepreneur groups: Innovators often come up with pioneering business ideas
- Computer fairs
- Science and science fiction shows and fairs

In sum: Look for Innovators anywhere their powerful intellect can be stimulated and where they can exercise their considerable communication skills.

How do you get a date with an Innovator?

Get the Innovator talking about anything he or she knows. Remember: The Innovator knows plenty. Simply start asking questions about his or her many areas of expertise and listen as the verbal volcano erupts.

A typical encounter with an Innovator might go something like this:

You: "What do you think of cloning?"

Innovator: "Hmm, fascinating concept. Who would imagine that clones—that is, cells, microorganisms, or organisms all derived from a single progenitor by asexual means—could have such profound implications on humanity?"

Now that your Innovator is on a roll, let him or her keep talking. The more he or she talks as you listen attentively, the smarter (and more attractive) you will appear in the eyes of your chatter-loving Innovator.

Hot Dating Tip:
Ask the Innovator a question about what he or she likes to do on a date.

When you ask a question about dating activities, the Innovator will soon convince himself or herself that he or she came up with the idea for both of you to do whatever was just said. Just go along with the plans; you'll definitely enjoy yourself.

Now let's observe how Anna, a forty-three-year-old public speaker, used the Innovator's natural loquaciousness and curiosity to hook up with her talkative love, Matthew.

Anna had met Matthew, a forty-eight-year-old Innovator, at a local chapter of the National Speakers Association (NSA)—an organization for professional speakers. Impressed by his dark Italian looks and exquisite taste in designer clothes, Anna was further pleased when she spoke with him during breaks: He turned out to be a complete charmer, an old-school European gentleman with refined tastes and courtly respect for women.

One problem: Many of the single women at NSA were also pining after Matthew. At almost every meeting, Anna had to wait in a long line of adoring females just to get a chance to speak with him. By the time it was her turn, Matthew was already running late to his numerous business commitments as a marketing consultant to several local companies.

As a student of the LoveType system, Anna knew what to do. At the next meeting, she was the first one to Matthew's table during the break, and she immediately plopped a copy of the LoveType quiz in front of him.

She said, "I'm doing some research on personality styles and relationship satisfaction for one of my speeches. I'm wondering if you could take this test and get back to me."

Before Matthew could answer, Anna slapped her business card on the table and immediately left.

"Wait!" cried Matthew, but she was already gone.

When Anna got home, she already had three messages from Matthew asking her what the LoveType quiz was all about and wanting to know when she was free to discuss it.

They met the next night, and the next, and the next. Matthew was impressed with the concept of relationship types and wanted to incorporate the idea in his consulting work. But best of all, he decided—after he talked himself into it— that he wanted to incorporate an intelligent, vivacious, and beautiful woman like Anna into his life.

What kind of videos would an Innovator enjoy on a date?

Innovators will be pleased with the following choices:

- *Rear Window* (1954). In this Hitchcock murder mystery, Jimmy Stewart plays a photographer with a broken leg who looks out his apartment window and solves a murder. Although immobolized by a leg cast, the resourceful Stewart uses the Innovator's favorite tools—intuition and logic—to catch the murderer in a tense showdown.

- *Contact* (1997). Is there intelligent life on other planets? This is just one of the intriguing issues you and your Innovator can discuss after watching Jodie Foster's brilliant performance as a radio astronomer who detects radio signals from deep space and risks her life to discover what they mean.
- *JFK (1991)*. Your Innovator's curiosity will be piqued by the conspiracy premise of this probing film—that Lee Harvey Oswald did not act alone in the Kennedy assassination and that various parties, including individuals connected to the CIA, may have been involved. This provocative film is sure to ignite debates long after the credits roll.
- *The Game* (1997). Michael Douglas stars in this reality-bending thriller in which nothing is what it seems. In the film, a self-absorbed businessman receives a role-playing birthday gift from his brother and finds himself running for his life.

How do you win the love of an Innovator?

Keep the Innovator talking. While the Innovator is chatting, and you are presumably learning more than you ever considered possible, both of you can enjoy just about anything couples normally do: fine dining, concerts, plays, the ballet, and movies.

Another important point: When dating an Innovator, make sure you display enthusiasm and support for his or her constant stream of ideas, inventions, and schemes. Because Innovators live by their ideas, they want their partners to share in their lofty plans and alternate worlds. At the same time, you should also be aware that Innovators can, and often do, change their minds when it comes to their grand visions.

Hot Love Tip:
Don't argue with an Innovator's fanciful schemes; just appear agreeable.

When an Innovator suddenly presents you with an un-realistic scheme, your best strategy is to remain calm and display guarded support for his or her ideas. If you argue with the Innovator, you will have the opposite effect of encouraging him or her further in a possibly foolhardy plan. The Innovator's need to play devil's advocate may urge him or her to press on with an idea just to prove you wrong.

On the other hand, if you show the Innovator that you support his or her intellect and abilities, everything will usually work out just fine.

Let's observe how Regina, a thirty-three-year-old cos-tume designer, successfully dealt with her Innovator boy-friend, Bob, a sweet, baby-faced forty-five-year-old stockbroker, when he made her an offer she could defi-nitely refuse.

One night after six months of dating, Bob popped the kind of question Regina wasn't expecting and didn't want to consider.

"Honey, I'm liquidating my investments and I'm going to start a business in Cuba. I'm moving there permanently in three months. Will you come with me?"

"Excuse me?" replied a stunned Regina.

"I've done it; I've developed an incredible blueprint for a combination amusement park and gambling center that will be a winner in Cuba. With the foreign money coming in and Castro loosening his reins on Communist dogma, this proj-ect—a combination of Disney World and Las Vegas—will bring us a fortune."

Regina was about to explode when she remembered the rules of handling an Innovator: Don't argue; appear agreeable.

"Oh, that's great, honey," said Regina, as she tried to keep herself from beaning Bob with a pan. The closest she wanted to get to Cuba was watching Desi Arnaz on the "I Love Lucy" show. "You work out the details, and get back to me when you have a firm plan."

As expected, Bob reconsidered his grand idea and dropped it a few weeks later. He never mentioned the Cuba scheme again.

On the night of their engagement four months later, Bob had nothing but praise for Regina, his wife-to-be: "I need your practical mind by my side, sweetheart. You are my calming influence and guide when my plans and visions need to be brought to reality. Will you be my wife?"

"I'll think about it and get back to you," Regina replied with a smile that said YES louder than words could have.

What kind of sexual relationship can you expect with an Innovator?

Innovators can be exciting lovers, although, like most Knowledge Seekers, they may be lacking in the warmth, cuddling, and affection departments.

They make up for it, however, with their excellent sexual technique and desire to try anything that works or could theoretically work in bed. Many Innovators enjoy reading the latest sex manuals, and mentally store sexual knowledge from every lover they have had. By the time they hit their thirties and forties, Experts can be virtual encyclopedias of sexual expertise.

One woman who dated an Innovator for three years had this to say about her lover's prowess: "He was like a car wash, coming at me from all angles, techniques, and styles—he was an incredible lover."

Hot Sex Tip:
Invite your Innovator to do library research and discover new sexual techniques or positions the two of you can try.

Present this assignment like a challenge: Tell your information-hungry Innovator that you would like to create a detailed storehouse of sexual knowledge that far surpasses that of any other couple. Now, with a gleam in his or her eye, your Innovator mate will eagerly begin to search for the best sexual techniques, positions, and bedroom accessories he or she can find.

Just remember: Sex with an Innovator can be intoxicating if you are open to being with a partner who has a voracious appetite for sexual experimentation, and who will not rest until the two of you have sampled every erotic pleasure you can dream up.

What kind of long-term relationship can you expect with an Innovator?

Life with Innovators is always stimulating and thought-provoking. These ultimate orators love to engage their lovers in conversation and debate any imaginable topic. Sometimes an Innovator can talk about four different things at once (and quite well), while thinking of at least four other topics he or she could bring up at any moment.

If you are in a relationship with an Innovator, expect to be challenged; Innovators enjoy intellectual stimulation of any kind. If you don't satisfy your Innovator's quest for mental excitement, he or she may lose respect and affection for you and start looking elsewhere for an "intellectual fix."

Female Innovators sometimes have difficulty with traditional female stereotypes because they possess traits not always considered to be feminine by society. Their witty, enthusiastic, competitive, and debate-loving nature can seem intimidating to some men.

On the other hand, men who are bright enough to understand and appreciate the female Innovator's teasing, "go for broke" style will be rewarded with a wonderfully exciting mate for life.

Whatever else it might be, a relationship with an Innovator is rarely dull. As the most risk-taking LoveType, Innovators revel in living and loving on the edge.

When you are with the "anything goes" Innovator, you never know whether you'll be residing in a thirty-two-room beachfront mansion after your Innovator achieves a tremendous financial coup, or sharing a two-room apartment with another couple when the Innovator's new company goes belly-up.

In either case, be assured that your quick-witted Innovator is already planning one more scheme to put you on top in the game of love, success, and happiness. Grab on to his or her coattails, and hold on for the ride of your life.

CHAPTER FIFTEEN

The General

(ENTJ): EXTRAVERTED INTUITIVE THINKING JUDGER

If You Are a General

You were created to be a leader, and you already know this. That is why you have already skipped all the sections in this book that don't directly pertain to you. You have little patience for small talk, redundancies, or things you already know.

As the most outspoken LoveType, you are used to getting your way, yet you also like to make sure that others share in a win-win scenario. You enjoy building a team of success-minded people who share your desire for the important things in life: innovation and achievement, power and performance.

When You Are in Love

Your presence and charisma are intoxicating to the opposite sex and guarantee that your date book will always be full. Your problem is not how to attract others, but how to select the right partner who can complement what you call your "perfect empire," the ideal life you are constantly striving to create.

As a competition-loving General, you are curious to see

if you can capture the affections of a beautiful person; the challenge the unattainable hunk or hunkess presents is exciting and stimulating. Although sexual chemistry is important, in the long run you, as a General, prefer a partner who comes close to matching your level of achievement and brain power.

Once you are in a relationship, you strive to create a lifestyle that is nothing short of magnificent. One of your favorite pastimes is brainstorming with your mate—coming up with grand ideas for making the two of you richer, healthier, and ultimately, happier than ever before.

Your Best LoveTypes
If You Are a Female General

Your best match is the male General or Traditionalist (ESTJ).

With the General, you are dealing with an equal, and a game of one-upmanship may occur in which both of you continually try to top the other: intellectually, emotionally, sexually, or in any other way. Most of the time this game is stimulating and enjoyable, although sometimes the constant competitiveness may wear thin and you may need time apart.

The Traditionalist male is a fine choice if you are attracted to the type of old-fashioned male who will open doors for you and provide you with financial and emotional security. You may be tired of playing the superheroine role, and it can be nice to relax and let this "ultimate protector" take over.

Make sure, however, that your Traditionalist is not too strong on the Sensing (S) preference. If he happens to be a strong Sensor, he may not be able to keep up with your wonderfully Intuitive mind, and you may find him way too boring.

If You Are a Male General

The female Scholar (INTP), Innovator (ENTP), Traditionalist (ESTJ), or General (ENTJ) is a sound selection

for you. You may butt heads with your General counterpart, but the energy and power both of you bring to the
relationship can more than make up for the heated arguments you will often find yourself in.

If Your Ideal Mate Is the General

Where can you meet a General?

As befits their name, Generals like to be in command
and on center stage. You can usually find them in the
courtroom as attorneys, in the boardroom as executive
officers, and in health clubs playing a competitive, take-
no-prisoners game of racquetball.

They are also the high-powered leaders of political,
charitable, and religious organizations. To find Generals,
go where the power is; they are bound to be there—at
the top or striving for the top. You will find them at
fine import shops, exotic car dealers, The Single Gourmet
(where club members enjoy haute cuisine), sailing clubs,
polo clubs, and at country clubs playing tennis and golf,
or relaxing in the clubhouse or by the pool.

To meet up-and-coming Generals, you can hang out at
law school and M.B.A. libraries and courtyards. For sea-
soned Generals, you can check out your local trial lawyers' association, or you can attend one of the numerous
groups that cater to entrepreneurs.

Good cities to find Generals include Washington, D.C.,
New York, and L.A./Hollywood.

How do you get a date with a General?

Engage your General in verbal banter—titillate his or
her mind with your words. Remember: This brilliant conversationalist loves to flex his or her spicy wit in stimulating discourse with an intelligent person. If you can offer
the type of clever and mischievous word play your General loves, you will definitely be on his or her good side.

Also make sure you dress your best. Among the Knowledge Seekers, Generals are the most fastidious about the way you look. They like to think they are capable of winning the affections of someone who is a fine catch and has the looks to match.

This doesn't mean that a General will automatically cast you out if you are not the perfect hunk or hunkess. If you dress for success, and if you have the kind of personality and mind power the General can respect, he or she will pursue you over more physically attractive but empty-headed people.

~~~~~~~~~~~~~~~~~~~~~~~~~~~~

Hot Dating Tip:
Stay cool, no matter how much the General challenges
you.

~~~~~~~~~~~~~~~~~~~~~~~~~~~~

Generals, more than any other LoveType, want to test you to see if you can put up with their direct, in-your-face style. If you can take it, they will definitely take you as a potential mate.

While researching an assignment for her political science class, Ruth, an ambitious prelaw student, made a few trips to the library of the largest law school in her community. On her first visit she spotted Avi, a striking law student with thick curls of jet black hair, a strong aquiline nose, and an outrageous sense of humor and self-command.

Ruth could tell Avi was her ideal LoveType, the General, by the way he spoke and carried himself. Whenever Avi made his presence known in the library, law students would appear out of nowhere to pay their respects and share a few jokes with this "killer lawyer-to-be."

Ruth made it a point to sit next to Avi, but she didn't make eye contact or start a conversation. She knew that Generals like to believe they're the ones making the first move, so she didn't want to make a mistake by being the first to display interest.

Her restraint proved wise when Avi opened up the conversation on her third visit: "Excuse, me; I'm curious about something," Avi said in a mock serious tone. "You're not a law student or lawyer, are you? I've noticed you here before. What are you doing here?"

Ruth coolly replied: "Not only sharks swim in the ocean. The rest of us need to use the library once in a while, too."

"So you think lawyers are sharks, do you?" replied Avi with growing amusement. This girl has a spicy wit, thought Avi. And she wasn't bad-looking, with her short blond hair and tailored suit.

"No, not all of them," replied Ruth with a half smile. "Only the ones with J.D. after their name."

"I see," said Avi. He couldn't help himself from grinning. She was his type, exactly: a self-assured and witty lady. "Well, would you let this shark buy you a drink?"

"Why not? Even sharks have to drink," replied Ruth smartly.

As Ruth had expected, Avi was attracted by her cocksure attitude and sarcastic touch, and he pursued her like mad. After resisting him in the beginning (she knew that Generals loved the chase), she gradually became more affectionate and finally said yes when Avi asked her to move in ten months later.

Another point: If you discuss the LoveType system with a General, make sure you know enough to answer questions about its research base and credibility. (Check out the "Notes on Sources" section at the end of the book.) Generals are typically the most skeptical of the LoveTypes and will want you to prove the scientific merit of the system.

If a General asks you a question about the LoveType system that you can't answer, don't get upset or flustered. Simply say, "I don't know the answer off the top of my head, but I'll get back to you about it."

Of course, you'd like to know the General's home phone so you can call him or her with the requisite information. Chances are, the General's curiosity will get the best of him or her, and you will have your darling's number. Now all you have to do is call the General for a date, but you'd better have the information you promised, because the General will definitely ask you for it.

What kind of videos would a General enjoy on a date?

Consider these intelligent, well-acted films:

- *Wall Street* (1987). This is, perhaps, the favorite General film of all time. Michael Douglas won an Academy Award for Best Actor as the impossibly powerful and crooked stock market manipulator who is eventually brought down by his own "greed is good" credo.
- *Reversal of Fortune* (1990). Generals will appreciate this cleverly structured film based on the notorious Claus von Bülow case. Paced with an offbeat sense of humor and a cool, penetrating performance by the Academy Award–winning Jeremy Irons as the man accused of attempting to murder his socialite wife, this film impresses and entertains.
- *Patton* (1970). The ultimate warrior is depicted in this ambitious and thoroughly satisfying biopic about Patton, the fearless American general who defeated Rommel in North Africa during War World II. George C. Scott won an Academy Award for Best Actor in the title role.
- *The Devil's Advocate* (1997). Your General will get a kick out of Al Pacino's modern take on Satan—as the flamboyantly seductive managing partner of a prestigious New York law firm who attempts to corrupt a young hotshot southern lawyer (played by Keanu Reeves).

How do you win the love of a General?

Above all, don't be intimidated by this person's formidable presence. With the General's keen mind, wonderful communication skills, and desire to "mix it up" verbally, this powerful personality can be threatening to most people.

Yet beneath the General's surface arrogance lies a loyal heart that can take care of you no matter what happens. If you have the patience and courage to look for his or her "soft spot," the General will reward you with a loyalty and understanding few people experience.

One caveat: The General will make you pay a price for admission into his or her gentle core. The price is that you must become accustomed to, and even enjoy, what appears to be conflict.

From the Generals' perspective, however, it isn't conflict, but merely the stimulating exchange of ideas in friendly discussion. Generals are attracted to people who engage them in logical debate and who have a razor-sharp wit.

Hot Love Tip:
Find the absurdity in the moment.

Generals like to point out the flaws and inconsistencies they observe in life and other people. You will score points with your General by engaging his or her barbed sense of humor as both of you skewer the pompous, the silly, and the hypocritical.

Although certain LoveTypes may find the General's approach to humor to be sarcastic and even cruel, for the General, it's natural to deflate those people who need to be deflated. It's all part of the General's tough-minded and competitive view of life: "If it doesn't kill you, it makes you stronger."

What kind of sexual relationship can you expect with a General?

A General can be hot and steamy, but not necessarily affectionate and cuddly. If a General cuddles with you, it's usually because your lover wants to stay warm—not because he or she wants to be "lovey-dovey."

The hard-driving General may seem a bit domineering in sex at times (most Generals prefer to be on top), but he or she can also provide a lot of excitement other Love-Types aren't able to generate. Some Generals like to play the opposite role in bed—totally submissive—because this is the one chance he or she has to relax and allow someone else to take charge.

〰〰〰〰〰〰〰〰〰〰〰

Hot Sex Tip:
Play the "Can You Top This?" game.

〰〰〰〰〰〰〰〰〰〰〰

Remember that Generals love to compete in everything, including sex. To spice up your sex life, try this tactic:

Tell your General that you would like to try a fun sex game for a thirty-day period. The rules: Each of you will come up with one new sexual technique, strategy, or position per week. Then, during the week, each person will have a chance to introduce his or her new strategy. Afterward both partners will rate how much they liked each sexual technique and then add up their ratings to determine the total satisfaction points for each technique.

At the end of the month the person whose strategies earned the most sex-satisfaction points is declared the winner, and the loser must do the bidding of the winner—sexually and otherwise—for one week.

Martha, a twenty-nine-year-old real estate agent, tried the "Can You Top This?" game with her fiancé, Roger, a thirty-

one-year-old real estate broker, and she was definitely im-pressed with the results.

At first Martha thought that Roger would selfishly rate his techniques as 100s and hers as 0s so that he would come out on top at the end of the thirty days. But Roger was actually quite fair and logical in rating her choices. He even gave her a 98 on the night she suggested a very interesting combination of leather and lace as a prelude to nonstop love-making that had the neighbors wondering.

When the thirty days were over, Martha was declared the winner, but in reality, both were winners. Their sex life was better than ever, and Roger seemed to get a kick out of his scanty attire and role as hand and foot servant to Martha for a week. Martha didn't seem to mind either; she was having too much fun.

Just remember: When it comes to sex, Generals usually bring a high level of technical expertise. They know how to please themselves and their partner because they have tried and evaluated many different sexual styles, and they know what works by trial and error. If you are will-ing to let the General teach you his or her tricks, you may be in for some erotic surprises.

What kind of long-term relationship can you expect with a General?

According to my research, their partners consider the General (both male and female) to be the most domi-neering of all the LoveTypes. The General's favorite re-sponse to an argument is: "If I want your opinion, I'll argue it out of you."

Although Generals can appear domineering, they would not agree with that observation. They would most likely say that yes, they do speak their mind, and yes, they are confident in their views, and yes, if you think that is intimidating, then "eat my shorts!"

In reality, Generals respect those who stand up to them, although few people do. To have a successful relationship with a General, you need to participate in the debate and argument he or she relishes. You also need to show this confident warrior that you understand and respect his or her unique take on the world. Always remember that the General sees life from a confrontational point of view, high need to control, and desire to engage others in controversial debate in the name of learning.

Male Generals make competent and commanding spouses and leaders of their families. Their argumentative and frequently impatient nature can become tiring at times, but their wit, intelligence, and drive to succeed more than make up for any personality flaws.

Female Generals bring their own special brand of femininity to a relationship—one that includes a dash of arrogance, independence, and enjoyment of confrontation. Only self-assured men who respect confident, independent women need apply.

In the long run, a high-achieving General can be one of the most exciting, stimulating, and upwardly mobile LoveTypes you can ever meet. If you give a General the opportunity, he or she can be a driven, success-minded spouse who will do anything possible to raise your marriage and family life to ever-increasing heights of success and prestige.

THE SECURITY SEEKERS

The Caretaker
(ISFJ): INTROVERTED SENSING FEELING JUDGER

The Administrator
(ISTJ): INTROVERTED SENSING THINKING JUDGER

The Dutiful Host
(ESFJ): EXTRAVERTED SENSING FEELING JUDGER

The Traditionalist
(ESTJ): EXTRAVERTED SENSING THINKING JUDGER

Mom, apple pie, and Chevrolet: All the good, old-fashioned sentiments and values are surely the province of that most traditional of groups—the Security Seekers, those who share the letters S and J (Sensing Judger).

If you are one of the Security Seeker LoveTypes, you are someone who values tradition, loyalty, security, and structure in your relationships.

But Will This Lead to Marriage?

As one of the Security Seekers, you may be asking yourself this question as you learn the LoveType system: Will this lead to marriage?

Yes, if that is what you want. As a Security Seeker, marriage—or at least a secure, long-term, live-in relationship—is usually foremost on your mind. You may be interested to know that, compared to the other three LoveTemperament groups, the Security Seekers get married the earliest in life, remarry the quickest if divorced or widowed, and tend to stay married the longest.

You, the Security Seeker, will gain the most from the LoveType system by turning it into your very own marriage plan. You will be able to create an outline of the type of marriage partner (and mother or father for your children) you desire, and then lay out the practical steps needed to win his or her hand in marriage.

With the LoveType system as your family planner, you will start doing the right things to achieve your goals. You will be on your way to having that dream house with the white picket fence, taking delight in the children and dogs that play in your front yard, and celebrating many years of marital bliss.

CHAPTER SIXTEEN

The Caretaker

(ISFJ): INTROVERTED SENSING FEELING JUDGER

If You Are a Caretaker

You are the closest thing there is to a perfect parent. Taking care of others in your sweet, giving, and gentle way is perhaps your greatest desire and is what keeps the rest of us feeling safe, warm, and cared for.

Starting and building a family are top priorities for you, often more important than a career or other interests. Although you may prosper in your chosen profession, very little in life gives you more pleasure than taking care of your children and the husband or wife you hold dear.

When You Are in Love

As a Caretaker, you believe love represents safety, responsibility, commitment, and ultimately, marriage and children. While those words may scare off certain Love-Types, for you, these words perfectly describe what you want from a romantic relationship.

Like other Security Seekers, you are cautious at the beginning of a relationship. You want to make sure your prospective mate will be a loyal, stable, and conscientious spouse and parent.

Once you make up your mind about your mate, you tend to sustain an unwavering devotion toward him or her. Even if the relationship is lousy, you may be reluctant to give it up because of the tremendous importance you place on your commitment to your partner. Sometimes you suffer because you obey the dictates of tradition and stay in a terrible relationship, even though your common sense screams at you to leave.

Your Best LoveTypes
If You Are a Female Caretaker

You can build a long-lasting relationship with the male Caretaker (ISFJ), Administrator (ISTJ), or Dutiful Host (ESFJ).

A male Caretaker will be a gentle partner who can match your caring ways and your desire to "mother" the important people in your life, especially your family. And a Dutiful Host will help you tremendously by taking over all the entertaining chores that you tend to avoid. His Extraverted nature will be a nice complement to your more withdrawn personality.

If You Are a Male Caretaker

You can prosper with a female Caretaker or Administrator (ISTJ). The duty-bound Administrator's calm, steady presence will help you maintain the right perspective when things get hectic and you are in danger of losing your cool.

If Your Ideal Mate is the Caretaker

Where can you meet a Caretaker?

Try some of these favorite Caretaker places, events, and activities:

- Cooking classes
- Craft shops and fairs
- Picnics and housewarmings sponsored by community groups
- Wedding receptions
- Horse shows and associations
- Children's stores, activities, and entertainment centers: Caretakers may be single moms or dads, or they may enjoy spending time with kids they know and love
- PTA (Parent-Teacher Association) meetings: Single parents often attend
- Yarn and needlepoint classes
- Pet clubs and shows
- Coed softball teams
- Bowling leagues
- County fairs
- Playgrounds
- Church picnics and socials
- Sierra Singles: a national organization that sponsors outdoor events for singles

Add to this list by thinking of all the places, activities, and organizations that cater to the needs of family, children, pets, the community, and preserving the traditions of a healthy and happy home.

How do you get a date with a Caretaker?

Walk a dog—borrow one if you need to—and show a lot of affection toward it in the Caretaker's presence. (Hopefully you really like the dog anyway.) Caretaker favorites include cute and cuddly dogs such as the golden retriever and cocker spaniel.

If dogs aren't your style, try spending time with a cute cat as your Caretaker looks on. If you don't have a pet and can't borrow one, compliment the Caretaker's four-legged friend or the furry creature you see in the area.

Betty, a divorced mother of four, met her great love, Hans, by appealing to his Caretaker personality and strong feeling for animals.

"Hans lived a block away from me, yet I couldn't figure out a way to get personal with him. He was a warm, loving man who always had a kind word for everyone, but he kept pretty much to himself.

"One thing I noticed about him: He had a great heart for animals. Hans would often bring stray or injured animals into his home to nurse them back to health.

"Based on my observations and conversations with people who knew him, I determined Hans was a Caretaker. He liked to spend most of his time alone (Introvert), was handy and practical around the house (Sensor), was very caring toward people and animals (Feeler), and was extremely organized and structured (Judger). He was my kind of guy, all right.

"Knowing how much Hans loved dogs, I decided to display my own interest in the canine world. I proceeded to walk my frisky Saint Bernard, Brandy, past Hans's house at the same time he walked his dog. Like clockwork, Hans always walked his golden retriever, Jeremy, every morning at 7:00 A.M.

"When Hans saw me with Brandy, he immediately said hello and we started a conversation about dogs. We enjoyed each other's company so much that we started walking our dogs together on a daily basis.

"Then, on our first official date, we brought Brandy and Jeremy with us, and we had dinner at a restaurant that allowed pets. We had a blast, and we're still going strong. Not only are we crazy about each other, but Brandy and Jeremy seem to be quite fond of each other as well. This is working out just fine."

Aside from animals, Caretakers also love anything to do with kids. Ask your Caretaker friend to join you at the toy store and help you buy gifts for your nieces or nephews. Or if you don't have any tiny relatives, buy toys for a boy or girl in your neighborhood.

Remember: Caretakers value caring and considerate people, and you will stand out in their eyes if you show them you are concerned about the "little people" in life: kids, animals, and the sick and elderly.

Hot Dating Tip:
Be nice and gentle; and get an introduction.

Smile a lot. Caretakers respond well to warm and caring people. But take it slow. Like other Security Seekers, Caretakers value security and tradition—they tend to scare fairly easily when strangers approach them without the proper introduction. If you can have someone introduce you (preferably a close friend or relative of the Caretaker), you will be off to a much better start.

What kind of videos would a Caretaker enjoy on a date?
Here are some films that will appeal to your Caretaker:

- *Sleepless in Seattle* (1993). Caretakers will be charmed by this contemporary film about a widowed dad (Tom Hanks) and an engaged woman (Meg Ryan) who are irresistibly drawn to each other after Hanks's character reluctantly goes on a national call-in show. Hanks and Ryan have excellent chemistry together in this lovable throwback to romantic comedies of yesteryear.
- *Ordinary People* (1980). The hankies will come out in this emotionally draining, but never false, drama about a family coping with their oldest son's death. Wonderful star turns by Mary Tyler Moore, among others.
- *Dances With Wolves* (1990). Although this Oscar-

winning Kevin Costner movie appeals to many Love-Types, Caretakers will be touched by the protagonist's search for his true home among the Sioux Indians.

- *Absolute Power* (1997). Caretakers will root for the wily burglar who quietly loves his daughter but ends up placing her life (as well as his own) in danger when he witnesses a murder at the White House.

How do you win the love of a Caretaker?

Show caring, tenderness, and respect. Although you may normally do this anyway, Caretakers are especially impressed by a nice, sensitive person. Bring out your gentle, family perspective when you are going out with a Caretaker. Talk about the kid brother or eccentric uncle you adore; mention how much you value your friends.

You can also woo your Caretaker with old-fashioned courtship: giving and receiving flowers and candy, taking long walks along the beach, and cuddling by the fireplace. The sentimental Caretaker will be yours if you can add a touch of romance and tenderness on your dates.

As Security Seekers, Caretakers are cautious and slow to make relationship decisions, but once they make them, they tend to stick with their choices. If you take your time, and treat the Caretaker like the perfect lady or gentleman she or he is, you can look forward to a long-lasting and caring relationship.

What kind of sexual relationship can you expect with a Caretaker?

As lovers, Caretakers are gentle and tender; not too experimental, but willing to please their mate. Unmarried female Caretakers may experience embarrassment or guilt during sex, especially if they come from traditional or conservative family backgrounds.

An important point: Don't rush the sexual part of the relationship when you are romancing a Caretaker. Caretakers are interested in getting to know you first—and determining where you fit in their long-term marriage plans—before they become amorous with you.

In fact, many Caretakers want the relationship to be close to marriage before they even think of sleeping with you. A Caretaker may want to meet your parents (and have you meet his or her parents) before he or she makes a sexual commitment to you.

Of course, some Caretakers (as can be said of any Love-Type) are exceptions to the general rule and can surprise you with their passion. For the most part, however, Caretakers want to take their time and become acquainted with you as a potential marriage partner—and make sure you are *the* one—before they have sex with you.

In the beginning of their relationship, twenty-eight-year-old Paul was tempted to take his girlfriend, Heather—a twenty-six-year-old beauty—to bed as soon as possible.

Handsome with curly blond hair, Paul was considered quite a lady-killer. As an up-and-coming fast-food entrepreneur with five franchises, he had plenty of offers from beautiful women. Paul knew Heather would surely succumb to his charms if he wanted her to.

But there was something different about Heather. It wasn't just her beauty—Paul had dated plenty of attractive women before—it was her personality. She was loving, gentle, and kind, and his ideal LoveType: the Caretaker.

Although he had to fight himself, Paul knew he needed to go slow with Heather when it came to sex. Consequently he and Heather agreed to a hands-off policy: no heavy petting or intercourse before marriage. Heather wanted to remain a virgin until marriage, and Paul respected her wishes.

After nine months of courtship, Paul proposed and Heather accepted. They are now expecting twins and enjoy a wonderful married life with exciting and mutually satisfying sex. Paul and Heather are glad they waited to have sex until they were joined for life.

What kind of long-term relationship can you expect with a Caretaker?

Caretakers are the epitome of the "perfect mother"; regardless of their gender, they take a special interest in catering to the needs of their spouse and children.

Because they have such a strong sense of duty and responsibility, Caretakers will often stay in a marriage that's gone astray. Once they commit to someone, Caretakers feel that leaving is the ultimate act of betrayal—something they could never do.

For those couples who desire it, the male Caretaker can make the perfect stay-at-home husband. He is the type of man who loves children and is as handy with a diaper as he is with a wrench.

Holly, a thirty-five-year-old pharmaceuticals saleswoman, couldn't believe her good fortune when she met David, a thirty-seven-year-old elementary schoolteacher and Caretaker, at a PTA function. As a hard-driving businesswoman and mother of two, Holly rarely had time for non-work-related activities, but she made an exception for PTA meetings. Not only did her daughters benefit from her attendance, but Holly also hoped to meet that rare breed, a Caretaker male.

Before meeting some of the dedicated male teachers at the PTA meetings, Holly had often wondered if such caring, loving, and family-devoted men actually existed. When she met David, a teacher and handsome widower, all her doubts were laid to rest.

David was a man who loved children and family life more than many mothers Holly had known. After his wife's death, he single-handedly raised four boys while maintaining his backbreaking commitment to school and volunteer activities.

During a break at a PTA meeting, Holly and David began talking about how alike their children were and were soon discussing how alike they were. They began their relationship with a cup of coffee and sanctified it three months later with a touching wedding ceremony that combined elements of Judaism and Christianity, representing their respective religions.

Now David is content to stay home and raise their two children as a house dad, while Holly pursues her career and continues to make more money for their family every year. They are delighted with their arrangement: Holly has found the career fulfillment she needs, and David loves raising a second family. And they both are delighted to have a loving, stable marriage and family life.

If you are fortunate enough to marry the right Caretaker, you will have a devoted and loving spouse for life. You will bond with someone who can be the ideal father or mother for your children, a tireless helpmate who will help transform your house into a home and your life into a joy-filled existence.

CHAPTER SEVENTEEN

The Administrator

(ISTJ): INTROVERTED SENSING THINKING JUDGER

If You Are an Administrator

You are the glue that holds the pieces of civilization together. Your trademarks are duty, discipline, responsibility, and organization. Without your dedicated and loyal efforts, many of the powerful businesses, institutions, and organizations that exist today would crumble to the ground.

When You Are in Love

As the most practical of the LoveTypes, you are not overly impressed with extravagant romantic gestures. Nor do you need constant stimulation and excitement on your dates. You are perfectly content with a home-cooked meal, an interesting video, and the company of your sweetheart.

You also tend to hold traditional values when it comes to male-female roles. Even if you are an enlightened feminist, deep down you may still believe that a husband should be a good provider for his family and that a wife should be able to run a neat and organized household.

Your strong need for security keeps you from taking

too many risks in initiating a relationship. You usually develop romantic relationships with people you have known for a long time: co-workers, friends of the family, or classmates. Because you are the ultimate "nest builder," you want to be absolutely sure your prospective mate is the type of person who will make an excellent caretaker and/or provider before you allow him or her to get close to you.

The qualities you expect from your mate are the things you value most: loyalty, security, and responsibility. You are not particularly impressed with your mate's potential or grandiose ideas; you want to find out what your mate can bring to a serious relationship right now—not five years from now. When it comes to relationships, your favorite motto is "What you see is what you get."

Your Best LoveTypes
If You Are a Female Administrator

You will be pleased with the male Administrator, the high-achieving Traditionalist (ESTJ), or the emotionally supportive Caretaker (ISFJ).

If You Are a Male Administrator

You will thrive with the female Administrator or Caretaker (ISFJ). The female Administrator's organized and duty-conscious nature may perfectly complement your desire for a traditional home. And the Caretaker—with her affectionate ways and "perfect mother" personality—may be just what you need to build the supportive and loving family life you want.

How Tony Found His Perfect Pie Baker

Tony, an Administrator, was widowed after ten years of marriage. Although only forty, he had just about given up on meeting another woman like his wonderful wife, Elaine—

the perfect friend and lover. Tony felt lonely, but he wasn't sure what to do about it.

After reading a manual on the LoveType system, Tony tried to put the program to work at his local singles club, but had a terrible time. He kept mixing up the LoveType questions and couldn't accurately LoveType the women he was talking to. Fortunately, Tony's bachelor brother, George, was experienced with the LoveType system and offered to help LoveType the women Tony was interested in.

With George's help, Tony was able to meet Leonora, a gentle, thirty-three-year-old preschool teacher who just happened to be his ideal LoveType—the Caretaker.

On their first date, Leonora baked Tony a delicious cherry pie. On their second, she helped clean his attic. Laboring together, they tossed out the junk Tony had accumulated over the last ten years. In return, Tony cut her lawn and waxed her car.

Soon they moved in together and started fixing up their new home. They decided to spend the rest of their lives together as companions and lovers—two Security Seekers building a stable and loving home.

If Your Ideal Mate Is the Administrator

Where can you meet an Administrator?

Administrators are quiet, unassuming people. In fact, they are often so quiet you may not even notice their presence. Because they usually like to stay in the background, the best place to find them is in a far-off corner, by themselves.

Look for the one person at a restaurant or nightclub who doesn't say much, the loner who hugs the dark corners of the room. Another sure bet: Look for the loyal person who is always caught holding a friend's drink or purse. The loyal, stable Administrator can always be counted on to help a friend and take responsibility when no one else wants it.

Administrators are usually attracted to any activity, organization, or place that smacks of duty, hard work, and responsibility. Check out community groups that focus on keeping the neighborhood safe and clean, charity fund-raisers such as car washes and bake sales, PTA (Parent-Teacher Association) meetings, patriotic organizations such as Daughters of the American Revolution, farming-related groups, government agencies, community coed sports teams, bowling leagues, chambers of commerce, the League of Women Voters, and military special events such as air shows and parades. (Administrators often make excellent military personnel because they are loyal, hardworking, and good at following orders.)

How do you get a date with an Administrator?

Have a need they can fill, or work with them toward a worthy cause, and Administrators will have a legitimate reason to become acquainted with you.

Go to the library and chat with the cute library clerk as he or she checks out your books. Visit a PTA meeting—there are usually several single parents—and ask the Administrators questions about their favorite topic: child rearing.

Pitch in at a charity car wash, volunteer for a political campaign, or participate in a neighborhood watch group, and meet plenty of hardworking, duty-conscious Administrators in the process.

Ask an Administrator about a practical matter—how to organize or clean a house, fix something, take care of children, or fill out paperwork—and chances are, this highly responsible individual will be willing to help. Once an Administrator agrees to help you, you will have the perfect opening to spend more time with him or her in a platonic, and eventually romantic, way.

What kind of videos would an Administrator enjoy on a date?

Your Administrator will be pleased with the following movies:

- *My Fair Lady* (1964). Administrators will enjoy watching Oscar-winning Rex Harrison as Henry Higgins. In this comedy tinged with social criticism, the strong and loyal Henry Higgins educates and falls in love with Eliza Doolittle, a former flower seller whom he passes off as a duchess.
- *Forrest Gump* (1994). Tom Hanks is perfect as the sweet-tempered, loyal, practical, and patriotic man-child who fits in perfectly anywhere he goes, performing his duty and doing what is right.
- *Dirty Harry* (1971). Stimulate your Administrator's secretly held desires for action and excitement (and retribution against the bad guys of society) in this classic "by any force necessary" cop thriller, starring Clint Eastwood.
- *Misery* (1990). When the decent qualities of an Administrator (duty, loyalty, sacrifice) are corrupted by madness, the result is this frightfully entertaining Stephen King film about a famous author who suffers an accident and becomes the prisoner of his number one fan. Kathy Bates won the Academy Award for Best Actress for her haunting portrayal of the obsessed fan.

How do you win the love of an Administrator?

In the beginning of your courtship, spend time with your Administrator at quiet places where you can be together without having to say much. Excellent choices include a park, moonlit beach, or movie theater. You can also try a quiet date at home: Feast on Mexican food and cuddle up in front of the VCR as you and your partner enjoy a video that emphasizes old-fashioned relationships.

Remember this important point: As soon as you start dating an Administrator, he or she is probably already considering what kind of husband/wife and father/mother you would make. The Administrator's desire to have a successful marriage and family life is an important part of the person's character and will shape his or her dating decisions. To win the Administrator's heart, he or she needs to believe that you will be a good provider and/or homemaker for the family you build together.

~~~~~~~~~~~~~~~~~~~~~~~~~

Hot Love Tip Number One:
Accent the traditional side of your personality, as follows:

~~~~~~~~~~~~~~~~~~~~~~~~~

Men: Talk about your career aspirations, how much money you want to make for your family, and what type of home you would like to own someday. Express your desire to be a first-rate father and role model for your children. Share your interest in building a secure and prosperous family life.

Women: Emphasize your domestic skills such as cooking, cleaning, and sewing. If you don't have any domestic skills, now is a good time to read a book or take a class. Talk about your desire for children, security, and tradition.

Caveat: The Administrator man is not for every woman, but his stable, conventional sense of home and family life can be very appealing if you are prepared to offer him some of the old-fashioned values he desires.

~~~~~~~~~~~~~~~~~~~~~~~~~

Hot Love Tip Number Two:
Cater to the Administrator's craving for timeliness, cleanliness, and organization.

~~~~~~~~~~~~~~~~~~~~~~~~~

Always be on time when you are dating an Administrator; to him or her, wasting time is as bad as wasting food. You can also make a good impression on the cleanliness-loving Administrator by being freshly scrubbed and smelling nice when you are around him or her. Also, make sure your home is clean and organized if you plan to invite your Administrator over.

~~~~~~~~~~~~~~~~~~~~~~~~~

Hot Love Tip Number Three:
Offer to clean your Administrator's home or ask
him or her to help clean your place.

~~~~~~~~~~~~~~~~~~~~~~~~~

If you really want to capture your Administrator's heart, appeal to his or her strong desire for order and cleanliness by offering to help clean your lover's place. As an alternative, you can ask the Administrator to help clean and organize your home. If he or she agrees, have some snacks and music ready and make it a pleasurable day.

Warning: Make sure your house is already fairly tidy (Perceivers take heed) when the Administrator arrives with mop, duster, and vacuum cleaner in hand. Even though your Administrator is coming to help spruce up your house, he or she doesn't want to see a *real* mess, at least from the Administrator's exacting perspective.

Once your house is up to par (from your viewpoint, not the Administrator's), invite him or her over. Let your Administrator loose as he or she uses incredible organization and cleaning skills to bring your house up to a housekeeping standard unattainable by the average person.

What kind of sexual relationship can you expect with an Administrator?

A typical sexual relationship with an Administrator will evolve slowly. Don't expect instant fireworks with an Administrator; he or she is the most cautious and conservative of all the LoveTypes when it comes to sex and romance.

Hot Sex Tip:
Introduce a new sexual position or technique in casual conversation first.

During your chat, stress how the new technique will enhance your relationship and bring you closer. Then remain quiet and allow the Administrator to process what you have just said. As an Introverted Thinker, your Administrator needs time to mull over new information before he or she acts on it.

Hot Sex Tip:
Make a Sex Schedule.

To help your Administrator feel secure about the new sexual activity, create a schedule for your lovemaking. Although certain LoveTypes may find such a structured approach to be a turn-off, many Administrators will feel comfortable and secure if they know exactly what (and when) to expect from their mate in the sex department.

Gladys, a thirty-eight-year-old day-care center owner, had a high sex drive and loved to try new things in bed. But her new boyfriend, Peter, a forty-year-old accountant and Administrator, was not the kind of uninhibited lover she had enjoyed in the past. He was, however, the perfect gentleman for her—respectful, intelligent, and a reliable provider. But he needed some bedroom lessons.

Knowing how much Peter valued logic and predictability, Gladys created a written schedule for their lovemaking, and designated one night per week as their "experimental time." During this time slot, each of them would write down their sexual fantasies and then try them out.

Although skeptical that such a contrived structure would work, Gladys was pleasantly surprised: Peter loved it. With a firm schedule and a list of the things he could try out in bed, he felt more comfortable and secure. And best of all, he felt more free to experiment and please both himself and Gladys.

What kind of long-term relationship can you expect with an Administrator?

Administrators believe in the "shoulds" and "oughts" of marriage: "Men and women should get married" and "Once married, husband and wife ought to stay married till death do they part."

According to research findings, Administrators tend to stay married the second longest, next to the Dutiful Host (ESFJ). Their structured, logical, and practical nature make them excellent candidates for the type of long-term, realistic commitment that marriage requires.

Once married to you, the Administrator will be like the Rock of Gibraltar, perennially supportive and solid. If you are interested in marriage the old-fashioned way—with conventional male and female roles—the Administrator can be your perfect choice.

CHAPTER EIGHTEEN

The Dutiful Host

(ESFJ): EXTRAVERTED SENSING FEELING JUDGER

If You Are a Dutiful Host

On those stressful days, we can thank God for that most wonderful of creatures—the one who nurtures and helps us unwind—the Dutiful Host. You are the gracious one, the master of ceremonies who delights in serving others and making sure they are well fed and well cared for.

When it comes to hosting any social occasion—a birthday party, an anniversary celebration, or a bar mitzvah—you can barely contain your excitement. As soon as the date for such an event is announced, your mind is already going a hundred miles a minute—planning, organizing, and thinking about how much fun you and your guests are going to have.

When You Are in Love

As a master host, one of your fondest dreams is making your wedding a smashing success: a cornucopia of people, food, music, and laughter—a lasting testament to your lifelong partnership.

Before you get to the wedding stage, you will probably experience a rousing and sometimes conflict-ridden relationship with your beloved. You are the type of person who is not shy about expressing your emotions in a relationship. Whether you are singing the praises of love or barking out resentments and criticisms, rest assured, your partner will know you are there.

Because of your invested feelings and sense of loyalty, you are reluctant to end long-term relationships that have gone sour. Fortunately, as you gain wisdom and experience, you will find the strength to say no to an incompatible partner and focus your abundant energies on nurturing a healthy and mutually rewarding relationship.

Your Best LoveTypes
If You Are a Female Dutiful Host

You will be well matched with the male Dutiful Host or Traditionalist (ESTJ). The Dutiful Host is your party-organizing counterpart, while the Traditionalist is a conventional male who will lend your household a strong, masculine presence.

If You Are a Male Dutiful Host

Your ideal LoveType is the female Dutiful Host or the equally affectionate, though more of a homebody, Caretaker (ISFJ).

The Caretaker is the ideal "mother" and your quieter half. While you like to take care of people in a fun and social way, she enjoys nurturing her family with a quiet, gentle touch—making sure your shirts are pressed and checking on the kids to see if their needs are being met.

If Your Ideal LoveType Is the Dutiful Host

Where can you meet a Dutiful Host?

The Dutiful Host is a natural at taking care of others. You will usually find them working as schoolteachers, nurses, receptionists, and administrators, as well as hosts and hostesses in restaurants, nightclubs, and other locales.

An excellent way to become acquainted with a Dutiful Host is to work or volunteer at the sites where they are helping others: hospitals, schools, mental health clinics, and churches.

You can also meet Dutiful Hosts wherever fine food, drink, and people are present: restaurants, The Single Gourmet (a club where singles meet at restaurants for dining and socializing), wine-tasting clubs, rotating singles dinner parties (where singles move from table to table during different courses), cooking classes, bar mitzvahs, and weddings.

Whenever one of Michael's friends or relatives invited him to a wedding, he made sure to attend. Not only did Michael, a thirty-two-year-old graphic artist, enjoy the jovial atmosphere, he also knew that he would have an excellent chance of meeting his ideal LoveType—the Dutiful Host.

At the last wedding Michael went to, he was introduced to Rachel, a striking twenty-three-year-old redheaded flight attendant who was one of the bridesmaids. Michael started a conversation with Rachel by remarking: "I'm sure you make a wonderful stewardess. You're doing a terrific job tonight taking care of the bride and making sure everyone's having a great time."

Rachel was delighted Michael noticed her efforts, which confirmed Michael's suspicion that Rachel was a Dutiful Host. Rachel was most impressed, however, with Michael's hospitable nature and desire to help out at the wedding reception. (He was serving drinks.)

Soon they were dancing, and guess what? The way things are going, their friends wouldn't be surprised if Rachel and Michael were the next ones marching down the aisle.

How do you get a date with a Dutiful Host?
Tell the Dutiful Host you are throwing a party and ask if he or she has any ideas on how to organize an outra-

geous bash that will keep people talking for months. Be prepared: The talkative Dutiful Host will not only offer you great party ideas, but he or she may even volunteer to be your master of ceremonies.

Another approach is to ask the Dutiful Host for advice or help on anything related to your home, family life, or kids. The Dutiful Host enjoys bringing good cheer, comfort, and relaxation into every home, and he or she will be content to help you, too.

Remember: The Dutiful Host is always volunteering for something, and your cause—developing a loving, lasting relationship—is as worthy as any other.

Tracy, a forty-two-year-old nurse, was crazy about Harry, a fifty-one-year-old Las Vegas singer and Dutiful Host. She had caught Harry's show seven times, and on each occasion had fallen more in love with his beautiful voice, charismatic personality, and sincere, helping nature.

She realized that Harry was the right man for her, but she also knew at least three other women who were after him, too. To beat out her competition, Tracy devised a clever plan that drew on her knowledge of the Dutiful Host's personality and his penchant for volunteering for good causes.

To implement her plan, she called the pastor at her home church and asked if he could use a singer like Harry for an upcoming fund-raiser. The pastor said yes, and Tracy excitedly called Harry's manager and arranged a meeting with Harry.

Harry, all six feet four inches and dazzling brown eyes, agreed not only to sing for the church fund-raiser, but also to contact other local entertainers who would sing as well.

During the course of their conversations and lunches, Tracy and Harry began a friendship that blossomed into lifelong romance.

What kind of videos would a Dutiful Host enjoy on a date?

You can get warm and cozy with a Dutiful Host by renting the following:

- *Like Water for Chocolate* (1992). In this tale of forbidden love, a young Mexican woman is prohibited from marrying her beloved but continues to express her passion for him (even though he is now married to her sister) by preparing magical meals that speak louder than words.
- *Emma* (1996). Dutiful Hosts will have fun watching the good-natured but meddling Emma—the mischievous young lady who is constantly trying to play matchmaker with her friends, with amusingly tangled results.
- *Grapes of Wrath* (1940). Dutiful Hosts will appreciate how a tough, determined mother tries to hold her family together in this classic, Academy Award–winning film about poor Oklahoman farmers who lose everything in the dust bowl and move to California to find a better life.
- *Moonstruck* (1987). An irresistibly wacky tale of romance and family, starring Cher (Best Actress, Academy Awards) as the Italian-American woman who is swept off her feet by her fiancé's brother.

How do you win the love of a Dutiful Host?

You can make a good impression on your Dutiful Host by inviting him or her to any restaurant, dance hall, or comedy club where people are enjoying themselves.

Or, better yet, take your Dutiful Host to action-packed parties and observe this social maestro in his or her natural habitat. Tell your Dutiful Host that you like to have a good time, and he or she will make sure you have one.

If you are responsible for planning the date, make sure you give your structure-loving Dutiful Host plenty of notice about the kind of experience you have in store for him or her: Tell your Dutiful Host where you are going, what to wear, what time to be ready, and so forth.

Once you have created a timetable for the date, don't deviate from it. Your Dutiful Host will love you all the more if he or she believes you can be trusted to follow through on your word and stick to your plans.

~~~~~~~~~~~~~~~~~~~~~~~~~~~~~~~~

Hot Love Tip:
On dates, steer the conversation to down-to-earth topics.

~~~~~~~~~~~~~~~~~~~~~~~~~~~~~~~~

Talk about practical and concrete topics such as the latest trends in fashion, finances, or entertainment. Dutiful Hosts, being the practical sort, like to talk about the news of the day. They aren't particularly philosophical, so you should avoid topics that require them to focus too much on intangibles.

~~~~~~~~~~~~~~~~~~~~~~~~~~~~~~~~

Hot Love Tip:
Before inviting a Dutiful Host over, make sure your home is clean and orderly.

~~~~~~~~~~~~~~~~~~~~~~~~~~~~~~~~

Before your Dutiful Host comes over, make a special effort to create an aesthetically pleasing environment: Make sure your house is tidy and clean, and fill the house with a pleasant-smelling air freshener or incense. Your Dutiful Host will definitely appreciate your preparation.

Maria, a thirty-six-year-old preschool teacher, did everything right when she started dating her Dutiful Host, Giovanni—a thirty-nine-year-old hairdresser.

Knowing the Dutiful Host's penchant for an aesthetically pleasing environment, Maria made sure her house was spotless whenever Giovanni came over for dinner. To set the mood, Maria would play soothing New Age music and carefully arrange the candelabra and jasmine-scented candles.

Everything about her place whispered order, beauty, and cleanliness.

Although conversant in many topics, Maria focused on practical subjects and talked about politics, finances, and fashion—subjects she knew stimulated Giovanni's Dutiful Host mind and that interested her as well.

As they spent more time together, Maria and Giovanni began building the foundation for a long-term relationship, one based on the Dutiful Host values of home, marriage, and family.

What kind of sexual relationship can you expect with a Dutiful Host?

Dutiful Hosts are verbally affectionate and love to talk in bed. Like all Stability Seekers, Dutiful Hosts are turned on by the five senses: They enjoy fine music, sumptuous food, pleasant scents (such as your perfume or cologne), the touch of their lover's skin, and a neat and clean home.

〜〜〜〜〜〜〜〜〜〜〜〜

Hot Sex Tip:
Make sex a complete sensory experience.

〜〜〜〜〜〜〜〜〜〜〜〜

Cater to your Dutiful Host's five senses. Begin by feeding him or her with your hands (chocolate is a favorite) as sexy music plays in a candlelit room filled with soothing scents. Take turns feeding each other as both of you savor the romantic ambiance.

Next, join your lover in a warm bubble bath filled with rose petals as you take turns scrubbing each other's back with a soft washcloth or firm bath brush. As you scrub and caress, tell your partner what part of his or her body you find especially sexy and irresistible. Tell him or her why you find it so arousing.

Now continue to look, listen, touch, taste, and smell, until both of you are filled with erotic fever.

Remember: The Dutiful Host is the most passionate of the Security Seekers and will make a wonderful erotic partner if you can create the necessary conditions to release his or her sexual desire.

What kind of long-term relationship can you expect with a Dutiful Host?

Research indicates that female Dutiful Hosts are highly rated as desirable partners: They are known to be caring, sociable, and loyal—qualities that many men desire.

Moreover, Dutiful Hosts, whether male or female, tend to have the longest marriages among the sixteen Love-Types. Yet despite their tendency toward lengthy marriages, female Dutiful Hosts (with male Dutiful Hosts not far behind) also rank high in *total number* of marriages.

The fact that Dutiful Hosts, on average, marry more times than other LoveTypes doesn't necessarily indicate they are bad marriage risks. The statistics can be explained by the fact that Dutiful Hosts typically marry young, and—if they divorce or are widowed—tend to remarry quickly. Dutiful Hosts are eager to remarry (and tend to stay remarried for quite a while) because they believe in the institution of marriage as well as the security, structure, and tradition it provides.

Their marriage pattern contrasts with that of other LoveTypes, such as the Social Philosopher (ENFP), who delay getting married (if they marry at all), and rarely remarry if divorced.

As believers in marriage, both male and female Dutiful Hosts make loyal and devoted husbands and wives—the type of mates who will do anything to keep their marriage and family strong. If you want someone who is a genius at entertaining and taking care of you and your family—someone who capably and warmly fulfills all the functions of a spouse and parent—then the Dutiful Host may be the perfect partner for you.

CHAPTER NINETEEN

The Traditionalist

(ESTJ): EXTRAVERTED SENSING THINKING JUDGER

If You Are a Traditionalist

You are a towering presence in the lives of many and are respected—near and far—for your ability to speak your mind without fretting too much about public opinion.

Of course, the same people who respect you may also be intimidated because they don't see your softer side: the part of you that is fiercely loyal to those who deserve it, and that will do anything to support and protect your friends, your family, and your country.

When You Are in Love

For you, love is a commitment that is taken very seriously. Once you fully commit yourself to a partner, you are determined to stay with that person "till death do you part."

You are also the type of person who likes to take charge of everything in your life, including your relationships. You are probably the one (unless you hook up with an equally strong-willed General or Traditionalist) who plans most of the dates and who eventually ends up running the household once you are married.

Because you tend to be straightforward—and some might even say rude—you may unintentionally hurt your partner's feelings. This is especially the case if your mate is one of the Feeling LoveTypes.

You, however, don't see your blunt tongue as a handicap to the relationship, nor do you intend to harm your partner. You simply see yourself as dealing with your mate in a realistic way that cuts through all the BS and allows both of you to go about the business of creating a successful relationship, marriage, and family life.

Your Best LoveTypes
If You Are a Female Traditionalist

You can meet men anywhere, anytime, but too many of them seem intimidated by your directness and straightforward attitude. No matter where you go, you keep running into skittish men who are not able to see past your "tough guy" exterior to find the pussycat inside.

Your wisest choice is the male Traditionalist or the General (ENTJ), provided he is not too strong on the Intuitive preference. If your General is a strong Intuitive, he may eventually become annoyed with your practical ways, and you may end up tearing your hair out over his wild plans and schemes.

On the upside, when you pair up with either of these men, you will probably enjoy a high standard of living. Both you and your partner are likely to be well educated, professional, and on the fast track toward career success. On the downside, you may experience some competitiveness, or one-upmanship, with your partner: A mental tug of war may ensue to determine which of you is the most successful or competent.

If You Are a Male Traditionalist

The female Administrator (ISTJ), Dutiful Host (ESFJ), Traditionalist, Expert (INTJ), and General (ENTJ) are your best LoveTypes. The first three will help build the "nest" or family life you desire based on traditional male-female roles and lifelong values of security, loyalty, and dependability. The latter two will offer you intellectual depth and a deeper appreciation for the finer things in life.

If you choose the General or Expert, try to find one who is not an exceptionally strong Intuitive. If your mate scores high on Intuition, she may overwhelm you with her fantastical ideas and endless dreaming, and you may wonder why she doesn't come down to earth.

If Your Ideal Mate Is the Traditionalist

Where can you meet a Traditionalist?

Traditionalists can be found at bars, nightclubs, sporting events, sports bars, shooting ranges, car shows, health clubs, and at outdoor activities (and as members of related clubs and organizations) such as hiking, skiing, camping, river rafting, and mountain climbing. To meet hardy, nature-loving Traditionalists, check out groups such as Sierra Singles—a national organization with local chapters for singles who enjoy the outdoors.

You will also encounter Traditionalists in positions of leadership at business organizations such as the Rotary Club, Lions Club, and Kiwanis Club. They often get involved with the chamber of commerce (you can meet them at the mixers), bowling clubs, beer-drinking associations, and business networking events.

Lauren, a thirty-nine-year-old travel agent, wanted to make business contacts as well as a romantic connection with her ideal LoveType: the Traditionalist male. To achieve both objectives, she joined her local chamber of commerce and, before long, spotted her ideal man in Jerry—a great-looking forty-five-year-old Irish redhead and luxury car dealer.

Over the course of several meetings, Lauren made small

talk with Jerry and discovered through their conversations that Jerry was both practical (S for Sensing) and logical (T for Thinking).

His talkative nature gave away the fact that he was an Extravert (E). And Lauren observed that Jerry was always in the same seat at exactly 7:00 P.M., come rain or shine; thus, she assumed, he was a structured Judger (J). Putting all four preferences together, Lauren determined that Jerry was indeed the Traditionalist (ESTJ), her perfect match.

After learning that Jerry was part of a governmental affairs task force that she was interested in, Lauren volunteered her time and was soon working closely with Jerry. They became friends, and before long their friendship blossomed into romance and then marriage.

Now Lauren and Jerry are expecting a girl, and they wonder if she will be a Traditionalist like her daddy and a skilled LoveTyper like her mommy.

How do you get a date with a Traditionalist?

Ask your Traditionalist for advice or protection. Tell your Traditionalist about a problem you have with your nosy neighbor or the dog that just won't stop barking. Ask him or her to help you with your business problem, home-decorating issue, or child-rearing dilemma.

As long as your request is within his or her sphere of influence, the Traditionalist will be glad to help and show you how powerful and successful he or she really is. Chances are, this person does indeed have a lot of influence and can be a comforting shoulder to lean on.

Once the Traditionalist offers advice or support, you can get to know him or her on a more personal basis and begin to develop a romantic relationship.

Hot Dating Tip:
Keep the conversation practical.

Traditionalists are practical communicators. They say what they mean and expect you to do the same. If you are a strong Intuitive, try to keep your musings and ramblings to a minimum. Traditionalists don't have a lot of patience with esoteric theories or fantastic visions; they want to talk about things they can see, touch, taste, smell, or hear—right now.

Talk about the Traditionalist's job (some people accuse them of being workaholics because they spend so much time at work) or about his or her interests in sports, entertainment, business, politics, religion, or family life. Traditionalists love to talk and will warm up to you as long as the conversation touches on the realities of daily living. (Save the talk about curing emotional or spiritual hunger for other LoveTypes.)

What kind of videos would a Traditionalist enjoy on a date?
Check out these quality movies:

- *Top Gun* (1986). Traditionalists will enjoy this Tom Cruise action-adventure film about the trials of skilled U.S. Navy pilots at an aviator training school.
- *Air Force One* (1997). Harrison Ford is the perfect patriot and steadfast American president who refuses to compromise even when Russian terrorists take over Air Force One and hold his family hostage. A fast-paced ride that refuses to compromise on its entertainment value.
- *Braveheart* (1995). Traditionalists will root for Mel Gibson as the courageous Scotsman who uses his sword and unyielding will to rally his people to freedom in this panoramic, beautifully detailed thirteenth-century saga and Academy Award winner (Best Picture and Best Director).
- *The Godfather* trilogy: original, *Part II*, and *Part III* (1972, 1974, 1990). The ultimate Traditionalist movies when it comes to the old-fashioned values of tradition, loyalty, and family. The ultimate gangster

movies when it comes to the dynamics of power, corruption, and bloodshed. And the ultimate winners when it comes to the Academy Awards.

How do you win the love of a Traditionalist?

Let the Traditionalist decide where to go and what to do on dates; then join him or her for the ride. Always remember that Traditionalists like to plan and take charge of just about everything, including their dating lives.

You don't have to be a doormat, however. Traditionalists appreciate mates who can stand up for themselves and speak their mind. Traditionalists, however, usually want the last word and can be very persuasive (and quite charming if they want to be). This is especially the case with the Traditionalist male—the most macho of the male LoveTypes.

~~~~~~~~~~~~~~~~~~~~~~~~~~~~

Hot Love Tip:
Save the "touchy-feely" attitude for another LoveType.

~~~~~~~~~~~~~~~~~~~~~~~~~~~~

Although Traditionalists are caring in their own way, they are not what you would call "touchy-feely" or overly sentimental. Their sympathy and compassion extend to what they believe is right, loyal, logical, and true.

Don't try to win a Traditionalist's affection by whispering sweet nothings—"Baby sweetums, you're my cuddly poochie"—into his or her ears. If you act gushy and sentimental, you're likely to get the opposite response in return.

A better approach is to display your interest, affection, and loyalty in logical and concrete ways.

Buy groceries for your Traditionalist and prepare him or her a nice meal. Go dining and carousing with your Traditionalist and his or her many friends as you enjoy stimulating discourse about the important news and gossip of the day. Spend time with your Traditionalist's family and listen attentively as your partner's dear old dad (or mom) recounts family stories (the ones he or she has already told a hundred times, but who's counting?) about loyalty, togetherness, and devotion.

In short, give Traditionalists what they want most: a socially fluent partner who will share day-to-day activities and who will talk about the real-world issues that affect them and the friends and family they love.

If you can accept their no-nonsense talk and straightforward attitude, you may be surprised to find yourself falling for the protective, "tough guy" image that Traditionalists (both male and female) project.

Her friends warned thirty-six-year-old Donna, a human resources manager, about Vince, a forty-two-year-old venture capitalist and "manly" man.

"Sexist, macho, and domineering" were the kinder words Donna's friends used to describe Vince. At first glance they appeared to be right. Vince had a tough—sometimes coarse— exterior honed by growing up in a tough neighborhood and clawing his way to the top of the business world.

To top it off, Vince had some typically macho habits and interests. He liked chewing tobacco, drinking beer, and watching football every Sunday.

"But I knew there was something more complex about him than his surface personality or what some of my friends (who are still single, by the way) thought of him," recalls Donna. "I was curious to find out what Vince was really like, so I had a mutual business friend introduce us. Upon meeting Vince, I talked with him at some length, and I determined he was the Traditionalist.

"Based on his LoveType, I knew he valued marriage and family, and that he would make a devoted husband and father with the right woman. After going out with him, he validated my conclusions and turned out to be a terrific guy.

"Now Vince is building us a beautiful home in the country,

and we're going to create a life together. This is the man of my dreams."

What kind of sexual relationship can you expect with a Traditionalist?

Some female Traditionalists, especially if they are paired with male Traditionalists, enjoy sex the traditional way with the man on top and in charge. Although they may act like lions in the corporate world, when it comes to their love lives, these Traditionalist women are perfectly happy with conventional sex roles: as soft, yielding, and nurturing partners.

Other female Traditionalists prefer to assert their natural leadership tendencies and play the dominant role during sex. They like to be in charge of everything, and sex is no exception.

Male Traditionalists tend to be very attentive toward their mates and will go out of their way to please them sexually. In fact, most male Traditionalists take enormous pride in their ability to provide for their women in every way—as breadwinners, fathers, husbands, and sexual partners.

Because they can be so performance-oriented and driven to please their mates, some Traditionalist men may not be able to fully relax and enjoy the type of deeply satisfying sex that is found in a give-and-take partnership. If that is the case with your Traditionalist man, try the following Hot Sex Tip:

~~~~~~~~~~~~~~~~~~~~~~~~~~~~

Hot Sex Tip:
Teach your traditionalist man how to relax and enjoy a true sexual partnership.

~~~~~~~~~~~~~~~~~~~~~~~~~~~~

As a prelude to sex, set aside thirty minutes for touching, caressing, and massaging each other with oil or lotion. Take turns giving and receiving sensual pleasure.

One rule: The person who is receiving the sensual attention must lie quietly without speaking or moving. The only time he or she will speak is to give directions: telling the other person how he or she likes to be touched— faster, slower, harder, softer, and so forth.

This is the crucial part. No matter how much your talkative Traditionalist tries to distract you with extraneous conversation, insist that he lie quietly and fully experience what you are doing to him. When it's his turn to touch and caress you, you will do the same.

This exercise will help your Traditionalist man experience lovemaking as a two-way communication that involves both giving and receiving. With practice, this exercise can significantly improve your sex life and bring the two of you closer.

What kind of long-term relationship can you expect with a Traditionalist?

Perhaps no other LoveType personifies the conventions of marriage as well as the Traditionalist. Skilled communicators about practical day-to-day matters and advocates of security and structure, the Traditionalist is the perfect choice for an "old-fashioned" marriage, in which duty, loyalty, and responsibility mean everything, in which husband and wife are joined together to protect and love each other, their children, their God, and their country.

Traditionalist males tend to be the most conventionally masculine—some might say macho—of the LoveTypes. Moreover, some Traditionalist males may act in ways considered to be crude, abrasive, or sexist by the rest of society.

But despite their potential flaws, Traditionalist males are usually highly rated as spouses—their wives are typically quite satisfied with their assertive, decisive, and protective Traditionalist husbands.

Although some women desire a more flexible and sensitive male, many women still yearn to be protected and cared for by a powerful man. These women want an "old-fashioned" Traditionalist man who will treat them like a lady: a man who will open car doors for them, bring them flowers, and give them the support and security they desire.

While male Traditionalists are usually accepted by mainstream society, women Traditionalists tend to swim against society's current more than any other LoveType because of their supposedly "masculine" ways. Because they are comfortable taking charge and being decisive and opinionated, some men (and women) may unfairly describe them as being "tough," "bitchy," or "butch."

Men, however, who are intelligent enough to respect the female Traditionalist's strengths and abilities will find themselves with an excellent life partner. In fact, research indicates that those who marry female Traditionalists have one of the highest ratings of marital satisfaction.

Other research findings indicate that male Traditionalists tend to marry the second most often (next to the wedding-happy female Craftsperson: ISTP), while female Traditionalists also tend to have a greater than average number of marriages.

Traditionalists have a high remarriage rate because they love being married; in fact, they can't stand *not* being married. Consequently, they marry early in life, and if they are widowed or divorced, they jump right back into the security and stability marriage offers them. Many Traditionalists would probably agree with Zsa Zsa Gabor (a Traditionalist herself) when she said: "I am not promiscuous; I marry all of my lovers."

When you prove your loyalty to them, you will find that Traditionalists are fiercely loyal in return and will stand by you in the face of the worst catastrophes. If you want an old-fashioned man who can provide you with financial security and a strong shoulder to lean on, or if you desire a woman who can take charge of your household and be an equal partner, the Traditionalist may be your perfect mate.

THE EXCITEMENT SEEKERS

The Gentle Artist
(ISFP): INTROVERTED SENSING FEELING PERCEIVER

The Craftsperson
(ISTP): INTROVERTED SENSING THINKING PERCEIVER

The Performer
(ESFP): EXTRAVERTED SENSING FEELING PERCEIVER

The Promoter
(ESTP): EXTRAVERTED SENSING THINKING PERCEIVER

Lights, camera—action!

Welcome to the fast-moving, spontaneous world of the Excitement Seekers. If you are one of these four Love-Types—if you share the letters S and P (Sensing Perceiver)—you are someone who values fun, excitement, adventure, and spontaneity in every aspect of your life, and especially in your relationships.

I'm Weary of Theories: How Do I Use the System to Meet My Honey?

As an Excitement Seeker, you were probably bored silly in school when your teachers droned on about theories. Face it: You want to learn something you can apply to your life *right now*. You don't have patience for theories or explanations if you're not sure they will make your life better in the present.

So you may not get too excited about the theories and

foundations of the LoveType system, or even about the research that substantiates it. But you will be excited by the practical LoveType tips explained in the next four chapters—special tactics that will help you find your soul mate, starting today.

It's time now to meet you and your partners in the excitement-seeking world. Ideally I would include lights, music, and interactive displays in this section to make your reading more appealing to your action-loving ways. Who knows? Maybe I'll write such a book in the future, just for you.

Meanwhile, start your engines, Excitement Seekers. The fun is about to begin.

CHAPTER TWENTY

The Gentle Artist

(ISFP): INTROVERTED SENSING FEELING PERCEIVER

If You Are a Gentle Artist

You are nature's balm: the soothing presence who calms us when we are stressed, who reminds us of the delightful spontaneity of childhood, and who shows us how to appreciate nature and all living things. But as easily as you bring happiness to others, you can bring sadness to yourself when you fail to see your strengths, focusing only on your limitations.

When You Are in Love

Love for you is an all-or-nothing experience. Because you tend to shut out the rest of the world so you can experience love more fully, you can be vulnerable to the whims of your beloved.

To please your partner and sustain the relationship, you may make life-altering changes such as moving, switching careers, or saying good-bye to your old friends. If your partner happens to be insensitive or demanding, you may suffer under his or her stinging rebukes and orders because you will do anything for love.

Devotion and flexibility are two of the most important

qualities you, as a Gentle Artist, bring to a relationship. Your genuine and almost innocent expression of love can make the right person (and yourself as well) very happy. But you must make sure you have chosen a compatible mate, because once you fall in love, you are riding a roller coaster that is almost impossible to stop.

Your Best LoveTypes
If You Are a Female Gentle Artist

You will do well with the male Gentle Artist, Craftsperson (ISTP), Performer (ESFP), or Wheeler-Dealer (ESTP).

The Performer's and Wheeler-Dealer's outgoing personalities will help coax you out of your sometimes too cozy shell. They will offer you the entertainment and spice you need to balance your low-profile personality.

If You Are a Male Gentle Artist (a very rare LoveType: less than 2 percent of the population)

You are well paired with your counterpart, the female Gentle Artist. She is a top choice for you because she matches your Introverted emotional nature and is likely to share your deep feelings about children, animals, and the outdoors.

If Your Ideal Mate Is the Gentle Artist

Where can you meet a Gentle Artist?

You can meet the Gentle Artist everywhere art, fashion, nature, children, and animals are present or discussed. Look for Gentle Artists at these places:

- Children's stores, activities, or entertainment centers
- Gardening clubs
- Pet shops, clubs, or shows
- Animal rights organizations (Gentle Artists are often quiet activists for animal rights) such as the Humane

Society, People for the Ethical Treatment of Animals, and Friends of Animals
- Flower shops
- Horse shows or associations
- Craft shops and fairs
- PTA (Parent-Teacher Association) meetings
- Environmental protection groups
- Sierra Singles: a national organization that offers outdoor activities and events for singles
- Fine department stores, especially at cosmetics or jewelry departments (Gentle Artists are either browsing or working behind the counter)
- Art stores and schools

Also, keep your eyes open for classes or workshops that cover any of the preceding subjects. If you know where to go, you may become a success story like Jasmine, a thirty-year-old interior designer who met her Renaissance man in one of the Gentle Artist's favorite hangouts: art class.

At thirty, Jasmine was tired of superficial guys and dead-end dates. As a new LoveType student, she decided to find her ideal guy, the Gentle Artist, by enrolling in an art class at her local community college.

As the students introduced themselves, she became fixated on George, a thirty-two-year-old sculptor who was branching out into painting. His eyes radiated kindness, and his jolly face was sweeter than molasses.

When George talked about himself, Jasmine recognized all the signs of a true Gentle Artist (ISFP): He was soft-spoken (Introverted), appeared practical and concrete in his speech (Sensor), talked with great emotion (Feeler), and jumped from one subject to the other (Perceiver). He was her man, all right.

After one particularly stimulating class, Jasmine struck up a conversation with George about famous impressionist artists. Realizing how much they enjoyed each other's company,

Jasmine and George began dating. They are still together after eighteen months, and both agree this is the best relationship they have ever been in.

How do you get a date with a Gentle Artist?

Talk softly and slowly so you don't scare this gentle, skittish creature. Remember: Gentle Artists are like beautiful deer who are ultrasensitive to their environment.

~~~~~~~~~~~~~~~~~~~~~~~~~~~~~

Hot Dating Tip:
Talk about the Gentle Artist's passions: children, the arts, animals, and nature.

~~~~~~~~~~~~~~~~~~~~~~~~~~~~~

Gentle Artists are interested in their immediate environment and what people are doing to make the world a more humane place for all living creatures. If you can talk honestly and compassionately about the subjects your Gentle Artist cares about most, you are sure to make a fine impression on him or her.

For six months, Sam—a supremely shy twenty-eight-year-old shipping and receiving clerk—had been eager to ask Caroline, a ravishing twenty-two-year-old receptionist, out on a date. Based on his brief conversations with co-workers who knew her, he had determined Caroline was his ideal Love-Type: the Gentle Artist.

The problem: They worked in different departments, and he couldn't think of any way to get to know her. Plus, being as beautiful as she was, he was sure she probably had a boyfriend. But he also knew that if he didn't at least try to meet this mesmerizing woman, he would have to give up women altogether and join a monastery. He had to make a connection with her.

Fortunately, an opportunity arose when Caroline's mixed-breed cat had kittens, and Caroline wanted to give a few away. Sam knew he could make a good impression on an animal-loving Gentle Artist such as Caroline if he adopted one of her kittens. He actually liked cats anyway and wouldn't mind having one in his apartment (especially if Caroline was around, too).

Although he was terribly nervous, Sam summoned up his courage and approached Caroline just as she was getting off for lunch. He said: "Excuse, me. Caroline, right? I'm Sam, from shipping and receiving. I understand you're giving away some kittens. I would be interested in meeting you, I mean, the kittens."

"Sure, here's my number," replied Caroline. "Call me to set up a time to see them. I'm sure you'll love them."

Two days later, Sam saw the kittens (he took the one called Tiger) and had lunch with Caroline afterward. During lunch, Sam and Caroline discovered they had a lot in common and enjoyed each other's company tremendously. They agreed to spend more time together, and during the next several weeks enjoyed quiet dates at the park or at Sam's place snacking, watching TV, and cuddling with each other and their cats.

Now Sam happily spends his nights with Caroline and the rest of their cat family. Luckily, Tiger, their frisky cat, doesn't seem to mind sleeping on the floor, next to the bed Sam and Caroline share as husband and wife.

What kind of videos would a Gentle Artist enjoy on a date?

You will find favor with your date by renting the following:

- *Beauty and the Beast* (1991). In this animation favorite, your Gentle Artist will find everything he or she wants in a film: witty dialogue, a captivating musical score, and a heart-melting story about a beauty who ultimately discovers her prince.
- *Roxanne* (1987). Gentle Artists will enjoy this tender remaking of the classic *Cyrano de Bergerac*. In this story of mistaken identity and unrequited love, Steve

Martin is a small-town fireman with an impossibly long nose who secretly woos a gorgeous astronomer.

- *Babe* (1994). An unlikely hero, Babe the piglet steals the show in this sweetly eccentric film about talking animals and Babe's quest to become a champion sheepdog. Touching, funny, and perfect for the Gentle Artist.
- *Shine* (1996). The true story of an Australian piano prodigy who suffers a nervous breakdown and, years later, is rescued from despair by a compassionate woman. Geoffrey Rush won an Academy Award for Best Actor in this heart-wrenching story of a mentally ill piano genius.

How do you win the love of a Gentle Artist?

First of all, don't offer too many compliments at once. Although your Gentle Artist may be worthy of praise in many areas, you may lose his or her respect if you allow your tongue to wag too much.

Gentle Artists will be suspicious of your flattering words because they often don't appreciate their own talents and attributes. If they don't believe they are worthy of admiration, they may think you are insincere for flattering them. It's a smart idea, therefore, to wait until future dates before you let your Gentle Artist know how highly you think of him or her.

―――――――――――――

Hot Love Tip Number One:
Set up dates that include animals or nature.

―――――――――――――

With your animal-loving Gentle Artist by your side, visit the zoo or circus, browse at pet shops or the pound, or take a dog to the park. You can also suggest outdoor activities such as hiking, camping in the woods, swimming in natural hot springs, or bathing in the ocean.

**Hot Love Tip Number Two:
Give simple, heartfelt gifts.**

The Gentle Artist loves giving and receiving gifts that have an artistic and sentimental quality to them. Try giving your Gentle Artist simple, creative gifts such as handmade cards, fruit baskets, special desserts, and embroidered pillows. Gentle Artists are more impressed by your genuine appreciation and concern than by the monetary amount of the gift.

Gabriela, a thirty-six-year-old graphic designer, used the Hot Love Tips to capture the affections of her Gentle Artist: Seth, a forty-one-year-old fashion consultant.

Seth, a second-generation Russian-American Jew, had a lot going for him. Sensational looking with an athlete's build and a cute ponytail, he was also very successful in the fashion business and earned a considerable income. He was also a decent man who contributed large amounts to charities, always anonymously.

Because of Seth's Gentle Artist nature and the heart-crushing divorce he had just experienced, Gabriela realized she had to tread carefully with him. Gabriela also knew Seth was very desirable to women: Both single and married women were constantly throwing themselves at Seth and showering him with lavish praise. Of course, as a Gentle Artist, Seth was wary of their compliments because he tended to downplay his successes.

Applying her knowledge of the LoveType system, Gabriela was kind and affectionate toward Seth, but she refrained from giving him compliments. Instead, she demonstrated her affection by bringing him homemade gifts such as paper cutouts with cute animal designs on them, and spending time with him on the beach—walking, holding hands, and talking.

"I love you," Seth gushed on one of their beach dates. "You're unlike any other woman I've ever known. You're a simple, down-to-earth lady, and you enjoy the things I'm passionate about. You're the best."

Gabriela was overjoyed by Seth's affection and felt equally tender toward him. She was looking forward to a wonderful relationship with her dream man.

What kind of sexual relationship can you expect with a Gentle Artist?

Gentle Artists are gentle, caring, and shyly adventuresome lovers. Their desire to please can sometimes make female Gentle Artists vulnerable to sexual predators who take advantage of their sweet, giving disposition. Fortunately, as they grow older and more experienced, female Gentle Artists become better at separating the sharks from the genuinely decent men.

When it comes to romance, Gentle Artists are soft and expert lovers because they are attuned to sensory pleasures and deep feeling. They may not say much when they hold and caress you, but you can feel their loving, soulful energy radiating from their eyes.

Hot Sex Tip:
Go slow with a Gentle Artist.

Gentle Artists can be somewhat shy when first making love to you. But if you are gentle and loving, your Gentle Artist will relax and allow his or her spontaneous nature to take over.

When you take your time with a Gentle Artist, you will undoubtedly find yourself with a wonderfully active and creative sexual creature in bed—a loving whirlwind who will astound you with his or her eager lovemaking.

What kind of long-term relationship can you expect with a Gentle Artist?

Gentle Artists, according to my research, are one of the LoveTypes most resistant to marriage; a significant percentage of them never marry. This is because Gentle Artists love to explore the unknown. When they stay in a relationship too long, Gentle Artists may feel they know their partner too well, and the all-important mystery is gone. Consequently some Gentle Artists prefer to remain single rather than be tied down to one partner and what they fear might be a lifetime of boring predictability.

When Gentle Artists do marry, however, they make tender, devoted, and loving spouses. They don't need to control things, and are instead interested in seeing that everyone lives peacefully and harmoniously.

Caveat: If you are involved in a long-term relationship with a Gentle Artist, make sure you don't take his or her sweet, soft-spoken ways for granted. Although your Gentle Artist may not complain out loud, he or she may be holding a lot of resentment inside. Ultimately a Gentle Artist may express his or her anger by leaving you without warning and without looking back.

On the other hand, if you treat a Gentle Artist with kindness and compassion, he or she will be by your side for life and offer you his or her contagious belief in the power of love.

CHAPTER TWENTY-ONE

The Craftsperson

(ISTP): INTROVERTED SENSING THINKING PERCEIVER

If You Are a Craftsperson

You thrive on raw action—a thrill-seeking type of life that revolves around your hobbies and interests, whether racing, skydiving, motorcycle riding, surfing, or anything that feeds your lust for excitement. Independence is your middle name, and seeking adventure is your game.

When it comes to trying new experiences, you are utterly fearless. You are always willing to undergo a fresh adventure whenever the urge strikes you. Of course, you often end up on your own because others may be afraid to join you on your daredevil stunts.

When You Are in Love

Your romantic relationships typically involve your favorite activities and hobbies—hiking, camping, surfing, auto repair, carpentry, landscaping, origami, pottery, painting—or anything else that stimulates your hands-on desire to be spontaneous or creative.

You especially enjoy arts and crafts because you like to work with your hands, and you get a kick out of seeing the tangible results of your creativity. You also love to hear words of praise from your mate when he or she genuinely admires a product you have painstakingly crafted.

As a Craftsperson, you want your partner to respect your need for autonomy—the desire for personal space and independence. Of course, if you spend too much time on your own, your mate may feel that you don't love him or her anymore. When this occurs, you may need to relax some of your personal-space requirements so you can have a closer relationship with your partner.

Your Best LoveTypes
If You Are a Female Craftsperson

Your smartest selections are the male Craftsperson, the Wheeler-Dealer (ESTP), or your exact opposite, the Growth Teacher (ENFJ).

If you choose the Craftsperson, you will be with a person who understands and accepts your need for space and autonomy, your desire for excitement and stimulation, and your passion for the hobbies that define your life.

If you select the Wheeler-Dealer, you will be with the type of mate who can "light your fire" with fun, spontaneity, and excitement. Of course, when paired with this social dynamo, you will sometimes wish he would slow down and relax with you once in a while.

When you are with the Growth Teacher, his creative and imaginative personality will surprise, intrigue, and challenge you. With him as your guide, your world will be much more than the hobbies you love. Even though you may not understand all of what he says, a lot of it will make sense and will leave you feeling better about yourself and the world around you.

If You Are a Male Craftsperson

Your best mate is the female Craftsperson, Gentle Artist (ISFP), or Growth Teacher (ENFJ). Both the Craftsperson and Gentle Artist are quiet, practical, and spontaneous women who will complement your carefree, independent nature.

The female Growth Teacher can also be a compatible match for you. She is the type of lady who will bring you out of your shell and inspire you with her warmth.

How Shirley Expanded Her Horizons and Met Malik

Shirley was a successful twenty-eight-year-old African-American ceramic artist who was unsuccessful in love. As a fun-loving Craftsperson, she could always have a blast no matter who she went out with, but she often felt she was wasting her time by going out with guys who wanted sex and nothing else.

After learning about the LoveType system, she began to look for a man who could offer her more, a gentleman who could help her grow. Her perfect candidate: the Growth Teacher. To find her Growth Teacher and develop her inner self at the same time, Shirley started going to psychology and spirituality seminars.

At first Shirley felt awkward—she had never attended any self-help events before—and she had assumed the people at these events would be too brainy and stuffy for her. Contrary to her expectations, she discovered that many of the self-growth folks were actually a lot of fun and surprisingly down-to-earth.

During a workshop on inner healing, she met Malik, a handsome thirty-five-year-old African-American psychologist and Growth Teacher. It turned out he was fascinated by her artistic talents, and she was equally inspired by his focus on inner strength and his volunteer work in the inner city.

Together they explored many aspects of life they had never experienced before. Shirley and Malik are now dating each other exclusively, much to the amazement of their friends who never expected that such different people would make a great match.

If Your Ideal Mate Is the Craftsperson

Where can you meet a Craftsperson?

Since Craftspersons enjoy hands-on hobbies, you can meet them at some of the following locations and activities:

- Car shows
- Needlepoint and crocheting classes, as well as hobby or craft fairs, are excellent locales for meeting the female Craftsperson
- State or County fairs
- Farming-related organizations
- Sierra Singles: a nationwide singles group that organizes activities and excursions in nature
- Automotive repair and auto-part shops are great for meeting the male Craftsperson
- Auto racing
- Hardware stores
- Gun shops and clubs
- Motorcycle clubs
- Hiking clubs

Or you can participate in any action-focused, down-to-earth activity or hobby. Consider any group or club activities that offer excitement and physical stimulation, or those that require artistic hand-eye coordination such as pottery or macramé.

Elizabeth—a forty-five-year-old personnel manager and Growth Teacher (ENFJ)—had to change some of her expectations in order to meet her ideal Craftsperson in Bill, a fifty-year-old forklift operator.

"In the past I never considered construction workers as potential mates, but I remembered what I had learned from the LoveType system—that a Craftsperson, a man who works with his hands, is one of my ideal matches.

"When my brother introduced me to Max, I still had some

stereotypes about dating a "hardhat." In the back of my mind I still thought blue-collar workers were mainly uneducated, sexist, and crude.

"Of course, some are, but as I got to know Max, I was impressed with his quiet, intelligent ways. He was also polite and funny—a real gentleman. I found myself attracted to him!

"Well, I gave him my number, and we started going out. Before long, I fell in love with Max's practical and spontaneous manner. We made love the first time in his '67 Camaro convertible, and it was incredible.

"As of last month, we've been happily married for three years, and we're more in love every day."

How do you get a date with a Craftsperson?

Show interest in the Craftsperson's favorite hobby or activity, whether it's auto repair, sculpting, watercolors, or needlework. Ask the Craftsperson to show you his or her handiwork.

Share in the Craftsperson's passion and joy as he or she wields creative magic over the simplest of things and teaches you the subtle elements of his or her craft. Once you display eagerness to enter the Craftsperson's world, he or she will want to get to know you better—in a romantic way.

Another good idea: Invite Craftspersons to do fun things that revolve around one of their favorite tools: their hands. Have a fingerpainting contest; give your Craftsperson a shiatsu (fingertip pressure) massage and ask him or her to reciprocate; join your Craftsperson for a piano duet at a nearby hotel lounge.

Remember: Craftspersons prefer dates that promise action, spontaneity, and hands-on fun. At the same time, they detest the conventional movie-and-dinner date, as well as dates filled with too much idle chitchat.

What kind of videos would a Craftsperson enjoy on a date?

Your action-loving Craftsperson will get excited with these adrenaline-pumping films:

- The *Mad Max* trilogy: *Mad Max* (1979), *Mad Max 2 (The Road Warrior)* (1981), and *Mad Max Beyond Thunderdome* (1985). Your Craftsperson will root for Mel Gibson as the loner—a fearless hero born for adventure in these futuristic thrillers.
- *Speed* (1994). In this fireball thriller, in which a madman has wired a bus so that it will explode if it goes under 50 mph, man of few words Keanu Reeves and courageous Sandra Bullock team up to save the day.
- *Die Hard* (1988). Atop an L.A. high-rise, trouble looms. Terrorists have taken hostages, and only one man can stop them. Bruce Willis is the wisecracking detective who uses his hands-on intelligence to outwit the bad guys and save the day in this thrilling action movie.
- *The Fugitive* (1993). An unjustly accused man on the run (Harrison Ford), a relentless U.S. Marshal (Tommy Lee Jones), and chase scenes that make you sweat in your seat combine to create one of the best action movies in recent years.

How do you win the love of a Craftsperson?

To win the Craftsperson's affections, make an effort to talk less and do more—the more spontaneous you are, the better.

If you want to enjoy a meal with your Craftsperson, don't simply call him or her and make a reservation at a local restaurant. Instead, show up at your Craftsperson's place and invite him or her to go fishing at a nearby lake or stream. At the end of day, pull out the bubbly and feast on your hand-won meal.

For fast-paced action, join your Craftsperson in the thrills of water-skiing, kayaking, or parachuting. For a more relaxed time, kick back and enjoy the Craftsperson as he or she tinkers on a 1965 Ford Mustang engine, practices on a Fender Stratocaster guitar, or bakes delicious, one-of-a kind, homemade brownies.

~~~~~~~~~~~~~~~~~~~~

Hot Love Tip Number One:
Always give your Craftsperson more space than you
think he or she needs.

~~~~~~~~~~~~~~~~~~~~

If your Craftsperson wants a day apart from you, agree to it. If he or she wants a week off, don't argue. Although you need to draw the line somewhere, it is better to err on the side of giving a Craftsperson too much space than too little, especially in the beginning of a relationship.

When Claire, a twenty-four-year-old M.B.A. candidate, started dating Kacey, a thirty-six-year-old race-car driver and Craftsperson, everything seemed perfect. Despite their busy schedules, they spent time together almost every day, either at the track where Kacey practiced, or at home making love and tinkering around the house. Kacey was so exciting and different from any man Claire had ever dated. Each day he delighted her with gifts, activities, and lovemaking tricks she had never experienced before.

Then the problems started. Kacey said he felt suffocated in the relationship and that he needed time alone to clear his mind. He informed Claire that he was leaving on a cross-state motorcycle trip with a bunch of old college buddies. He would be gone four weeks, and he would miss Claire's graduation ceremony—one of the most important moments of her life.

Claire was tempted to explode: "Don't you love me? How could you leave me like that and miss my graduation? You're a selfish and inconsiderate loser! I'm leaving!"

Fortunately her knowledge of the Craftsperson's nature kept her from lashing out at Kacey. Claire knew that her man valued his space and independence more than anything, even more than a particular relationship. Although she was nanoseconds away from exploding with anger and jealousy, she bit her lip and said nothing as Kacey left for his trip. It was one of the hardest things she had ever done, but she maintained her self-control.

Two weeks later, Kacey returned (just in time for her graduation) and acted like a new man: He apologized for leaving and promised he would make it up to her. He did: He was attentive, loving, and more crazy about her than ever. He even suggested they move in together. He confessed: "Claire, I couldn't stop thinking about you, and I told myself I had to get back to you as soon as possible. You are wonderful; you're the most flexible and nonpossessive woman I've ever met. Any other woman would have been incredibly mad if I left her the way I left you, especially with your graduation coming up. But you know me, you know my needs, and I love you for it. This is going to work."

Claire smiled to herself. It hadn't been easy, but she had done the right thing. She had her man back, and she knew what it took to keep her exciting Craftsperson happy and in love.

What kind of sexual relationship can you expect with a Craftsperson?

Craftspersons are practical and spontaneous in their approach to sex. They don't waste time talking about it, and don't pay attention to old-fashioned rules such as waiting for the man to make the first move. If they want you, they will let you know, and the fireworks will begin.

When dating a Craftsperson, don't bother with flowery romantic gestures such as poetry, candlelight dinners, cards, and moonlit declarations of love. Although some Craftspersons may find such notions amusing, they are not likely to become aroused by what they consider to be "touchy-feely" sentimentality.

~~~~~~~~~~~~~~~~~~~~~~~~~~~~~~~~

Hot Sex Tip:
Appeal to your Craftsperson's sense of sexual adventure
and excitement.

~~~~~~~~~~~~~~~~~~~~~~~~~~~~~~~~

Suggest lovemaking in the woods, behind a barn, on top of the stove. Add an element of risk (of being caught, for instance), and the novelty-loving Craftsperson will experience an erotic rush.

Unlike the Meaning Seekers—who are often more caught up in their fantasies of sex than the real thing—Craftspersons are more in tune with the immediate pleasurable sensations of lovemaking: the sight, sound, smell, taste, and feel of sex. You can arouse a Craftsperson with soft music, ceiling mirrors, perfume, and incense. Use massage with lotion and light gentle kisses as a prelude to sizzling intercourse.

Another important point: The Craftsperson respects individual sexual freedom and expression and is willing to try almost anything as long as no one gets hurt. The Craftsperson firmly believes that as long as two consenting adults have a mutually satisfying sex life, that is all that matters.

If you can keep up with his or her unconventional and freedom-loving ways, grab on to a Craftsperson and let the good times roll.

What kind of long-term relationship can you expect with a Craftsperson?

Craftspersons may find it difficult to stay in a committed relationship because their wandering, spontaneous nature leaves them yearning for constant adventure and novelty—and eternally seeking that fresh, exciting love.

Craftspersons, however, are not like Security Seekers, who want to remarry because they believe in the structure of marriage and want the security it provides. Craftspersons are more likely to move spontaneously from relationship to relationship—getting married, divorcing, and then remarrying without extensive planning or forethought.

When a Craftsperson does permanently settle down with someone, he or she likes to build a life around favorite hobbies and activities.

Male Craftspersons may engage in a myriad of typically "masculine" pursuits such as skydiving, race-car driving, contact sports, or carpentry. The female Craftsperson may share similar passions, but due to society's disapproval ("Girls should play with dolls . . ."), will most likely keep these interests to herself and not involve her mate as much.

Overall, Craftspersons can be quite unpredictable in a long-term relationship. Sometimes they are very enthusiastic and expressive about a new project they are working on; other times their quiet reserve can drive their partners crazy.

Now for the good news: Because they are firm believers in the right of everyone to pursue whatever activity they like in their own space, Craftspersons are perhaps the most tolerant and egalitarian of the LoveTypes. As long as you respect their individuality and desire for personal space, Craftspersons can make excellent mates— fun-loving and easygoing partners who are a joy to be around.

CHAPTER TWENTY-TWO

The Performer

(ESFP): EXTRAVERTED SENSING FEELING PERCEIVER

If You Are a Performer

You love to be around people, entertaining and bringing them (and you) as much love, laughter, and enthusiasm as you can. As the Performer, you crave the spotlight, and you enjoy socializing with all the people you can pack into your ever-expanding circle of fun. The one thing that makes you sad is being alone, but fortunately for you, you are not alone very often. For the true Performer, life is a nonstop party.

When You Are in Love

There are no limits to your expressions of love, tenderness, and sexual intimacy. Being with your lover can easily turn into an around-the-clock extravaganza of food, drink, high jinks, passionate lovemaking, exotic trips, and anything else you can cram into a day.

Whether you are partying or relaxing, you always want to maintain a feeling of harmony between you and your mate. Because you loathe conflict, you may become extremely uncomfortable if you fight with your partner. If you feel there is too much disharmony in your relationship, you may pack your bags unexpectedly, leaving your ex-mate pondering what went wrong.

When you do stay, you tend to smother your partner with gifts, favors, money, and affection. Your lover might be intimidated by your generosity because he or she knows it's impossible to repay you.

Despite occasional setbacks in matters of love, you rarely get down for long—to you, love is an endless out-pouring of fun and affection. You are indeed the love tonic that many people have been searching for all their lives.

Your Best LoveTypes
If You Are a Female Performer

Your preferred LoveType is the male Performer or Wheeler-Dealer (ESTP). Life with either can be a blast; a never-ending stream of invitations, parties, and exciting social events. You will probably have a huge wedding since both of you know so many people.

If You Are a Male Performer

Your best LoveType is the Performer or Gentle Artist (ISFP). The Gentle Artist can provide you with the ten-derness your life may lack. And your lively Performer mirror image will match your high energy and keep the home fires burning.

If Your Ideal Mate Is the Performer

Where can you meet a Performer?

"Let's dance!" You guessed it: The Performer can be found holding court wherever there are lights, action, music, and people.

Try bars, swing dance clubs, comedy clubs, restau-rants, nightclubs, dance classes, parties, gambling meccas (Las Vegas and Atlantic City), theaters (many actors are

Performers), and acting classes at your local community college.

As a quiet Gentle Artist, April, a seamstress, rarely went anywhere after coming home from work. She would spend her spare time cooking for married friends who came over or taking care of her sister's twin toddlers. But at twenty-nine, she was still single, and her one great wish in life—marriage and family—seemed a galaxy away.

Fortunately, April's best friend, Sally, was a LoveType student and introduced her to the system. "A great LoveType for you is the exciting Performer," said Sally. "If you want to meet him, you need to go to places like nightclubs, parties, or comedy clubs. Even if nothing happens, you'll at least get out of the house for once and have a lot of fun."

Gathering her courage and all her willpower, April started going out with Sally for Tuesday nights at the Improv, their local comedy club. On Tuesday nights, all the cute young comics did their stand-up in the hope of being discovered.

April quickly discovered her Performer, a twenty-seven-year-old comic named Tim. He was tall and lanky, very intelligent, and had incredible wit. And he seemed to like Sally, always making eye contact and smiling at her during his breaks.

One night Tim came to their table and started regaling April with his tales of being an East Coast guy trying to meet West Coast women. Laughing so much she was in tears, April gave Tim her phone number, and they started going out.

Now April and Tim have been together for eleven months and are planning to move in together next year.

How do you get a date with a Performer?

Allow yourself to get in touch with that fun-loving side of you, the part of you that is like a Performer. To resonate on the Performer's intense, exciting emotional level, you need to access that spontaneous kid in you who used to enjoy himself or herself no matter what.

Hot Dating Tip Number One:
Appeal to the Performer's love of nightlife.

Mention all the night spots or restaurants you have been to or heard about and listen as the Performer rates them, adds another dozen to your list, and maybe even invites you and your friends to join him or her there.

Hot Dating Tip Number Two:
Ask your Performer for advice on how to party.

Performers like to help others—especially when it comes to promoting social events. When you get the Performer involved in putting together a social event, there is no limit to his or her ability to create an atmosphere of uninhibited fun.

Mention your desire for a Mexican fiesta, and before you know it, your Performer will grab your hand and take you to buy beer, tacos, and Mexican hats. Next stop: your neighborhood copy center where the party-animal Performer will print up hundreds of multicolored flyers for the bash. Even if you don't have hundreds of friends to invite to your party, you'll soon realize that your Performer friend *is* the party.

What kind of videos would a Performer enjoy on a date?
Your Performer will love these entertaining flicks:

- *Saturday Night Fever* (1977). This is the film that catapulted John Travolta to stardom and personified the seventies disco era: a gritty coming-of-age tale about a teenage dance king who ultimately realizes there

is more to life than Saturday nights at the neighborhood disco.

- *Birdcage* (1996). When their son marries into a conservative family, a gay couple scrambles to convince
their new in-laws that they, too, are straight and traditional. Robin Williams and Nathan Lane provide
dignity and madcap humor in this hilarious farce.
- *City Slickers* (1991). An engaging comedy about city
men who head out west and join an old-fashioned
cattle drive to regain their sense of adventure.
- *The Fabulous Baker Boys* (1989). Performers will
enjoy this bittersweet story about the Baker brothers,
traveling lounge pianists whose lives get turned upside down when they team up with the sultry, tough-
talking singer played by Michelle Pfeiffer.

How do you win the love of a Performer?

Performers like to have fun and be positive in everything they do. It's in your best interest, therefore, to
avoid talking about any potentially unpleasant topic
(your mean boss or domineering sibling, for example).
Even though the topic may seem humorous, light, or interesting to you, remember that Performers look at life
differently from you; they want everything to work out
harmoniously. You will do yourself and your date a big
favor by keeping this point in mind and avoiding (at least
until later) any subject that could upset the easygoing
Performer.

Except for the preceding caveat, go out and enjoy yourself. Want to dance all night? It's all right with the Performer. Want to engage in hysterical antics and pranks? No
problem. Want to go to Las Vegas (or Atlantic City) on a
lark? "Let's get it on!" says the Performer.

Rousing dates with the Performer include grand openings anywhere, celebrity events, the theater, concerts,
parties, barhopping, and wherever you can find bright
lights, excitement, drama, jokes, and lots of people. If

there is no party going on, be assured, the Performer will start one.

Just remember: The key to the Performer's heart is through his or her irrepressible sense of humor, desire to have fun with lots of people, and craving for excitement and spontaneity. If you are an outgoing type, go ahead and enjoy nightly frolics with your Performer. If you are a more Introverted type, let your Performer entertain you, while you show him or her how to relax with your quiet and reflective ways.

If you allow your Performer free rein to express his or her joy for life, you may find yourself with a thrilling partner who will entertain you for a long, long time.

What kind of sexual relationship can you expect with a Performer?

The Performer's Extraverted, outgoing nature, as well as their attention to detail, make them perceptive and successful seducers. On top of that, their emotional flamboyance and charisma can be very hypnotic to the opposite sex.

Performers crave variety and excitement in their sexuality. Different positions, sex toys, wigs, and costumes all appeal to this novelty-loving LoveType.

But remember this: Despite their apparently wild persona, Performers do not usually enjoy impersonal sex. They like to feel a certain degree of tenderness (although it doesn't have to be life-lasting) before they allow their sexual desires to take over, giving you the ride of your life.

Normally, Dianne, a twenty-seven-year-old illustrator, would be too shy to try acting. She knew, however, that acting class was a great place to meet her ideal LoveType, the Performer, so she decided to give it a try. During the next several weeks, Dianne became acquainted with the leading man of her life—Chad, a sexy twenty-eight-year-old actor with electric blue eyes.

As they acted together during class exercises, Dianne felt drawn to a mysterious and animalistic energy Chad exuded; she had never felt this way about a man before. After class one night, she agreed to join Chad for drinks at a nearby bar and grill.

Talking, flirting, and touching, Dianne felt mesmerized by Chad's looks and charisma. A good-night kiss outside Dianne's apartment quickly turned into a passion-filled embrace and delirious lovemaking on her living room floor. It was a night of unplanned ecstasy.

Although it was beautiful in its own right, Dianne thought their encounter would be a one-night stand and nothing else. But Chad really showed some class. At the end of the night, he apologized for the hasty introduction to lovemaking and said he wanted their relationship to develop more slowly because he really liked her.

Of course, Chad didn't have a chance to slow things down, because Dianne wouldn't let him. She seduced him on their next date, and their next, and their next. Pretty soon they were making love everywhere: the bathtub, the beach, the backseat of Chad's car.

Not only were they sexually compatible, but their personalities meshed nicely: They reveled in each other's company and, after six months of pure passion, moved in together. They are still happily together and enjoying two-times-per-night lovemaking sessions that would make Masters and Johnson blush crimson.

What kind of long-term relationship can you expect with a Performer?

Although Performers have many positive qualities, there are also some drawbacks to this LoveType. My research indicates that Performers are the second most resistant to marriage (next to the Wheeler-Dealer), and the second most promiscuous (next to the Wheeler-Dealer).

Because of their sociable (Extraverted) and spontaneous (Perceiving) nature, Performers find it difficult to be tied down to only one person; they want to explore the fruits of what life and sex have to offer. Thus, even though Performers may find themselves in a relationship or marriage, they are often tempted to stray.

If they do stray, their sensitive side makes Performers feel guilty, and they will often go to great lengths to make amends—with flowers, professions of love, and flashy gifts and trips. If your Performer mate is being especially charming, giving, and endearing toward you for no apparent reason, be on the alert: He or she may be hiding something.

Of course, you don't want to jump to conclusions or be overly suspicious or possessive (that is sure to drive him or her away), but you want to be smart about the situation. Give your Performer the benefit of the doubt, but don't allow this wily charmer to fool you with his or her blinding charisma.

Despite these findings, it is true that a large percentage of Performers can be faithful once they fall deeply in love with someone. As Feelers, they have a great capacity for caring and genuine love, and they can express it better than any other LoveType, with the possible exception of the Social Philosopher (ENFP).

To be content in a relationship, Performers need to feel they are free (within limits) to spend time doing what they want with the people they enjoy, without having to face the repercussions of jealousy or possessiveness from their mate. As long as you respect and encourage the Performer's natural spontaneity and zest for life, he or she will reward you with faithfulness, enthusiasm, and optimistic love.

Realize this: When you are with the right Performer, you will enjoy a relationship that is chock-full of good times. Your Performer mate is perfectly capable of making you feel that everything is right with you and your world.

CHAPTER TWENTY-THREE

The Wheeler-Dealer

(ESTP): EXTRAVERTED SENSING THINKING PERCEIVER

If You Are a Wheeler-Dealer

You are the type of person who makes things happen. Your lively, engaging, and charismatic style is bound to raise the excitement level in anything you do. You are also an expert at observing people and making uncanny judgments about their personalities. If you are so inclined, you can use this information to get what you want from others. Others may call you manipulative, but in your own mind, you are simply skilled at operating in the game called Life.

When You Are in Love

To you, love represents excitement and never-ending pleasure. You want a partner who can join you on a roller coaster of sensual delights as both of you enjoy the bounty that life has to offer.

If you set your eyes on someone you *really* want, you don't hesitate: You are capable of instantly turning on your irrepressible charm and joy-loving personality to capture his or her affections. As a lover, you are patient, practiced, and always eager to please. You pride yourself in making sure your partner pleads for more.

When it comes to relationships, predictability bores the hell out of you. If you had your way, your primary relationship would always be changing—transforming itself and yielding one action-packed adventure after another.

After a while your mate may give up trying to change your freewheeling ways, and he or she will wisely accept the fact that you were born to be fun-loving and uninhibited, and neither heaven nor earth will change you. Of course, you don't mind what your mate or anyone else thinks; you are perfectly happy with your lifestyle and wouldn't give it up for anything.

Your Best LoveTypes
If You Are a Female Wheeler-Dealer

You get along well with the male Wheeler-Dealer or Innovator (ENTP). You are impressed by the Innovator's intellect and ideas, but you think he sometimes gets too carried away with his theoretical plans. Consequently, you might be better off with an Innovator who is not an exceptionally strong Intuitive.

If You Are a Male Wheeler-Dealer

You can prosper with the female Wheeler-Dealer, Craftsperson (ISTP), Gentle Artist (ISFP), or Performer (ESFP).

You will also do well if you choose your exact opposite, the Mystic Writer (INFJ), because she can help you appreciate the need for helping people and improving the world, instead of merely sampling life's goodies without giving anything back.

If Your Ideal LoveType Is the Wheeler-Dealer

Where can you meet a Wheeler-Dealer?

Like the Performers, you can run into Wheeler-Dealers wherever there are people and excitement—anywhere fun is about to happen. You can meet Wheeler-Dealers at parties, promenades (where people walk up and down a main boulevard as a social activity), health clubs, concerts, casinos, horse races, restaurants, and street fairs.

You can also find your Wheeler-Dealer mate at sports bars, house parties, happy hours, athletic events, jazz clubs, dance clubs, and anyplace you are likely to find plenty of people and fast-paced action.

Finally, look for Wheeler-Dealers in their natural habitat: at clubs, companies, organizations, and other settings where they can exercise their considerable talents in the arts of promotion, marketing, and public relations.

It took Karen, a forty-six-year-old librarian, thirty years of dating the wrong guys before she finally developed her personalized LoveType program. Her number one goal: to meet her ideal LoveType, the Wheeler-Dealer.

For her girlfriends, going out to Wheeler-Dealer hangouts such as sports bars and happy hours was not a problem. But for Karen, as a Mystic Writer and devout Christian, it was definitely a problem.

She didn't like the drinking and sexually charged atmosphere at bars and nightclubs; she believed the men she met there would not share her spiritual values. Yet at the same time, she found the men she met at her small community church (the few of them who were single) to be boring and unappealing.

When Karen came to me for advice after attending a Love-Type seminar, I helped her design a dating program to suit her special needs and desires. She wanted a Christian man with strong moral values, so I suggested she join a singles group at the biggest church in her city—a church that had an action-packed social calendar for a large group of singles.

I further suggested that she volunteer to serve on any committees that planned and promoted social events for the singles group. This way she would have an excellent chance to meet the Wheeler-Dealer men (Christian, single, and her type) who typically lead such committees.

Following this plan, Karen met and started dating three devoted Christian men within six weeks. All of them were exciting, charismatic Wheeler-Dealers who used their extraordinary powers of persuasion and considerable people skills in service of the Lord.

Now Karen's problem is not where to meet her LoveType, but how to make up her mind about the quality Christian men she is dating. It's a nice problem to have.

As long as you can put yourself in the right place—where Wheeler-Dealers can display their flashy promotional skills—they will do the rest. After all, Wheeler-Dealers are usually confident in approaching the opposite sex: They are the ones who often make the first move.

The next person who tells you how dazzling you look, and how much you resemble a movie star, may just be a Wheeler-Dealer, that master persuader who is putting the moves on you without you even knowing it. Be ready for them because they are ready for you.

How do you get a date with a Wheeler-Dealer?

Take what they say with a grain of salt. Many Wheeler-Dealers, whether they admit to it or not, have the potential to be master persuaders who can get you to believe almost anything—whether it's true or not. They don't usually mean any harm; they just like to see how far they can go before getting caught.

It's important to set the boundaries at the beginning of the relationship. Don't permit the charming and smooth-talking Wheeler-Dealer to get away with telling you anything less than the absolute truth. When you suspect the Wheeler-Dealer is not being completely honest with you, look in his or her eye and say: "I know you're not telling me the truth. You have to be straight with me."

Don't be afraid of losing the Wheeler-Dealer if you do this. On the contrary, he or she will want to go out with you because you have now earned the ultimate currency in the Wheeler-Dealer's eyes—respect. The Wheeler-

Dealer will give you the respect you have asked for, and he or she will be truthful with you in the future. Remember: A Wheeler-Dealer can make a great dating partner and soul mate.

~~~~~~~~~~~~~~~~~~~~~

Hot Dating Tip:
Mention a few exciting social or leisure activities you have enjoyed, or a few exotic locales you have visited or would like to visit.

~~~~~~~~~~~~~~~~~~~~~

Wheeler-Dealers hate to be outdone when it comes to excitement. Before you finish your next sentence, your new friend will be excitedly telling you about his or her most pleasurable and passionate experiences. To prove it, your Wheeler-Dealer will invite you to his or her favorite places and activities to show you "something you've never seen before."

Since Wheeler-Dealers pride themselves on being master persuaders, let them work hard to convince you that the activity or place they are talking about is the "most exciting experience you'll ever have."

Once you have your Wheeler-Dealer excited and flustered, reluctantly agree (or at least pretend to be reluctant) to go along with his or her suggestions. Wheeler-Dealers like to think that they convinced you to go with them, even though you may have been eager to go anyway.

What kind of videos would a Wheeler-Dealer enjoy on a date?

You and your Wheeler-Dealer mate will have fun with the following:

- *One Flew Over the Cuckoo's Nest* (1975). Wheeler-Dealers will identify with the carousing, loudmouthed, spontaneous lunatic (or sane man, depending on your point of view) played by Jack Nicholson in this Academy Award winner.

- *Bugsy* (1991). The true story of the playboy gangster and reckless visionary who founded Las Vegas. Warren Beatty is perfectly cast as the hunky hood who carries on with his violent and lusty ways until the mob catches up with him.
- *Dirty Rotten Scoundrels* (1988). Charming, lovable, and definitely rascals, Steve Martin and Michael Caine are master con men who compete against each other to defraud a wealthy damsel in the French Riviera.
- *Terminator 2: Judgment Day* (1991). Two ultimate warrior machines—the morphing evil cyborg and the good cyborg (played by Arnold Schwarznegger in top monosyllabic form)—duke it out as the future of the Earth hangs in the balance. A speed-thrill sci-fi film that packs enough excitement to keep your Wheeler-Dealer glued to the screen.

How do you win the love of a Wheeler-Dealer?

Join the Wheeler-Dealer in his or her favorite social activities: Head to parties, dance clubs, or comedy clubs; have fun scuba diving, water-skiing, or gambling; relax in the mountains, on the beach, in hot springs, or anywhere else the Wheeler-Dealer suggests.

Allow your Wheeler-Dealer to entertain you, enthrall you, and make you laugh until you cry. Quick with a joke, story, or amusing repartee, a Wheeler-Dealer can make even a monks' convention seem like a twenty-four-hour comedy club.

Hot Love Tip:
Don't be possessive.

Wheeler-Dealers hate possessive mates. You can raise your stock with a Wheeler-Dealer if you demonstrate your trust and nonpossessiveness. Don't be the type of boyfriend/girlfriend who raises a fuss when the Wheeler-Dealer scampers off with a multitude of friends for a girls' (or boys') night out.

At the same time, you need to stand firm occasionally when you sense your Wheeler-Dealer is thinking of cheating on you. It's a delicate balance, but one that is crucial to keeping the Wheeler-Dealer comfortable and committed to a relationship.

Isabel, a thirty-nine-year-old mechanical engineer, was able to find that balance when she reined in her Wheeler-Dealer's wandering ways and made their relationship a lasting one.

When they first started going out, Isabel and Alfonso, a thirty-two-year-old marketing vice president, had a relationship that was like a magic-carpet ride. Almost every day, Alfonso would bring her a new gift or treat. One night he rented a limousine, and they cruised the beach. On another occasion he sent her a note to meet him at the airport. They flew to Paris for dinner and jetted back the next morning. It was amazing!

There was one chink in Alfonso's armor. Isabel suspected he was a womanizer and that he was keeping secrets from her. Her intuition told her that Alfonso's late-night business meetings and weekend trips weren't all about business.

Normally, Isabel was not a possessive woman. But with Alfonso, the Wheeler-Dealer and expert seducer (after all, he had seduced her like a pro), Isabel knew she had to be careful. Methodically and carefully, she began to notice inconsistencies in Alfonso's schedule and demeanor.

One night Isabel met Alfonso at a restaurant and calmly and rationally confronted him with her evidence. Using information she had gleaned over the course of two months, she told Alfonso she knew that he had been cheating on her with at least two other women.

At first he tried to deceive her, but she kept probing no matter how convincing he sounded. Finally Alfonso capitulated and admitted that he had indeed been seeing two of his former girlfriends.

Because she was familiar with the traits of a Wheeler-Dealer personality, Isabel handled the situation beautifully. Instead of making a scene—crying or yelling—she acted in a way that would impress Alfonso's logical, practical nature. After coolly telling Alfonso that she was no longer interested in seeing him, she quickly left the restaurant and refused to take his calls for three weeks.

Alfonso was now a changed man. Not only was Isabel one of the few women who could resist his charms, but he sensed that she had an internal lie detector that could catch him any time he lied. For the first time in his life, he was truly impressed with a woman's intellect and strength of personality. He decided she was the one woman he could, and would, be faithful to because she had too much to offer. He knew he would be a fool to lose her.

As Isabel learned, having a relationship with a Wheeler-Dealer can be a fantastic experience if you are able to walk the fine line between giving your Wheeler-Dealer personal freedom and keeping him or her faithful and true. If you can maintain this delicate balance, the always charming Wheeler-Dealer can be one of the best life companions you could ever have.

What kind of sexual relationship can you expect with a Wheeler-Dealer?

Different, wild, and exotic—and that's only the foreplay. Like the song, Wheeler-Dealers were born to be wild.

When it comes to sex, Wheeler-Dealers revel in the sensual pleasures of the moment; they seek excitement, surprise, and variety. My research indicates that, not only are Wheeler-Dealers the most promiscuous of all the

LoveTypes, they are also the most open to nontraditional sexual activities.

Like the Social Philosopher (ENFP) and Performer (ESFP), Wheeler-Dealers are sexually aroused by role-playing, fantasies, exotic positions and locales, and anything else that arouses their intense need for sensual and erotic stimulation.

If you can offer your Wheeler-Dealer at least a modicum of sexual variation and experimentation, you will enjoy a faithful and exciting lover. Your Wheeler-Dealer will realize that the other benefits of the relationship (your caring, intelligence, companionship, and the like) will be enough to compensate for the variety (in sexual partners) that he or she is sacrificing by being monogamous with you.

What kind of long-term relationship can you expect with a Wheeler-Dealer?

According to my research, Wheeler-Dealers are the LoveType most resistant to getting married—they have the highest percentage of never-marrieds. They are also the most promiscuous LoveType: Some Wheeler-Dealers are notorious for carrying on numerous affairs, regardless of whether they are single, living with someone, or married.

One more thing: When it comes to romantic relationships, Wheeler-Dealers are not especially sentimental; consequently, their words and deeds may seem impersonal and even coldhearted to more Feeling types.

As Extraverted realists (Sensors), Wheeler-Dealers invest themselves in a relationship only if they are certain they will receive equal value in return. If a Wheeler-Dealer believes someone isn't worth the energy invested, he or she will disappear in a hurry and move on to the next relationship, sometimes without even saying good-bye.

It isn't easy to stay with a Wheeler-Dealer, especially when he or she thinks like a playgirl or playboy. Yet despite the potential pitfalls, having a romantic relationship with the Wheeler-Dealer can be well worth the effort.

Where else can you find someone who can light up any room with his or her mere presence, who is entertaining and gregarious without even trying to be, and who can convince Eskimos to not only buy ice, but invest in ice stocks? When you are with the right Wheeler-Dealer, you will have a perpetual smile on your face, and you'll be ooohing and aaahing as you wonder what amazing, wonderful thing this master of persuasion and excitement is going to do next.

Bon appétit.

PART THREE

PUTTING THE LOVETYPE SYSTEM TO WORK FOR YOU

In the next five chapters you will learn the essential steps of the LoveType system: going where your ideal Love-Type is, making a great first impression, LoveTyping your potential dates, and making the date.

No matter what your dating difficulties are, the Love-Type system has your answers. If you are the type of person who:

- Doesn't know where to meet your soul mate, check out Chapter Twenty-four, "Going Where Your Ideal LoveType Is," and learn how to set up a weekly schedule that takes you where you are most likely to find your ideal LoveType.
- Is shy around attractive members of the opposite sex and finds it hard to break the ice, read Chapter Twenty-five, "Making a Great First Impression," and learn time-tested tips for making initial contact and making your potential partner feel at ease and eager to know you.
- Is frustrated with the uncertainty of dating and wants a simple way to identify your ideal mate, read Chapter Twenty-six, "LoveTyping Anyone, Anywhere,"

and learn how to pinpoint your ideal LoveType in a short period of time (and have a lot of fun doing it).

- Can easily meet people, but have a hard time getting dates with your ideal type, investigate Chapter Twenty-seven, "Making the Date with Your Future Soul Mate," and learn how to get a date with your future soul mate by appealing to his or her core values, beliefs, and preferences.

- Doesn't have the opportunity to meet other singles because of your tight schedule or limited social circle, peruse Chapter Twenty-eight, "Cutting-Edge Love-Type Dating Strategies," and learn how to meet your soul mate without leaving the comfort of your own home, by using LoveType personal ads and Love-Typing potential dates on the Internet.

CHAPTER TWENTY-FOUR

Going Where Your Ideal LoveType Is

When Rolodexes bulge and schedules overheat, people start to wonder: Where do I find my soul mate, and how do I find the time to meet him or her?

Open up most dating books and you will peruse a laundry list of places to meet eligible singles, ranging from car washes to singles events. One problem: The list is often as long as there are singles to meet. In today's busy world, few people can afford the time to participate in an endless number of activities and events in the unlikely chance of unearthing Mr. or Ms. Right.

Sound hopeless?

Not so, says the LoveType system. In this chapter you will learn Action Step One of the LoveType system and discover how to save valuable time and energy by going to those places where you are most likely to meet your ideal LoveType.

Instead of wasting your life at generic singles traps, you can efficiently meet your ideal LoveType at his or her preferred hangouts and hot spots, favorite events and activities.

Action Step Number One:
Go Where Your Ideal LoveType Is

Begin by making a list of all the prime places and activities for meeting your best LoveType as described in each chapter. If you have more than one ideal LoveType, use a separate sheet of paper to list the best places for each LoveType.

Participate in Structured Activities and Join Groups That Meet on a Regular Basis

When deciding where to go and what to do, place special emphasis on activities and groups that occur (or meet) on a regular basis—structured situations that allow you to become acquainted with your ideal LoveType over time. Classes, discussion groups, weekly club meetings, and the like are excellent options that provide sustained contact with the men or women you want to know better.

If, for example, your ideal LoveType is the hands-on Craftsperson (ISTP), sign up for car-repair classes, join a gun club, or participate in a pottery class. If he or she is the intellectual Expert (INTJ), become a member of your neighborhood chess club or join an astronomy organization that meets weekly.

Structured activities are ideal because they allow you to LoveType people at your own pace. Instead of feeling pressured to LoveType someone the first, and only, time you meet, you can slowly and casually become acquainted with someone's personality style over the course of days, weeks, or months.

At the same time, the person you are getting to know is taking his or her time getting to know you; in this way, romance has a chance to blossom naturally and at a comfortable pace.

KNOWING WHERE TO GO IS HALF THE BATTLE

When you use the LoveType system, you don't have to be in the dark: You know exactly where to find your ideal LoveType.

Without this important knowledge, meeting your ideal Love-Type in the outside world can be a difficult endeavor. Here's why:

Certain LoveTypes are rare in society; you probably won't see much of them unless you participate in the handful of activities they enjoy. These rare birds include the Idealistic Philosopher (INFP—3 percent of the population), Mystic Writer (INFJ—2 percent of the population), Expert (INTJ—2 percent of the population), and Scholar (INTP—3 percent of the population).

Of the sixteen LoveTypes, eight are Introverted. Because Introverts tend to have small social circles and spend a lot of time at home alone, they can be difficult to meet. To make contact with them, you need to engage in the few outside activities they enjoy.

There is one final advantage to hanging out at your ideal LoveType's favorite places: You immediately become part of his or her environment, and he or she becomes accustomed to you. When you are on someone's home turf, his or her anxiety about meeting you lessens, and you have ready-made common ground to initiate a conversation. (At a chess club, you can always say something like: "Can you show me that Kasparov opening?")

Establish a Consistent Weekly Schedule

Once you know which activities and events you want to participate in (and the LoveType you want to meet), set and keep a weekly schedule.

If you are looking for an artsy Idealistic Philosopher, you might attend a poetry-reading class on Tuesday night and a fiction-writing class on Saturday morning. If your choice is the razzle-dazzle Performer, you might drop in on a comedy-improv class Wednesday nights and try dance lessons on Friday nights.

Create a chart or database with the basic information

about the activities or events you have selected: type of activity (event), location, meeting time, the LoveType who usually goes there, how many total people (and how many of your ideal LoveType) you meet there, how much you enjoy each experience, and so forth. This record will help you determine exactly how many eligible and compatible singles you are meeting at each location and what personal value you are obtaining from each event or activity.

As you spend more time at the right places (where you enjoy yourself and have a great opportunity to meet your ideal LoveType), you may find yourself going out with one or more people who happen to be your preferred LoveType. In time you may discover that one of these guys or gals is *the* one—the person who automatically clicks with you and who promises to be a loving and loyal mate.

As a student of the LoveType system, Gloria, a thirty-one-year-old divorced mom of two, knew who her ideal match was: the family-loving male Caretaker (ISFJ), the ultimate husband and father. She also knew where to find him—at activities related to home, children, and family.

Combining her desire to spend quality time with her two-year-old daughter, Amy, and her interest in meeting her Caretaker soul mate, Gloria enrolled Amy in Gymboree: a weekly educational play program for kids and their parents.

Three weeks into the program, she met her Caretaker match in Jesse, a forty-three-year-old high school basketball coach and divorced father of three. Not only was he a sensitive and loving parent, he was also a beautiful man with a mischievous smile.

Now they spend most of their time together—along with their happy herd of children and pets—enjoying their passion for the outdoors (camping, riding horses, and mountain climbing) as well as the beginnings of a loving relationship.

Develop a Mind-set of Curiosity and Self-Improvement

Decide that during the next thirty days you will try one new adventure per week; every seven days you will visit a new place or engage in an interesting activity you have never experienced before (where you also have a good chance of meeting your ideal LoveType).

With this curious mind-set you might find yourself at a sci-fi convention, pottery class, poetry group, or business club meeting. Regardless of where you go, make sure you have a legitimate interest or curiosity in the event, activity, or organization you have chosen to be a part of.

When you feel you have a good reason to be there (even if it's just because you are curious about how a certain LoveType lives), you will be confident about yourself and what you have to offer. You won't feel that you are chasing others or putting your life on hold as you desperately seek your soul mate.

Your main goal in going to these places is to learn new things that will help you become a better and happier person. Although you are always open to meeting your ideal LoveType, your driving desire is to learn and grow. Meeting your potential soul mate is simply an added bonus.

With this approach, you not only feel good about yourself, but you will meet your ideal LoveType faster than you ever imagined. You will discover the universal truth: Others are attracted to you when you exude an aura of self-confidence, curiosity, and comfort. When people sense that you are relaxed and not desperate to meet them, they will be naturally and irresistibly drawn to you.

CHAPTER TWENTY-FIVE

Making a Great First Impression

Have you ever been tongue-tied when talking to an attractive member of the opposite sex? Can you recall a time when that alluring someone was in your presence, and your heart did more thumps than a Native American war dance? You tried to say something coherent, interesting, and charming, but the only sounds that spilled from your mouth were: "Argh, ice ta mit ya."

Don't feel bad. It happens to millions of singles daily throughout the world. According to social psychologists, one of the greatest fears we have is the fear of strangers, especially when that stranger happens to be so irresistible that we trip over our tongue just to say hello.

If talking to a desirable member of the opposite sex makes you feel like crawling under the covers, you are about to receive some relief: The LoveType cavalry is coming. In this chapter you will learn Action Step Two—Making a Great First Impression—and five easy-to-use contact tips for successfully presenting yourself to the person you want to meet.

IF YOU'RE A WOMAN AND HESITATE TO MAKE THE FIRST MOVE
Should you or shouldn't you? That is the dilemma facing women

today when they consider whether they should approach men they are interested in.

Retro dating guides advise women to act as they did in the 1950s: to be passive recipients of men's affections. Don't approach him, don't call him, don't return his calls, act disinterested. If a woman doesn't play the "hard-to-get game," these guides suggest, she will lose the respect and interest of the man she craves. If he doesn't dump her right away, he will make her life miserable, cheating on her and treating her with no respect.

If you are not sure whether to take the initiative in dating, consider this:

Not all men are created equal. Some men, such as the Traditionalists (ESTJs), are more likely to be conventional in their sex roles. This type of man may indeed feel insulted, or at least uncomfortable, when a woman initiates romance: asking him out on a date, offering to pay, and so forth.

On the other hand, men who are Feeling and Introverted, such as the Caretakers (ISFJs) and Idealistic Philosophers (INFPs), are likely to appreciate a woman who takes the dating initiative. Because of their typically quiet and shy nature, these men may not approach a woman, no matter how interested they are. If a relationship with one of these men is to happen, it's up to you to make the first move.

Smart Tip: Find out the LoveType of the man you are interested in before you decide which dating strategy to use, passive or active. Depending on his LoveType—and what you learned about his relationship preferences in the preceding chapters—you may decide to approach him and ask him out, or you may position yourself so he comes to you.

Action Step Two: Making a Great First Impression

Social psychologists have found that men and women form an initial judgment of each other within the first sixty seconds. Your goal in the LoveType system is to use those sixty seconds to make a positive first impression on your new acquaintance as you begin to gather information about his or her personality style.

In Action Step Two you will learn five powerful strategies—simple-to-use tactics to help you make a great impression and spark that all-important first contact with an intriguing stranger.

• *Communicate nonverbally as you enjoy your day.*

Researchers have discovered that body language or nonverbal behaviors (facial expressions, body posture, breathing rate, walking style) play a crucial role in how people respond to each other. Your nonverbal signals convey a vast amount of information to other people, whether you realize it or not.

For example, if you display a hunched-over posture, darting eyes, and rapid-fire speech, others may see you as socially anxious and insecure.

On the other hand, if you maintain good eye contact, a straight posture, a relaxed and confident walking style, a well-modulated rate of speech, and, when appropriate, a smile or a wink, others will regard you as a self-confident and approachable person.

The best way to develop attractive body language is to work on your state of mind first: Allow yourself to relax and truly enjoy yourself when you are out. When you take pleasure in your own company, your nonverbal signals will automatically convey your sense of self-comfort, and others will be attracted to you.

At the same time, make sure you practice the universal signal that indicates availability: eye contact. According to research, intermittent eye contact works best to attract the opposite sex; that is, you glance at someone for a few seconds, look away, then look back again.

This type of "hit and run" eye contact will create a playful and relaxed environment in which the other person can respond if he or she is interested. If he or she offers eye contact and/or a smile after you look at him or her a second time, you have a "go ahead" signal; you can now answer with a smile of your own and perhaps a word or two.

Another point: Notice how people react to you when you intentionally alter your nonverbal behavior. See what happens when you play with your hair, twirl your sunglasses, or glance over your shoulder with a smile. Do people smile at you or give you a curious look? Do they come over and talk with you? Concentrate on repeating those nonverbal signals that create the best reactions in others and that make people want to get to know you better.

- *Display contrast to accent your individuality and create an aura of mystery.*

You can attract positive attention from the opposite sex by being subtly and intriguingly different from everyone else.

When you are at a loud party or night spot, speak quietly. Whisper to the person you are interested in and make him or her lean forward to hear what you have to say. In this way you communicate both intimacy and challenge: You are a sensitive person who speaks quietly, and the type of confident person who is used to attracting people into your space.

If the person you like is walking in a straight line, you might zigzag past him or her. If he or she is sitting, you might silently stand next to him or her. The key is to offer novelty and uniqueness without saying a word. You allow your body to communicate the message: "I'm different and special. Would you like to meet me?"

If you are going to a social event where everyone is dressing in trendy clothes, you might show up wearing classic-cut trousers, suspenders, and wing-tip shoes (if you're a gentleman). Or you might put your hair up in a French twist and don an elegant black cocktail dress and black pumps (if you're a lady).

Your goal here is not to dress up merely to impress others, but to express a part of your personality that is authentic and unique. "Who is he?" "Who is she?" are the questions other singles will ask when you make your intriguing appearance.

• *Maneuver your space to jump-start an interaction.*

You can create social interactions by the way you position yourself at parties, nightclubs, restaurants, or any public place. Place yourself in a location where people have to pass by you on their way to the entrance, exit, bathroom, or dance floor. Or find the one spot that is in the center of the action, where you will be seen by everyone in the place.

Now that you are centrally located, practice giving up your space to people you would like to know better. If you are at a crowded bar or table, offer your seat to the handsome hunk or fine-looking damsel who is dying to sit down. If you are blocking the way to the bathroom, make eye contact, smile, and gracefully move out of the way as intriguing strangers walk by. When you maneuver your space like this, you are not only expressing sensitivity toward others, but you are also providing an excellent segue into a conversation that can catch romantic fire at any moment.

• *Start conversations with upbeat, open-ended questions.*

Open-ended questions are those that begin with how, when, why, what, and where. Open-ended questions are especially useful for starting conversations because the other person can't get away with a simple yes, or no. He or she needs to think about an answer and offer more than just one word.

When you use this approach to jump-start an interaction, make sure you keep the questions fun, positive, and in the moment. Focus your queries on the things you are most curious about or interested in. If you are genuinely intrigued by an idea or by something that is going on in your immediate environment, chances are the person you want to meet will pick up on your energy and respond in a positive manner.

For example, if a member of your reading group is perusing the latest best-seller, you might say, "That's a terrific book, but I think his first novel was his best by far. What do you think of his earlier work?"

Remember: You don't have to be witty, funny, or brilliant to break the ice with open-ended questions. All that's required is that you be sincerely interested in a topic or situation and that you communicate that curiosity to the other person in the form of an open-ended question.

• *Comment on the environment.*

An excellent conversation opener is to comment on your immediate environment. For example, if you are at a jazz concert, tell the guy or gal next to you how much you admire the improvisational style of the musicians. If you are waiting for a seat at a deli counter or sushi bar, tell the attractive person next to you about the culinary delicacies that await him or her. Always be positive, and stay in the moment.

During a museum outing with her singles group, Beth, a thirty-seven-year-old travel agent, had her eye on one of the members: Neal, a good-looking thirty-five-year-old airline pilot. Normally insecure with hunky men like Neal, Beth relied on the LoveType contact tips to initiate an encounter.

As she enjoyed her day at the museum, Beth made sure to engage in brief eye contact with Neal each time he passed by her on his way to an exhibit.

By the time Neal had passed her a third time, Beth decided it was time for her move. As Neal stood still, lavishing his attention on a Picasso, Beth zoomed past him and spoke

softly over her shoulder: "I think Picasso outdid himself here."
Without waiting for a response, Beth continued to walk
toward another exhibit.

"Excuse me, are you an art student?" asked Neal nervously
as he tried to stop her from leaving. He had been observing
Beth throughout the day, and he was intrigued by this mys-
tery woman. He knew she was a member of the singles
group, but he didn't even know her name.

"I could be if I had the right teacher," replied Beth with a
mischievous smile. It turned out Neal was the perfect teacher
as Beth joined him for the rest of the afternoon, receiving
art-appreciation pointers and eventually sharing dinner with
him. They loved the time they spent together and are now
dating exclusively.

Get Out There and Practice, Practice, Practice

As you develop your social contact skills, think of the
LoveType system as a fun, grand experiment. Think of
this as your opportunity to experience uninhibited joy
again—to be that kid who loved to tease, flirt, and joke,
and who captivated and effortlessly drew people into
your world.

Starting today, incorporate the following contact tips
into your daily social agenda:

Make eye contact and display socially inviting nonverbal signals when you spot someone you would like to
know better.

Display contrast—speak softly in loud places, dress up
when people are dressing down—and offer a part of yourself that whispers mystery and uniqueness.

Manipulate your space—display your sensitivity and
awareness of others as you draw them into your personal sanctum.

Ask open-ended questions about the things that intrigue you, and wait for your new friend to jump into
the conversation.

And when the opportunity presents itself, ignite a conversation by commenting on the environment as it unfolds before you.

With this chapter as your guide, you will soon be attracting more quality and interesting people than ever before. As these romantic candidates pour into your life, you will be ready to take the final Action Steps outlined in the next two chapters: LoveTyping your potential dates so you know exactly which one is ideally suited for you, and making that first date with your future soul mate.

CHAPTER TWENTY-SIX

LoveTyping Anyone, Anywhere

As animated discussion and streams of laughter fill the air, you see him across the room. Making eye contact, displaying contrast, and maneuvering your space, you encourage him to respond, and he does: with a smile, a wink, and a few words of greeting.

You know you are at the right place—a social event jammed with the exact LoveType you would like to meet. You have exchanged glances with him at similar functions, but now your gut tells you it's time. Time to explore the possibilities, time to answer *the* question: Is he really my ideal LoveType, the type of man who will be compatible with me in a lasting, loving relationship?

You've already learned the first two Action Steps in the LoveType system—placing yourself in the right place and making a great first impression. In this chapter you will learn the most important step in the LoveType system, Action Step Number Three: LoveTyping the people you want to meet so you can identify your soul mate.

Action Step Three: LoveTyping Your Potential Dates

Your goal in Action Step Three is to accurately LoveType the person you are interested in as easily, quickly, and smoothly as possible so you can determine two essential points: whether he or she is really compatible with you, and if so, what the best strategy is to win his or her heart.

There are two ways to LoveType someone: the Direct Approach and the Assumptive Approach. Let's start with the Direct Approach.

The Direct Approach: Straight to the Chase

The Direct Approach is fast, convenient, and easy-to-use. All you have to do is ask four basic LoveType questions during the course of a conversation:

1. "Do you tend to get more energy from your own thoughts or from other people?"
2. "Are you more practical or more imaginative?"
3. "When making decisions, which do you rely on more—your head or your heart?"
4. "If you had a choice, would you prefer a structured, scheduled lifestyle or a flexible, spontaneous one?"

Use the person's responses to determine his or her four personality preferences (just as you did when you took the LoveType quiz) and his or her LoveType. Now all you have to do is look up his or her LoveType description (assuming you haven't already memorized it) in the appropriate chapter, and you have the information you need to know to win his or her love.

RECRUITING LOVETYPE "SPIES"

You can gather a great deal of LoveType information simply by talking to people who know the person you like. Displaying a natural curiosity, you can ask Direct LoveType questions, such as "I'm curious about Betsy: Do you think she's more practical or more imaginative?"

Ideally you would recruit people who are also your friends, people who would give you the straight scoop about Betsy while keeping your interest in her confidential. Your goal is to discreetly gather information from as many sources as possible—reliable data about this person's preferences, attitudes, and behaviors so you can accurately LoveType him or her.

Introducing the Direct Questions

When using the Direct approach, you have the option of asking the four questions all at once or staggering them over the course of a long conversation or several meetings with a person.

If you decide to ask them all at once, you might tell your new friend that you have read a book about relationship styles, and you would like to determine his or her unique type.

A better option might be staggering the questions, asking one per week, or one each time you see the person. If you use this method, make sure you segue into each question as naturally as possible by first talking about a related topic. For example, you can talk about your friends or social life before you ask: "How about you? Do you like to hang out with a lot of acquaintances or just a few close friends?"

Decide which option works best for you. Some people like to take their time, asking one direct question during each encounter with a person because they feel more natural doing it this way. Others don't want to waste any time; they want to immediately determine if someone is compatible with them.

Although the Direct Approach is easy to use and effective for determining someone's LoveType, you should primarily use it as a training tool—as a primer to help you become comfortable using the LoveType system.

Once you have memorized the four basic questions

and know how to determine someone's personality preferences, you should move on to the graceful and powerful Assumptive Approach, which offers the ultimate advantage of allowing you to LoveType someone unobtrusively, without the person ever realizing what you are doing.

The Assumptive Approach: The Low-Key Way to LoveType Your Potential Dates

With the Assumptive approach you don't ask direct questions to ascertain someone's LoveType. Instead you make an educated assumption about your potential mate's LoveType based on information you gather in an indirect manner—by asking subtle questions or by observing him or her.

When you use this method, your conversational partner won't feel pressured or overwhelmed by too many intrusive questions about his or her personality.

On the contrary. Both of you will have a fun and natural conversation as your friend reveals his or her LoveType through verbal and nonverbal cues. When this is done properly, your new friend will never realize you are using a dating system to win his or her love.

In the sections that follow, you will learn two Assumptive options: asking your new friend indirect (open-ended) questions, and observing how this person interacts in the outside world.

Asking Indirect (Open-Ended) Questions

As you learned in Chapter Twenty-five, open-ended questions are those that don't require a yes or no answer. The advantage of asking open-ended questions is that you can casually LoveType someone in a playful manner—without giving the impression that you are trying too hard to figure him or her out.

Instead of feeling that they are under a microscope

and being "analyzed" (as can sometimes occur when you use the Direct Approach), the people you talk to will experience a sense of curiosity and intrigue when you ask the right open-ended questions. Best of all, they will freely offer you all the information you need to Love-Type them quickly and accurately.

The key to effectively using indirect questions is to weave them into a conversation at appropriate times, as naturally as possible. Warm the person up first by chatting about topics that gracefully lead to the open-ended questions you want to ask.

If, for example, you want to discover whether someone is a practical Sensor (S) or an imaginative Intuitive (N), you can begin by talking about your job, then segue into discussing the exorbitant compensation and perks that some of the top U.S. corporate executives receive. Then you can ask, "If you received a ten-million-dollar bonus, what would you do with the money?"

If the person mainly talks about using the money to improve the world and develop exciting innovations and inventions, then he or she is the creative, future-thinking Intuitive (N).

But if he or she talks primarily about paying off bills, accumulating property or possessions, or reveling in the sensory delights such money could offer, then he or she is the concrete, down-to-earth Sensor (S).

To find out more about someone's LoveType preferences, ask these questions:

For Determining the Introvert/Extravert Dimension
I'm curious; how do you balance your social life with all your other activities?

This is a good question to pose after you have discussed a person's daily activities. You can express surprise that this person is able to do so much during the day (a good bet since most people are very busy nowadays), and then segue into talking about his or her social life.

If the person is an *Introvert*, he or she may respond with, "What social life?" Or the individual will otherwise indicate that he or she doesn't go out very much and is comfortable spending a lot of time alone.

But if your new friend is an *Extravert*, he or she will tell you plenty of ways to balance a busy career and social life. And this person will gleefully recount his or her social exploits.

For Determining the Intuition/Sensation Dimension

Warm the person up by talking about work and career. Then pop this question:

If you had unlimited resources, what would your perfect office look like?

If the person answers with a large helping of imagination (a combination bedroom/office with miniature waterfall, hot tub, and robot maid/secretarial service), then he or she is likely an *Intuitive*. If the person responds in a concrete and practical manner (his or her office contains a matching mahogany desk, credenza, and bookcase; AV cabinet; plush carpeting; a large window; and a fully equipped computer work station), then he or she is probably a Sensor.

For Determining the Thinking/Feeling Dimension

You can start a discussion about fun things to do and then transition into talking about movies. Then ask:

What is your all-time favorite movie? (Then ask why it is his or her favorite.)

Pay attention to the words your new friend uses to describe his or her favorites.

If he or she uses words like "tearjerker," "inspiring," "emotional," "full of great relationships," or "really touching," then this person is likely a Feeler.

On the other hand, if this person focuses on the intricate plot, dazzling special effects, quality acting, or novel script, then he or she is probably a Thinker.

For Determining the Judging/Perceiving Dimension

You can lead into the following question by talking about hobbies, leisure activities, and travel. Then you can ask:

What would you do if you learned you had won a free weekend trip to a local resort and had to leave the next morning or you would lose the trip? Would you go?

Many Perceivers (especially if they don't have children) would answer that they would adjust their schedules and quickly make arrangements to go on the trip. Most *Judgers* would try to reschedule the free trip, or they would decline because they need sufficient advance warning and planning before they make any trip.

Questions That Tap into More Than One Dimension

A smart strategy is to use open-ended questions that shed light on more than one personality dimension at a time. In this way you can quickly and efficiently pinpoint someone's LoveType with a minimum of conversation. Again, it's important to introduce topics that naturally and effortlessly lead to the questions you want to ask.

For example, after discussing the need to balance career and personal life, you can ask:

If you had the power to do anything, what would your ideal day be like?

With this wonderfully broad but intriguing question, you can access all four dimensions:

1. *Introverts* would want to be alone, or with a partner or a few close friends. *Extraverts* would want to spend the day with as many friends and loved ones as possible.

2. *Intuitives* would fill their day by engaging in creative activities such as writing, or coming up with ingenious

plans, inventions, and schemes. *Sensors* would do practical things such as fixing up their home, shopping, or catching up with the day's sports scores.

3. *Thinkers* would enjoy thinking about or dealing with things in their environment. *Feelers* would spend time pursuing intimate experiences with loved ones.

4. *Perceivers* would do things spontaneously and tend to change their schedules—one day they would get up at 7:00 A.M. and make love till noon, another day they would wake up at 8:00 A.M. and tinker around the house all morning. *Judgers* would do things in a set order and stick to a precise schedule—up in the morning by 8:00 A.M., breakfast by 8:15 A.M., jogging by 9:00 A.M., and so on.

Other information-rich questions that tap into several dimensions at once are:

- *What makes you happy?*
- *What do you find beautiful?*
- *What would you do if you learned you only had one day to live?*
- *What would you write on your epitaph?*
- *What is the proudest moment of your life?*
- *Why do you strive for success?*
- *How do you strive for success?*
- *What would you like to have with you if you were stranded on a desert island?*
- *How do you know when you are successful (or happy)?*
- *If God (or a superior being) created a perfect world, what would it be like?*

There is no limit to the creative ways you can assess someone's personality with open-ended questions. Starting today, review the four dimensions (see Chapters Three through Six) and write down all the open-ended questions you can think of to discover information about each dimension. Also think of open-ended questions such as the preceding ones that can tap into more than one dimension at a time.

Before long you will have a storehouse of fun and interesting questions you can ask anyone, anytime—queries that will evoke a ton of LoveType information in a short period of time.

Observing Your Future Soul Mate

One of the most fun and effective ways to LoveType someone is through a focused and detailed observation of his or her appearance, habits, preferences, and behavior.

With the LoveType approach, you can observe someone over time and easily determine if he or she is a practical Sensor (S) or a dreamy Intuitive (N), an Introvert (I) or an Extravert (E), a Thinker (T) or a Feeler (F), a flexible Perceiver (P) or a structured Judger (J). It's easy once you know what to look for.

Check out how people walk, talk (observing their verbal content, rate, and tone), and dress, what they like to read (and how), what they carry with them, what (and how) they eat and drink, what they enjoy doing for fun, how they handle objects, how they react to other people and to sudden changes in the environment, and so on.

The number of LoveType clues is unlimited. When you adopt the mind-set of a LoveType supersleuth, you will become increasingly aware of every mannerism, habit, and behavior that can give you valuable information about a person's LoveType.

When you use the observational approach, your goal is to accurately LoveType (and prescreen) someone *before* you spend much, if any, time with him or her. This approach saves you the time, energy, and frustration of harboring a romantic interest toward someone who may ultimately be incompatible with you. And it gives you a tremendous feeling of confidence that you can comfortably and efficiently identify the right type of man or woman—the LoveType who is most likely to click with you in a long-term relationship.

That cute businessman with the wavy hair is reading a tattered fantasy novel during his lunch hour. Could he be an imaginative Intuitive (N) who feels trapped in a boring, money-is-everything profession? A good chance.

He's also eating by himself, as usual. Could he be the inward-focused Introvert (I)? A strong probability.

Isn't this interesting? Almost every time a homeless person approaches him, this guy gives up several dollars with a smile on his face. Could this charitable businessman be the sentimental Feeler (F)? Quite likely.

And why does he customarily order a new and different drink when he is only half finished with the old one? It's almost as if he were constantly trying to change something—to experiment, to experience. Could he be the spontaneity-seeking, "change is everything" Perceiver (P)? Bingo.

You haven't said a word to this gent, but you have already made tentative assumptions about his four Love-Type preferences, INFP, the Idealistic Philosopher. Keep observing him and you may soon have enough hard data to corroborate your initial hypothesis.

Your aim when using the observational approach is to obtain as many clues as possible for each of the personality dimensions. In this way you will gather enough information to come to a definite conclusion about someone's LoveType, merely by observing him or her over time.

Refer to the following traits when you use the observational version of the Assumptive LoveType approach. If you want a quick summary of important Assumptive personality traits, take a look at Appendix D:

The Assumptive Traits: Subtle Signs of Personality
Your new friend is probably a(n):

1. *Introvert (I)* if he or she has a few friends and acquaintances and tends to leave social events early.
Tip: Introverts occupy much of their time alone at home, where they can relax with their own thoughts.

2. *Extravert (E)* if he or she has many friends and/or acquaintances and is usually one of the last to leave a social event.

Tip: Extraverts like to spend time outside the house, where there is plenty of opportunity for social interaction.

3. *Intuitive (N)* if he or she prefers thinking, reading, or talking about the future, new discoveries, and the possibilities of life. For example, he or she may enjoy conversation about a better way to express feelings, or he or she may like spending a lot of time reading science fiction novels.

Tip: Intuitives like to use metaphors, analogies, and word pictures to communicate.

4. *Sensor (S)* if he or she prefers thinking, reading, and talking about practical, concrete, and "here and now" subjects. For example, he or she may like to talk about making the perfect margarita, or he or she may enjoy reading about the latest fashion trends.

Tip: Sensors like to communicate by citing readily observable and measurable facts, statistics, and concepts.

5. *Feeler (F)* if this person places great importance on being sensitive toward others and enjoys talking about feelings, relationships, and personal matters.

Tip: Feelers avoid arguments and heated debates because they don't want anyone's feelings (including their own) to be hurt.

6. *Thinker (T)* if this individual seems somewhat detached and impersonal and doesn't appear overly interested in interacting with others on a personal, emotional level.

Tip: Thinkers enjoy stimulating and controversial arguments and debates to exercise their analytical minds. They don't take these discussions personally.

7. *Judger (J)* if this person likes to thoroughly cover one conversational topic (or finish one activity) before starting another.

Tip: Judgers like to adhere to a regular schedule, and you will usually see them at set times. They are rarely late for appointments (unless a Perceiver is holding them back).

8. *Perceiver (P)*: if this person's conversation rapidly flows from one subject to another, or if he or she begins many tasks and activities that are left unfinished.

Tip: Perceivers are always changing their plans, and you never know when they will show up. They are often running late (and catching hell for it from the Judgers).

Using the Assumptive Approach to LoveType Anyone You Meet

As you become acquainted with the characteristics of each of the preferences (Introversion, Extraversion, and so forth), you will discover how easy it is to pinpoint someone's preferences and determine his or her LoveType.

Let's say you are really interested in the guy who works in the marketing department of your company. He is devastatingly cute, but you want to make sure he is your ideal LoveType before you invest a significant amount of time, energy, and social risk.

So you apply the Assumptive Approach and begin observing him and talking to people who know him. You learn that:

1. He always eats lunch with at least four or five people, and he is usually the one who does most of the talking. (Extravert)
2. His hobbies are working on classic cars and collecting stamps. His favorite topics of conversation are fine food, traveling, and sports. (Sensor)
3. He is very logical and straightforward about making decisions—he can fire employees without thinking twice. (Thinker)
4. His co-workers always kid him about being late for work—he is rarely on time, but he is such a good producer that nobody seems to mind. (Perceiver)

Based on these observations (and others), you may conclude that he is the flamboyant Wheeler-Dealer (ESTP), the master promoter and seducer; a charming rascal who loves excitement, stimulation, and variety in life and who believes in action, not theory.

Now you can quickly determine whether this exciting Wheeler-Dealer is your ideal LoveType by checking your LoveType recommendations. If he is one of your top selections, you can peruse Chapter Twenty-three for tips on how to get a date with him and win his heart. (How about leaving the adventure-loving Wheeler-Dealer a free pass to a raging night spot you have heard about? Include a note telling him to meet you there at 8:00 P.M., but don't tell him your name. He'll be dying with curiosity.)

With the information you have learned in this section, you are now ready to practice the Assumptive method with people you already know on a casual basis: the secretary at work, the classmate who sits next to you. See how many preferences you can determine simply by observing this person or by asking him or her open-ended questions. The more you practice, the quicker you will be able to accurately LoveType the people you want to meet.

How an Expert Found Her General with the Assumptive Approach

Loretta, a forty-seven-year-old patent attorney and Expert (INTJ), was tired of going out with weak, spineless guys: men who didn't have the guts to tell her they were married or otherwise unavailable, men who were scared to be with a strong woman, men who believed "commitment" meant making sure they made it to their buddy's basketball game.

Fed up with traditional dating methods, she listened carefully when her friend Cecilia recommended the LoveType system and raved about the Assumptive Approach. Although skeptical at first, Loretta decided to give the LoveType system a try.

"I'm the kind of person who wants the facts, all of them.

*I don't accept anything just because somebody tells me it's
so. At first I thought the LoveType system was just a bunch
of BS, some silly psychology theory that put people into
boxes.*

*"Yet the more I studied the LoveType system and began
to understand its strong research base, the more I trusted it.
I especially liked the idea of the Assumptive Approach—it
gave me the power I wanted to prescreen a guy even before
I talked with him.*

*"Once I became comfortable with the system, I tried it on
a guy I was kind of interested in who lived in my condo
complex. I had been observing him for some time, so I tried
the Assumptive Approach.*

*"I knew he was very talkative and usually surrounded by
friends; therefore I assumed he was an Extravert. Also, when
I overheard his conversation, he appeared to have a good
imagination (Intuitive) and he seemed rather straightforward
and logical about things (Thinker). Finally, I noticed he was
at the pool for his swim every morning at the same time; he
rarely missed. I guessed he was a Judger.*

*"Putting it all together told me he was an ENTJ, the Gen-
eral, which happened to be my ideal LoveType according to
the system. I just had to meet him.*

*"One night when he was at the pool, I sat next to him and
we struck up a conversation. We started talking about our
personal lives, and he told me he was a successful corporate
attorney and had recently divorced. Ironically, he had been
interested in meeting me, but he thought I was already involved because he always saw me with a man. The man he
thought was my lover was actually my brother.*

*"After two hours of conversation, I felt like I had known
this guy for years, and he felt the same way. As an ENTJ,
the General, he was my ideal LoveType, a self-confident man
with whom I could really debate important topics—a real
man who was not intimidated by a powerful woman like
me.*

"Before long, we started dating, and within six months we

were engaged. We got married last year, and I love him more every moment we're together."

Remember that LoveTyping someone is an ongoing process—as you get to know a person better, you will refine your assumptions until you have an accurate picture of his or her true love style. For this reason it's always a good idea to use more than one method for LoveTyping the person you are interested in.

If you initially LoveType someone using the observational option, you might verify your assumptions later by asking open-ended questions. If you LoveType someone with open-ended questions, you may want to back up your conclusions by asking more direct questions later.

If all else fails and you can't get a good grasp of someone's LoveType, you can always give your new friend the LoveType quiz at a nearby restaurant and make a date out of it.

Get Your Friends and Family into the Act

It doesn't have to be all you; your family and friends can be an excellent resource to help you find your ideal LoveType.

Give your people a brief course on the LoveType system: Let them know who your ideal LoveType is, and teach them to identify that person by using the Direct or Assumptive Approach.

You will be pleased at how helpful family and friends can be when they have a specific guideline of the Love-Type you want to meet. If you build a good family/friend search network, you may even be able to bypass steps one through three and move directly to step four: Making the Date.

CHAPTER TWENTY-SEVEN

Making the Date with Your Future Soul Mate

So far, so good. You have made it to the right "restaurant" (the best place to meet your ideal LoveType), finished your appetizer (made a great first impression), gobbled down your main course (LoveTyped your honey), and you are now ready to savor the delicious dessert at the end of the LoveType feast: making a date with your future soul mate.

In this chapter you will learn the final and easiest of the four LoveType Action Steps: Making the date. If you have been following the steps in the last three chapters, you are now in the perfect position to ask your ideal LoveType out on a date or prepare yourself to say yes when he or she invites you.

Action Step Four: Making the Date

There are two parts to securing a date with the love of your life: tapping into your friend's LoveType interest, and connecting your partner's LoveType interest to setting up a date with you.

Let's see how these two mini steps work in unison.

Mini Step One: Gear the Conversation to Your Friend's LoveType Interest

One of the benefits of the LoveType system is that it gives you ready-made conversational material that will interest and excite your prospective soul mate. Once you know someone's LoveType, you also gain valuable knowledge about that person's most deeply held values, interests, and preferences.

As you prepare to meet your ideal LoveType, make sure you review the chapter that corresponds to him or her. For example, if your perfect mate is the Caretaker (ISFJ), you know from the section "How Do You Get a Date with a Caretaker?" that he or she is interested in people who are concerned about the vulnerable in life: animals, children, the sick, and the elderly.

And you also know from the section "How Do You Win the Love of a Caretaker?" that the Caretaker is especially impressed by a gentle, caring, and tradition-loving family person.

Now you can enhance your Caretaker's interest and affection toward you by talking about the things he or she is most interested in: selecting the ideal pet, raising children in the appropriate way, and building a strong family life (which hopefully includes you).

Brag about your kids, pets, parents, siblings, and closest friends. Express a desire to meet, and get to know, your Caretaker's kids, pets, parents, siblings, and closest friends.

Your goal here is not to be inauthentic or to compromise your true identity, but to access the parts of your personality that resonate with what the Caretaker loves best. When you do this, you will exude the natural charisma that is manifest when you are true to yourself and when you are genuinely interested in the world of another.

Mini Step Two: Connect Your Partner's LoveType Interest to Setting Up a Date with You

Your final step is to make a connection between your Caretaker's major passions—the ones you just discussed—and the pleasures of spending time with you in a romantic way.

For example, you could ask the Caretaker to accompany you to a pet store to look at puppies, followed by a trip to the park to watch children play. Or you could express interest in the Caretaker's house-decoration plans, and wait for the Caretaker's invitation to watch him or her create a home masterpiece. Add some snacks and an evening stroll, and voilà, you are on your first date!

You may be surprised at how easy it is to get a date (and possibly a life partner) once you know how to tap into your LoveType's deepest preferences, values, and interests. Very few people know how to do this naturally because they are attuned only to their own needs and interests, not the real passions of the person they are with.

But you are different. You are a student of the Love-Type system, and you understand the tremendous value of accessing your sweetheart's most powerful needs and emotions en route to developing a mutually satisfying and love-filled relationship.

How Bridget Gambled on Love and Won Her Soul Mate

Bridget, a forty-four year-old business owner, had her sights set on Nicholas—a studly forty-eight-year-old systems analyst and Innovator (ENTP).

After observing Nicholas over the course of several weeks at their local entrepreneur group, Bridget confirmed he was an Extraverted (he was quite talkative), Intuitive (he always came up with far-out ideas during the group), Logical (he was very straightforward), Perceiver (he jumped from one topic to another). Perfect: Nicholas was the risk-loving, talk-a-mile-a-minute Innovator (ENTP)—her perfect LoveType.

Next step: Capture his LoveType interest. Realizing that Innovators are geniuses at coming up with novel plans, schemes, or inventions, she asked for Nicholas's advice on how to expand her greeting-card business. Thoughts flew like sparks on iron as Nicholas excitedly came up with new twists Bridget had never considered.

Sensing the time was right, Bridget casually invited him to her office for coffee and further discussion on business innovations. Nicholas agreed, and soon they were having a blast talking about everything from solar energy to summers in Egypt.

To seal the deal, Bridget appealed to Nicholas's risk-loving nature. She said: "I've just learned a foolproof system for winning at roulette, and I was thinking about heading to Vegas this weekend. Do you know anything about roulette?"

Unable to resist such a challenge, Nicholas invited himself to come along as part of her gambling team. Spending a luxurious weekend at Caesar's Palace, the couple made love, made money, and eventually made a plan: If everything kept working out as it had, they would move in together by the time they doubled their bankroll.

Unfortunately, on their last trip, Bridget and Nicholas's luck turned; they wound up losing all of their previous winnings and then some. They decided professional gambling was not for them and agreed to come up with another money-making venture that would provide them with more fun, thrills, and excitement than ever before.

Creating Your Ninety-Days-to-Love Program

Now that you have been introduced to the basic Love-Type skills, it is time to create your personalized dating plan: a powerful blueprint that, within ninety days, can put you in the position of meeting and developing a lasting relationship with the love of your life.

Steps to Take within the First Fifteen Days:

1. Based on the recommendations in Part Two, create a list of all the places you are likely to meet your ideal LoveType.

2. Review the four basic LoveType questions, as well as the most important characteristics and traits of your ideal LoveType and any other one you are interested in meeting.

3. Practice Action Steps Two, Three, and Four (making a great first impression, LoveTyping your potential dates, and making the date) with a friend or acquaintance. Role-play as if your friend were an attractive person you wanted to meet.

Days Sixteen through Thirty:

1. During the next two weeks, visit at least three of the places where you are likely to meet your ideal Love-Type. Take a friend with you who can provide support and companionship, but don't cling to your friend's side. After you are comfortable with your surroundings, go off on your own so you appear approachable and friendly.

2. During the time you are there, pick at least three people and practice LoveType Action Steps Two and Three: making a great first impression and LoveTyping your potential dates using the Direct Approach (asking the four LoveType questions).

At this stage, it's okay if the people you interact with are not your ideal: You are only here to practice. Your initial goal is to become comfortable asking the LoveType questions and gauging someone's answers so you can determine his or her LoveType.

Days Thirty-one through Sixty:

Use the Direct Approach and Action Steps One through Four to meet a minimum of three attractive singles per week. Out of those three, go out with the person (or persons) who most resembles your ideal LoveType.

Days Sixty-one through Ninety (and beyond):

1. Learn the Assumptive questions and personality traits described earlier. Practice Assumptively LoveTyping people anywhere you happen to be, either with open-ended questions or by observing them.

2. Using Action Steps One through Four and the Assumptive method, strive to meet at least three attractive singles per week. Make a date with the person (or persons) who is closest to being your ideal LoveType.

Regardless of which approach you use (Direct or Assumptive), make it a fun habit to LoveType as many people as you can during the course of your day, whether or not you would consider dating them.

It's perfectly okay to LoveType married people, kids, or elderly folks—the more you practice the system with as many different kinds of people as possible, the more confident you will be in your LoveTyping skills. When the right person does come along, you will be relaxed and comfortable using the LoveType system to draw him or her close to you.

One final point: During your LoveType campaign, be sure to keep careful records of your results. Remind yourself that you will continue your mission until you find the person of your dreams.

You are now ready to become a successful LoveTyper. Good luck, and may the next ninety days (and beyond) be the most fun you have ever had.

CHAPTER TWENTY-EIGHT

Cutting-Edge LoveType Dating Strategies

As you put the LoveType system to work in your dating life, you may find yourself in one of those moods. You know the ones. When you don't feel like leaving the house. When you don't feel like fighting traffic and crowds to hang out at your ideal LoveType's favorite haunts. When you don't feel like being socially perky and asking the LoveType questions (or making LoveType observations) of the people you meet.

Sometimes (or a lot of the time if you're Introverted or shy) you just want to stay home and relax. You want your compatible mate to come to you for a change. Why not? Why doesn't your soul mate just pick up that phone and call you? "Hi, I'm the compatible LoveType you have been waiting for all your life. Do you want to meet me?"

Sounds far-fetched?

Not necessarily, especially if you use the LoveType strategies you are about to learn in this chapter. Here you will become acquainted with two cutting-edge variations of the LoveType system—LoveType Personal Ads and Finding Your Ideal LoveType on the Internet—that can help you identify and meet your compatible Love-

Type, quickly and easily, from the privacy and comfort of your own home.

With these approaches, you don't have to be a flaming Extravert or supersmooth talker; all you need is a pen or computer, and you will have an excellent opportunity to meet your ideal LoveType—without stepping outside your door.

Create a LoveType Personal Ad

As a lark, thirty-year-old identical twins Sherrie and Celeste decided to place a joint LoveType ad in three local singles publications. The ad read as follows:

> *We're twin sisters looking for their Mr. Rights.*
>
> *Hi, I'm Twin Number One: Thirty years old, a quiet [Introvert], attractive, imaginative [Intuitive], and caring [Feeling] lady who has the wind at my feet and is ready to explore the universe [Perceiving]. I'm looking for my real soul mate: a thirty- to forty-five-year-old nonsmoker who is also quiet [Introvert], imaginative [Intuitive], caring [Feeling], and enjoys a spontaneous [Perceiving] lifestyle. Good looks a plus, but not essential.*
>
> *Hi, I'm Twin Number Two: good-looking and a thirty-year-old, quiet [Introvert], practical [Sensing], logical [Thinking] woman, who—unlike my twin—respects order, organization, and structure in my life [Judger]. You are a successful, family-minded, outgoing [Extravert], thirty-five- to forty-five-year-old man, who is practical [Sensing], logical [Thinking], and please, please, please, organized and neat [Judger]. It's okay if you smoke.*
>
> *After six weeks of placing the ads, the twins received dozens of quality responses from men who fit their criteria. Now Sherrie and Celeste spend their weekends going out with their prospective Mr. Rights. They are having an avalanche of fun, all thanks to placing LoveType personal ads.*

According to dating experts, personal ads will play an increasingly larger role as more and more singles use them to bypass the increasingly isolated society we live in. As a LoveType practitioner, you can apply what you have already learned to create personally tailored messages—LoveType personal ads—that target your ideal LoveType.

Here are the steps for creating a LoveType personal ad that works:

Step One: Write a Personal Ad with Your Ideal LoveType in Mind

First, decide which LoveType you want to target through a personal ad. If you were given more than one LoveType recommendation, you will want to write a different ad for each LoveType.

When you write the ad, pretend that you are speaking directly to your perfect mate. Be explicit in stating the exact LoveType you are looking for.

You can use two approaches to write a LoveType personal ad: the Preference Approach and the Major Traits Approach.

THE PREFERENCE APPROACH

Write down one word or phrase for each of the four preferences in your LoveType. Do the same for the Love-Type you are aiming to meet through the ad.

Rather than using the actual technical terms for the preferences (such as Introvert or Extravert, for example), use informal language that is easy to understand. Instead of saying that you are looking for an "Introvert," use the words "soft-spoken," "quiet," or "stay-at-home type."

Use a thesaurus to help you come up with words that represent each of the preferences. For example, if you are looking for a Feeler, put "sensitive" or "passionate" in the ad. If you want to meet an Extravert, insert "outgoing" or "sociable."

Study the following example of an ad written by an

Expert (INTJ) woman who wanted to meet her ideal mate, the Traditionalist (ESTJ).

> *Thirty-two-year-old quiet [Introvert], imaginative [Intuitive], intellectual [Thinking] brunette with a disciplined [Judger] lifestyle seeks take-charge [Extravert], down-to-earth [Sensor], logical [Thinking] man, forty-five to fifty-five, who enjoys a stable, secure [Judger] lifestyle.*

This ad helped Tara, a twice-divorced mother of two, meet her ideal mate in Henry, a forty-seven-year-old vice president of finance, when she placed her personal ad in a local singles publication. Thanks to Tara's decision to place a LoveType personal ad, Henry and Tara recently celebrated their one-year wedding anniversary and are expecting a daughter next year.

THE MAJOR TRAITS APPROACH

With this approach, instead of using synonyms for the preferences, you list the major traits of your LoveType and your ideal LoveType. For example, if your main squeeze is the Dutiful Host (ESFJ), you will find the following traits listed in Appendix B:

value harmony in their relationships
display goodwill toward others
are the perfect hosts
are great party organizer
are very family-oriented

If you wanted to design an ad using those traits, you would write something like: "(Insert your own LoveType traits here) woman seeks attractive, thirty-five- to forty-five-year-old, family-oriented gentleman, master host, great party organizer, and humanitarian."

Regardless of whether you use the Preference or Major Traits approach in writing your ad, you can insert any

factors you'd like to screen for, including age, health habits (smoking, drinking preferences), career, income, and
whether you want someone who has children.

For more help in creating a great personal ad, you
can read *Playing The Personals*, by Claudia Beakman and
Karla Dougherty.

Step Two: Place Your Ad in LoveType-specific publications
The best publication for your personal ad is the one
most likely to attract the highest number of responses
from your ideal LoveType.

Before you advertise in a publication, do your home-
work. Find out how the publication's readers break down
along the lines of gender, profession, socioeconomic
background, lifestyle preferences, and hobbies. Your goal
is to have enough information to answer the question:
Will running my ad in this publication generate enough
responses from my ideal LoveType to make it cost-effective
for me to advertise here?

Compare the demographic information you obtained
from the publication with what you know about the Love-
Type you are interested in. If the readership of a particular publication tends to have a substantial number of the
traits and characteristics of your ideal LoveType, go
ahead and place the ad. If not, look elsewhere.

If, for example, your ideal LoveType is the high-achieving
General, you will probably want to advertise in an up-
scale publication that caters to the culturally and eco-
nomically elite, to those ambitious individuals who have
a taste for high finance and the finer things in life.

On the other hand, if your ideal LoveType is the Mystic
Writer, you will want to advertise in a publication that
attracts a more arts-oriented, literary, and humanities-
minded readership.

Classified rates vary widely, and the cheapest is not
necessarily the best. It is better to pay more for an ad
that reaches a significant number of your ideal LoveType
than it is to pay less for an ad that doesn't.

Step Three: Place the ad

Once you have written your ad and have determined where you want it to run, your last step is to place the ad and wait for your LoveType replies to start arriving.

Personal Ad Action Plan

Here is your Action Plan for meeting your ideal Love-Type using personal ads:

FIRST FIFTEEN DAYS

First decide which LoveType you would like to meet and which personal ad approach (Preference or Major Traits) you want to use.

Depending on which approach you select, write down the four main preferences of your ideal LoveType or their main personality characteristics (they value competence, they are great party organizers, and so on), then do the same for your own LoveType.

DAYS SIXTEEN THROUGH THIRTY

Start writing personal ads that target people who possess the characteristics of your ideal LoveType. After you have written at least three differently worded ads for your chosen LoveType, select your best one. Polish your words until the ad presents the strongest, most compelling message you can create to attract your ideal mate.

DAYS THIRTY-ONE THROUGH FORTY-FIVE

Make a list of the best publications for your LoveType ad. Then place your ad in at least three of the publications you have listed.

DAY FORTY-SIX AND BEYOND

Track your results and create a permanent record of them. Note the name and type of publication, number of responses, the LoveType of the respondents, and the end result (phone call, date, relationship). By keeping meticulous records, you can adjust your personal ad program and only place ads in the best publications: those that draw the highest quality and greatest number of responses from the LoveType you are searching for.

Cruising the Internet for Your Ideal LoveType

Martha, a Social Philosopher, is ready to go "cruising" tonight for Mr. Right. Plugging in her Macintosh PowerBook, she gets to work. First she checks her e-mail and smiles at the electronic messages left by three men she met last night at the Electronic Tavern. There's a message from Party-Tech, a Performer LoveType, Plato2000, a Social Philosopher, and SPOCK-MERGE, an Expert. All of them want an intimate encounter (maybe cybersex?) with Martha in a private chat room. Sounds tempting, but she isn't ready for that just yet; she's in a more romantic mood.

Quickly she enters her favorite chat room, PsychTalk, where she can communicate with fellow Meaning Seekers. While she's in there, several interested men send her immediate messages wanting to talk with her privately. She gives one of them her e-mail address and suggests he send her his favorite poem.

Surfing the World Wide Web (WWW), she travels to Japan and has sushi (in her imagination, of course) with a Japanese businessman who happens to be an Administrator (ISTJ), not really her LoveType at all. Next stop, Paris, and she hits the jackpot: In an Artists with Feeling discussion group, she meets Jacques, a sensitive, imaginative artist—her Social Philosopher soul mate. Their talk flows easily on the computer screen as they banter about life, love, and art.

As the night ends, they vow to exchange love letters, continue their nightly love talks, and if destiny so desires, someday meet face-to-face. Martha is in love. And it all happened on her computer screen.

Everyone is getting excited about the Internet these days—that "information highway" made up of a vast network of computers. The Internet is an electronic society that connects millions of people worldwide with the stroke of a computer keyboard.

Experts predict the Internet will revolutionize the nature of dating. For the first time in history, singles worldwide can meet each other effortlessly, painlessly, and efficiently by talking to each other via their computers.

Internet dating offers interesting parallels to dating in the real world. In traditional dating, two people meet face-to-face and agree to spend time together: sharing an activity and engaging in conversation.

In Internet dating, two people agree to converse with each other by typing words on their computers. In the process, they may also agree to simulate (by typing descriptive sentences) a multitude of dating activities, including dining, dancing, and even making love.

For some people the romance remains in their imagination; others decide to consummate their love by meeting in person. Some Internet daters travel hundreds or thousands of miles to meet their beloved. It can definitely pay off: Plenty of successful long-term relationships and marriages have taken place after men and women met on the Internet.

Finding Your Ideal LoveType on the Internet

You can apply LoveType strategies and ask LoveType questions to meet your perfect match on the Internet. Like using personal ads, LoveTyping potential mates on the Internet offers a significant dating advantage: You can meet people from the privacy of your home without having to transform yourself into a talkative, outgoing Extravert.

Moreover, because Internet users are already accustomed to being asked a myriad of questions by other users, you will find that you can LoveType potential mates faster and easier on the Internet than almost anywhere else.

Everyone asks personal questions on the Internet.

There is something about the anonymity of the Internet that creates a feeling of openness—people don't see each other, and they only know each other by their screen names. When you are on-line, you can immediately Love-Type a man or woman who piques your fancy without worrying too much about awkward or embarrassing moments.

Getting started with your Internet LoveType dating program is easy. Just take the following steps:

Step One: Choose an Internet service provider

These are the services that connect you with the Internet and provide areas where you can meet, date, and correspond with other singles. The following are fine choices:

America Online (800-827-6364)
Prodigy (800-776-3449)
Genie (800-638-9636)
Delphi (800-695-4005)

Step Two: Become familiar with, and start using, the dating options on the Internet

The most important options are as follows:

E-MAIL

All providers give you the feature of sending and receiving electronic mail (e-mail). You can send LoveType quizzes to people you meet on-line, recipes for a cake, love letters, or anything else you want. E-mail is almost instantaneous and saves you the cost of postage.

INTERNET NEWSGROUPS

Imagine a tall bulletin board with thousands of special-interest areas that give you detailed information on where and how to meet the kind of people you want to know. Now condense that image into the size of a computer, and presto! You have Internet newsgroups: information areas in which people leave messages, news items, gossip, club information, and a host of other announcements.

Here you can find information about a wide variety of organizations and special interests such as scuba diving groups, writing clubs, and self-development classes, as well as all kinds of singles groups, including those that cater to people who are divorced, overweight, and recovering substance abusers, for example.

Now that you know how to identify your ideal Love-Type, you can scan the various newsgroups to find groups or activities that cater to the LoveType you are interested in meeting. Request information, and get involved in the group(s) of your choice.

Another idea: Post a message on one of the singles newsgroups and announce that you are starting a Love-Type singles group. (See Appendix E for more information on how to start one.) You can decide to run your group on the Internet, or you can invite prospective members to a convenient location where they can socialize face-to-face.

Personal ads are also becoming increasingly popular on newsgroups. You can place your own LoveType personal ad (often for free), or you can answer the ads of singles who appear to have the LoveType characteristics you desire in a mate.

The main benefit of newsgroups is that many of the people you meet (as opposed to the national and international connections likely in chat rooms) will be local. If you meet someone you like through a newsgroup, chances are you will be able to meet and date him or her, conveniently and without much delay.

Angie met Brad through a beginning surfers' club listing he placed on an AOL (America Online, an Internet provider) newsgroup. After exchanging e-mail (and scoring the Love-Type quiz he sent her), Angie discovered that Brad was ex-

actly the kind of guy she had always been attracted to: an action-loving, "devil-may-care" Wheeler-Dealer.

In the past, Angie's Introverted personality and reclusive job as a freelance technical writer prevented her from going out very much and meeting the type of exciting Wheeler-Dealer men who turned her on. And now that she had met Brad over the Internet, she was going to make the most of her opportunity.

After several phone conversations, Angie and Brad agreed to meet. They spent a wonderful day at Huntington Beach, and Angie made an interesting discovery: She learned that one of her stereotypes about fun-loving Wheeler-Dealers— that they were usually not supereducated—were entirely wrong. Contrary to her previous perceptions, she learned that Brad was well educated (he held an M.B.A. from Stanford) and conversant in many topics.

They dated for a while, and even though things didn't work out in the end, Angie is glad she decided to give Love-Type Internet dating a try. Now she is placing her own ads on Internet newsgroups, and she is on the lookout for more Wheeler-Dealer surfers.

CHAT ROOMS

These are designated areas, like clubhouses, where you can meet people who share special interests. You can communicate by typing your comments and reading the immediate responses of the people in the designated areas known as "rooms." You can easily scroll down a list of hundreds of special-interest rooms that have names like College Professors Looking for Love, Romantic Forties, and Irrepressible Flirts.

Of course, not all chat rooms deal with dating or romance. You can try special-interest rooms that have sports, news, religious, or academic discussion groups. Who knows? You may meet your ideal LoveType in a group discussion about ending world hunger or making the perfect approach shot in tennis.

Once you ask the LoveType questions and determine

that your new acquaintance is your ideal match, you can take the initiative and suggest moving into a private chat area. This is a private area (screen) where you can talk (type messages) with your prospective paramour in complete privacy. In this private chamber you can enjoy a mock date or even steamy lovemaking.

LEARN As MUCH AS YOU CAN ABOUT THE INTERNET

Read simple-to-understand books about the Internet and become acquainted with its terminology. As you become familiar with the intricacies of the Internet, you will find even more opportunities for applying the LoveType system to the fascinating world of cyberdating.

Your Ninety-Day (and beyond) Internet LoveType Dating Plan

FIRST THIRTY DAYS

Investigate several Internet providers, and select the one you like best. Read one or two basic books on how to use the Internet.

DAYS THIRTY-ONE THROUGH SIXTY

Browse through several Internet newsgroups, and get involved with those groups and activities that tend to attract your ideal LoveType. Drop in on several chat rooms, and practice LoveTyping the men or women you meet. Try to avoid any serious on-line relationships at this point; your goal is to enjoy yourself and become comfortable with the Internet.

DAYS SIXTY-ONE THROUGH NINETY (AND BEYOND)

Go for it: Place LoveType personal ads (or ads that recruit members for a new LoveType singles club) on those newsgroups that cater to singles. Party and mingle in special-interest chat rooms where you are likely to meet your ideal LoveType and send LoveType quizzes (by e-mail) to your male or female admirers. And when the time is right, enjoy private romantic interludes and/

or cybersex with that special someone. Have fun en route to meeting your ideal LoveType.

I would like to finish this section by telling you about one of my proudest success stories during my career as a LoveType coach. The story of Sophia, a lonely ghost-writer, nicely illustrates the way formerly lonely and frustrated singles can use the LoveType system to find their soul mate.

Sophia was an Idealistic Philosopher (INFP) and one of the shyest people I have ever met. Although Sophia was a wonderfully caring woman, she had a rotten self-image, mainly based on her belief that she was the ugliest woman in the world. She wasn't a beauty in the traditional sense, but she had an inner beauty that could radiate if she would only give herself the chance.

At thirty-one, Sophia had dated very little and was terrified of being rejected by men. After trying matchmakers, dating services, and everything else in between to meet Mr. Right, she finally decided to give the LoveType system a try. I suggested she use the Internet as her low-pressure entry point into the world of LoveType dating.

Though initially petrified, Sophia soon found herself in her element: the world of written worlds. As a shy Introvert, she was able to put her words into written form better than anyone she knew. Poetic, majestic, coy, flirting. She was all of these and more during her initial chat sessions on that great equalizer, the Internet.

She dated dozens of men on the Internet over the course of six months: top executives, computer nerds, college boys, even exotic dancers. With her knowledge of the LoveType system, she would quickly screen out the incompatible men and spend time with the few men who were her ideal LoveType.

During a group chat session on poetic expression, she finally met her love match in thirty-three-year-old Thomas, a fellow Idealistic Philosopher. He was everything she was, and everything she wanted in a man: introspective, imaginative, creative, emotional, and spontaneous. He was a well-respected psychiatrist and philanthropist, a man whose vision in life was to better humanity and share love.

Thomas lived relatively close for an Internet relationship (two hundred miles away) and desperately wanted to meet Sophia; he constantly told Sophia how much he loved her. Sophia felt that same way about Thomas, but her fear of rejection kept her paralyzed. She was afraid to consummate their on-line relationship by meeting Thomas in person.

Finally, after my counseling and the urging of other Love-Type students, Sophia took the plunge and agreed to meet Thomas, her dream man.

Afraid he would run when he saw her in person, Sophia was prepared for a fast getaway. When she finally saw Thomas at the restaurant they had arranged for their rendezvous, she felt like crying. He was so good-looking.

He'll never love me; he's too handsome, were Sophia's first thoughts as she backed away from him and ran to the bathroom.

"Wait, Sophia!" yelled Thomas, as he got down on one knee, and with his right hand took out a diamond ring. " 'She walks in beauty, like the night,' " he said, his brown eyes shining. "Will you be my wife?"

Could this be? thought Sophia. Thomas was reciting a line from the Lord Byron poem he had e-mailed her after their first on-line session. And he was proposing to her, knowing what she looked like, knowing who she was. It was really happening.

As the tears trickled down Sophia's cheeks, she rushed into Thomas's arms. Passionately they embraced with the tenderness of two Idealistic Philosopher souls coming together after an eternity apart.

It's Time to Unmask Your LoveType Soul Mate

Congratulations. You have now graduated as a student of the LoveType system. In the months to come, you will experience many ups and downs, but fortunately, you will have more ups than downs.

You will meet some jerks, and you will meet wonderful, sincere, and giving people. You will meet men and women who appear great at first sight, but whose glossy image evaporates once you place them under the magnifying glass of the LoveType system and unmask their true personalities.

And you may just find that special person who totally complements you: that lovely LoveType who appears to be on the same wavelength, who offers strength where you are weak, and who promises to be a faithful and devoted companion for the rest of your life.

When you find your soul mate, you may be surprised at the package he or she came in. Maybe you knew this compelling creature for a long time, but you never took the time to uncover his or her true identity as your special and ideal LoveType.

Or perhaps your sweetheart is someone you met in a casual encounter—a person who looks just like anyone else, but once you pull off his or her psychological disguise, you realize this is your one true love.

With the LoveType system as your gentle guide, you will soon be on your way to a lifetime of love and happiness. May your love be deep and your happiness everlasting.

The LoveType Quiz and the Sixteen LoveTypes

Take the following quiz to determine your LoveType, or give it to your potential mate to confirm his or her LoveType.

The LoveType Quiz

Although you may see yourself in both answers to a question, choose the answer that describes you best.

1. I tend to draw more energy from:
E) other people
I) my own thoughts.

2. When I'm at a social gathering, I tend to have more energy:
E) toward the end of the night, and once I get going, I may be the last person to leave.
I) toward the early part of the night, and then I get tired and want to go home.

3. Which sounds more appealing?

E) going with my date to a place where there are lots of people and social interaction, such as a nightclub or party.

I) staying home and doing something special with my date—such as watching an entertaining video and eating my favorite take-out food.

4. When on a date, I'm usually:

E) quite talkative throughout.

I) more quiet and reserved until I feel comfortable.

5. In the past, I have tended to meet most of my dates:

E) when I'm doing things in the outside world: at parties, nightclubs, work, recreational activities, chance meetings, or when friends introduce me to their friends.

I) through private methods such as personal ads, video dating, or sometimes by personal introductions from close friends and family.

6. I tend to have:

E) many acquaintances and many (or a few) close friends.

I) a few close friends and/or a few acquaintances.

7. In the past, my loved ones and partners tended to say this about me:

E) "Can't you be quiet and still for once!"

I) "Can you come out of your shell, please?"

8. I tend to gather information more through:

N) my imagination and expectation of what is possible.

S) my realistic sense of the here and now.

9. I tend to trust:

N) my leaps of intuition.

S) my direct observation and hands-on experience.

10. When I'm in a relationship, I tend to believe:
   N) there is always room for improvement.
   S) "if it ain't broke, don't fix it."

11. When I'm comfortable with a date, I prefer talking about:
   N) the future, improving or creating things, and the possibilities of life; for example, I may talk about a new scientific discovery or a better way to express my feelings.
   S) practical, concrete, and "here and now" subjects; for example, I may talk about the fine points of wine tasting or the exciting trip I'm about to take.

12. I am the kind of person who:
   N) likes to see the big picture first.
   S) likes to grasp the details first.

13. I am the type of person who:
   N) prefers to live in my imagination instead of reality.
   S) prefers to dwell in reality instead of my imagination.

14. I usually:
   N) tend to fantasize a great deal about a date I'm about to go on.
   S) tend to fantasize sparingly and simply allow the date to turn out the way it's going to.

15. I tend to make decisions:
   F) first with my heart, then (perhaps) with my logic.
   T) first with logic, then (perhaps) with my heart.

16. I tend to be better at noticing:
   F) when people need emotional support.
   T) when people are being illogical.

17. When breaking up with someone:
  F) I often let my feelings get in the way, and it's very hard for me to let go.
  T) although I can feel hurt, once I make up my mind, I am usually quite straightforward about putting my ex-partner out of my mind.

18. When dating someone, I tend to value:
  F) emotional compatibility: expressing affection and being sensitive to each other's needs.
  T) intellectual compatibility: communicating important ideas; discussing and debating matters objectively.

19. When I disagree with my partner:
  F) I do everything I can to avoid hurting his or her feelings, and I may not say anything if it will hurt too much.
  T) I usually speak up and set my mate straight because right is right.

20. People who know me tend to describe me as:
  F) warmhearted and sensitive.
  T) logical and straightforward.

21. I see most of my encounters with people as:
  F) being friendly and important in themselves.
  T) having a purpose.

22. If I had the time and money, and a friend invited me to an exotic location and gave me one day's notice, I would:
  J) have to check my schedule first.
  P) pack my bags without a second thought.

23. When on a first date, I:
  J) get upset if my date is late.
  P) don't worry about it since I'm usually late myself.

24. I prefer:
- J) to know, in advance, what's going to happen on my dates: where I'm going, who is going to be there, how long I will be there, how I should dress.
- P) to let the dates happen spontaneously without much (if any) advance planning.

25. I prefer a life that revolves around:
- J) schedules and organization.
- P) spontaneity and flexibility.

26. Which is more common?:
- J) I'm on time and everyone else is late.
- P) everyone else is on time, and I'm late.

27. I am the type of person who likes to:
- J) make up my mind and come to definite conclusions.
- P) keep my options open and continue gathering information.

28. I am the type of person who:
- J) likes to work on one thing at a time until completion.
- P) enjoys working on several things at once.

Scoring

For each set of seven questions, add up your answers and put the numbers on the appropriate lines below. Then circle the higher number for each pair.

Your LoveType

—	—	—	—	—	—	—	—
E	I	N	S	F	T	J	P

The Sixteen LoveTypes

Here are the sixteen LoveTypes and their descriptive phrases. Find the LoveType that pertains to you (or your potential mate):

1. *The Idealistic Philosopher (INFP)*: INTROVERTED INTUITIVE FEELING PERCEIVER: *"Love is the perfect place: quiet, peaceful and kind."*
2. *The Mystic Writer (INFJ)*: INTROVERTED INTUITIVE FEELING JUDGER: *"Love is in my mind, heart, and soul."*
3. *The Social Philosopher (ENFP)*: EXTRAVERTED INTUITIVE FEELING PERCEIVER: *"Love is mysterious, inspiring, and fun."*
4. *The Growth Teacher (ENFJ)*: EXTRAVERTED INTUITIVE, FEELING, JUDGER: *"Love is being consumed by my loved one."*
5. *The Scholar (INTP)*: INTROVERTED INTUITIVE THINKING PERCEIVER: *"Love is just another idea."*
6. *The Expert (INTJ)*: INTROVERTED INTUITIVE THINKING JUDGER: *"Love can be analyzed and perfected."*
7. *The Innovator (ENTP)*: EXTRAVERTED INTUITIVE

THINKING PERCEIVER: *"I invent love in my mind first."*

8. *The General (ENTJ):* EXTRAVERTED INTUITIVE THINKING JUDGER: *"Love is enhanced by power, influence, and achievement."*

9. *The Caretaker: (ISFJ):* INTROVERTED SENSING FEELING JUDGER: *"Love is a goal worth sacrificing for."*

10. *The Administrator: (ISTJ):* INTROVERTED SENSING THINKING JUDGER: *"Love is based on duty and responsibility."*

11. *The Dutiful Host (ESFJ):* EXTRAVERTED SENSING FEELING JUDGER: *"Love is based on serving others."*

12. *The Traditionalist (ESTJ):* EXTRAVERTED SENSING THINKING JUDGER: *"Love is grounded on the rock-solid values of family, tradition, and loyalty."*

13. *The Gentle Artist (ISFP):* INTROVERTED SENSING FEELING PERCEIVER: *"Love is gentleness, nature, and devotion."*

14. *The Craftsperson (ISTP):* INTROVERTED SENSING THINKING PERCEIVER: *"Love is action."*

15. *The Performer (ESFP):* EXTRAVERTED SENSING FEELING PERCEIVER: *"Love is savoring and reveling in the passions of now."*

16. *The Wheeler-Dealer (ESTP):* EXTRAVERTED SENSING THINKING PERCEIVER: *"Love should always be exciting and stimulating."*

The Main Characteristics of the Sixteen LoveTypes

INFPs (Idealistic Philosophers):

Enjoy the arts, philosophy, and psychology.
Must have a crusade (or mission) in life.
Are sensitive.
Are idealistic.
Are generally easygoing until their values are violated.
Tend to have high expectations regarding their loved
  one.

INFJs (Mystic Writers):

Are intrigued by psychology, philosophy, mysticism,
  and spirituality.
Are great listeners.
Are deeply compassionate.
Are usually quiet.
Have streaks of extreme stubbornness.
Love reading and writing.

ENFPs (Social Philosophers):

Have a great interest in relationships, ideas, and discovering the meaning of life.
Are people-affirming.
Are outgoing.
Are charismatic.
Tend to start many things (including relationships) but may not finish them.

ENFJs (Growth Teachers):

Are excellent communicators and persuaders.
Can be effective leaders and motivators.
Can be jealous and possessive if they feel their mate is taking them for granted.
Love to give their friends advice on anything and everything.
Are very emotionally supportive.

INTPs (Scholars):

Are fascinated by theory.
Can be like absentminded professors—forgetting and losing things, but still able to come up with brilliant ideas and observations.
Are generally easygoing and flexible companions.
Can be oblivious to the emotional needs of their relationship.
May alternate between quiet and argumentative.

INTJs (Experts):

Have a detailed theoretical concept of love.
Value competence in their mates.

Are among the most highly educated of the LoveTypes.

Are usually accomplished in the world of science and/ or ideas.

Constantly strive for self-improvement and compe- tence.

ENTPs (Innovators):

Can talk a mile a minute on almost anything.

Are geniuses at coming up with novel inventions, plans, or schemes.

Are multifaceted individuals.

Are high-rolling risk takers.

Like to have several things going at once (and are able to do them all quite well).

ENTJs (Generals):

Are powerful personalities.

Are usually well accomplished in their chosen field.

Are masterful communicators.

Are ambitious and hold high standards for themselves and their mate.

Have "trial lawyer" personalities: enjoy spirited debate and are able to argue both sides equally well.

ISFJs (Caretakers):

Have a strong sense of duty.

Are usually concerned about the little people in life: kids, animals, the sick, and the elderly.

Believe in order: "A place for everything and every- thing in its place."

Find happiness by serving practical human needs and

taking care of their families (they make great nurses, teachers, and moms/dads).

ISTJs (Administrators):

Are responsible.
Are loyal.
Are quiet.
Dislike flashy romantic gestures or "touchy-feely" expressions from their mates.
Are rock-solid dependable.

ESFJs (Dutiful Hosts):

Value harmony in their relationships.
Display goodwill toward others.
Are great party organizers.
Are the perfect hosts.
Are very family-oriented.

ESTJs (Traditionalists):

Display a take-charge personality.
Value authority and chain of command.
Enjoy a raucous sense of humor.
Are excellent protectors and providers for their families.
Seek the stability and structure of marriage and family life.

ISFPs (Gentle Artists):

Have strong artistic tendencies.
Love animals and nature.

Are gentle and caring lovers.
Are quiet.
Are flexible.

ISTPs (Craftspersons):

Enjoy working with their hands.
Are people whose lives and relationships revolve around their hobbies.
Place great value on their personal space.
Believe in the philosophy of "live and let live."
Can be unpredictable, ranging from raging enthusiasm to quiet reserve.

ESFPs (Performers):

Are natural entertainers.
Are often known to be smooth charmers and seducers.
Are the prototypical "nightclub crawlers" and incredibly fun people to spend time with.
Display eternal optimism.
Hate conflicts in relationships; may quickly leave if there is significant discord early in the relationship.

ESTPs (Wheeler-Dealers):

Crave excitement, stimulation, and variety in everything, including relationships.
Can be expert seducers.
Believe in action, not theory.
Are often master promoters.
Can be manipulative.

A Summary of Your Best LoveType Match(es)

The LoveType recommendations in this book are based on research findings compiled by me and other researchers in the fields of Jungian typology and compatible relationships. Although certain pairings have been shown to be superior, there are a number of combinations for which there is not enough data to make a firm recommendation one way or the other.

Therefore, your best bet is to first try to meet your recommended LoveType if you can find that person. If you have difficulty meeting your ideal LoveType, the next best thing is to choose your dates based on compatibility on certain important preferences (see Chapter Two) or similarity on the LoveTemperaments.

Research has shown that you maximize your chances of having a compatible relationship when you date someone who is from the same LoveTemperament group as you. For example, if you are one of the Meaning Seeker LoveTypes (INFP, INFJ, ENFP, ENFJ), you are usually better off dating another Meaning Seeker because you will tend to be compatible with this person and share similar values, goals, and preferences.

Regardless of whether you date your recommended

LoveType or not, you will still want to select your dates based on a number of additional factors such as physical attractiveness, career, income, and educational level, as well as compatibility on religious and moral values, personal habits (smoking and so forth), and other personality factors (good sense of humor and the like).

In summary: Use the LoveType pairings in this section for the purpose they were intended—as recommendations. Ultimately you are the one who will reap the rewards when you choose your future soul mate. Take your time and have fun.

You Are a:	*Your Best Match(es) Is/Are:*
INFP: *Idealistic Philosopher*	
Male	Idealistic Philosopher (INFP)
	Mystic Writer (INFJ)
Female	Idealistic Philosopher (INFP)
	Social Philosopher (ENFP)
	Growth Teacher (ENFJ)
	Mystic Writer (INFJ)
INFJ: *Mystic Writer*	
Male	Idealistic Philosopher (INFP)
	Mystic Writer (INFJ)
Female	Mystic Writer (INFJ)
	Idealistic Philosopher (INFP)
	Scholar (INTP)
	Wheeler-Dealer (ESTP)
ENFP: *Social Philosopher*	
Male	Social Philosopher (ENFP)
	Idealistic Philosopher (INFP)
Female	Social Philosopher (ENFP)
	Growth Teacher (ENFJ), provided the Growth Teacher is not a very strong Judger (J)

ENFJ: Growth Teacher

Male

Social Philosopher (ENFP)
Growth Teacher (ENFJ)
Idealistic Philosopher (INFP)
Craftsperson (ISTP)

Female

Growth Teacher (ENFJ)
Craftsperson (ISTP)

INTP: Scholar

Male

Mystic Writer (INFJ)

Female

Expert (INTJ)
General (ENTJ)
Innovator (ENTP)

INTJ: Expert

Male

Scholar (INTP)
Expert (INTJ)

Female

Expert (INTJ)
Traditionalist (ESTJ), provided the Traditionalist is
not a very strong Sensor (S)

ENTP: Thinker

Male

Scholar (INTP)
Wheeler-Dealer (ESTP)

Female

General (ENTJ)

ENTJ: General

Male

Scholar (INTP)
Innovator (ENTP)
General (ENTJ)
Traditionalist (ESTJ)

Female

General (ENTJ)
Traditionalist (ESTJ), provided the Traditionalist is
not a very strong Sensor (S)

ISFJ: Caretaker
Male

Caretaker (ISFJ)
Administrator (ISTJ)

Female

Caretaker (ISFJ)
Dutiful Host (ESFJ)
Administrator (ISTJ)

ISTJ: Administrator
Male

Administrator (ISTJ)
Caretaker (ISFJ)

Female

Administrator (ISTJ)
Caretaker (ISFJ)
Traditionalist (ESTJ)

ESFJ: Dutiful Host
Male

Caretaker (ISFJ)
Dutiful Host (ESFJ)

Female

Dutiful Host (ESFJ)
Traditionalist (ESTJ)

ESTJ: Traditionalist
Male

Traditionalist (ESTJ)
Dutiful Host (ESFJ)
Administrator (ISTJ)
General (ENTJ)
Expert (INTJ), provided the
General and Expert are not
very strong Intuitives (N)

| Female | Traditionalist (ESTJ) |
| | General (ENTJ), provided the General is not a very strong Intuitive (N) |

ISFP: Gentle Artist

| Male | Gentle Artist (ISFP) |

Female	Gentle Artist (ISFP)
	Performer (ESFP)
	Wheeler-Dealer (ESTP)
	Craftsperson (ISTP)

ISTP: Craftsperson

Male	Craftsperson (ISTP)
	Gentle Artist (ISFP)
	Growth Teacher (ENFJ)

Female	Craftsperson (ISTP)
	Wheeler-Dealer (ESTP)
	Growth Teacher (ENFJ)

ESFP: Performer

| Male | Gentle Artist (ISFP) |
| | Performer (ESFP) |

| Female | Performer (ESFP) |
| | Wheeler-Dealer (ESTP) |

ESTP: Wheeler-Dealer

Male	Wheeler-Dealer (ESTP)
	Gentle Artist (ISFP)
	Craftsperson (ISTP)
	Performer (ESFP)
	Mystic Writer (INFJ)

| Female | Wheeler-Dealer (ESTP) |
| | Innovator (ENTP), provided the Innovator is not a very strong Intuitive (N) |

The Assumptive Personality Traits

Use the following list of traits to determine your new friend's LoveType with the observational version of the Assumptive Approach.

For more information on the eight Jungian preferences, see Chapters Three through Seven and the recommended reading list at the end of the book.

Here are the eight Jungian preferences and their Assumptive traits:

I. **Introversion: Your new friend is an Introvert if he or she:**
   1. Enjoys staying home a lot, usually alone, reading, writing, thinking, or relaxing.
   2. Has a few close friends and/or a few close acquaintances.
   3. Talks little—or talks a great deal for a short burst of time—and then is tired.
   4. Recharges his or her batteries by spending quiet time alone.
   5. Tends to go to social events early and leave early.

II. Extraversion: Your new friend is an Extra-vert if he or she:

1. Likes to participate in regular social activities with a large group of friends and/or acquaintances.
2. Likes to spend time outside the house, where there is plenty of potential for human interaction.
3. Enjoys talking a great deal.
4. Draws a great deal of energy from social interaction.
5. Tends to be one of the last to leave a social event.

III. Intuition: Your new friend is an Intuitive if he or she:

1. Likes to use metaphors, analogies, and word pictures to communicate.
2. Is rarely satisfied with things as they are; is always striving to improve the world.
3. Prefers thinking, reading, or talking about the future, making new discoveries, and learning about the possibilities of life.
4. Is not overly skilled at practical matters such as balancing a checkbook, and prefers performing imaginative tasks: writing a sonnet or originating a great business idea.
5. Enjoys abstract humor such as double entendres and malapropisms.

IV. Sensing: Your new friend is a Sensor if he or she:

1. Likes to communicate by citing readily observable and measurable facts, statistics, and concepts.
2. Accepts life at face value and believes in the phrase "What you see is what you get."
3. Prefers thinking, reading, and talking about practical, concrete, and "here and now" subjects.

4. Is skilled with the details and practicalities of life, and not as interested in the "pie-in-the-sky" topics that dreamers think and talk about.
5. Enjoys "down-to-earth" comedy—practical jokes, pratfalls, and slapstick.

V.   Feeling: Your new friend is a Feeler if he or she:
1. Enjoys talking about feelings, relationships, and personal matters.
2. Avoids arguments and heated debates because he or she doesn't want anyone's feelings to be hurt.
3. Tends to be good at noticing when people need emotional support.
4. Wants to feel, at the end of a conversation, that the other person likes and supports him or her, and that they are now closer as a result of their shared communication.
5. Is impressed by people who are warm and personable.

VI.   Thinking: Your new friend is a Thinker if he or she:
1. Seems somewhat detached and impersonal and doesn't appear to be too interested in interacting with people on an emotional level.
2. Enjoys stimulating and controversial arguments and debates to exercise his or her analytical mind. He or she doesn't take these discussions personally.
3. Tends to be good at noticing when people are being illogical.
4. Wants to know that valuable information has been exchanged in a conversation and that the underlying objective of the communication has been achieved.
5. Is impressed by people who are smart and know what they are talking about.

VII. Perceiving: Your new friend is a Perceiver if he or she:

1. Likes to communicate by switching rapidly from one subject to another.
2. Is always changing his or her plans, and you never know when he or she will show up.
3. Is usually running late.
4. Has a tendency to be messy or disorganized (from other people's perspectives).
5. Enjoys working on several things at once—although may not always finish them.

VIII. Judging: Your new friend is a Judger if he or she:

1. Likes to thoroughly cover one conversational topic before starting another.
2. Likes to adhere to a regular schedule, and you will usually see him or her at set times.
3. Is rarely late for an appointment.
4. Is often compulsively neat and organized (from other people's perspective) or striving to be that way.
5. Likes to work on one thing at a time until completion.

Start Your Own LoveType Singles Group

In my experience working with singles, perhaps the most common complaint I hear is that they are tired of being lonely. They want to meet that special someone, but ironically, many singles exacerbate their loneliness by trying to connect with the opposite sex on their own—without the help and support of friends and family.

That is why I recommend that you stop trying to do everything yourself and start a neighborhood LoveType singles group (if you don't already have one in your neighborhood).

A LoveType singles group is a network of ten to fifty single people in your community who have studied, or are studying, the LoveType system. These individuals know their personal LoveType and the LoveType of their ideal mate. To practice their LoveTyping skills and meet potential mates, they meet once, twice, or four times a month at a convenient location.

Here is the blueprint for starting a smooth-running LoveType singles group.

Step One: Recruit members

Contact all your single friends, acquaintances, and relatives, and ask if they would like to participate in a Love-

Type singles group. Tell them about the myriad benefits they will receive upon becoming a member. They will:

- Discover their own LoveType and learn fascinating things about their relationship and lifestyle preferences.
- Learn who their ideal LoveType is likely to be.
- Learn how to meet their ideal LoveType anywhere they go. As members of a LoveType club, they will have credibility when they talk to new people and invite them to LoveType meetings.
- Meet and mingle with eligible, compatible singles at the LoveType meetings, as well as participate in fun group activities such as hiking, dancing, outdoor sports, parties, and potlucks.

Step Two: Assign tasks and roles

Decide who is going to fill each of the important roles for the group, including president (coordinates and oversees all the meetings and activities), treasurer (handles group funds), and secretary (fulfills recordkeeping duties such as maintaining a member database and making sure dues are paid on time). Assign roles and tasks based on your members' personality strengths and weaknesses, according to their LoveTemperaments.

For example:

The Meaning Seekers are excellent at making people feel comfortable, appreciated, and loved. Assign them to the hospitality committee where they will greet new members and take care of people who are upset, worried, or lonely.

The Knowledge Seekers are skilled at creating systems for doing things. Let them take care of any planning or technical requirements such as determining the best location for meetings, setting up the best database for the club, and so forth.

The Security Seekers are the pillars of the club. They make sure the practical things get done on time. Have them collect the dues, send out notices, organize materials, and make sure meetings run efficiently and on time. God bless the Security Seekers.

The Excitement Seekers, if you are lucky enough to have any as members, are geniuses at promotion. When you have an active Wheeler-Dealer or Performer member, your club will be known far beyond your community.

Step Three: Take care of the practical matters—better yet, have the Security Seekers handle them

Set parameters for the club: where will you meet, how often, will dues be charged? If so, how much? How long will the meetings be, who will speak at each meeting, will there be guest speakers?

Find a location (preferably free) to meet. Someone's home is fine in the beginning.

Make copies of the LoveType quiz in this book. I grant you permission to copy and administer the test, and use it only for nonprofit purposes related to LoveType singles club activities such as LoveTyping new members. You, however, do not have permission to use it for any profit-making ventures. (Charging dues for LoveType club activities is permissible.)

Give every member the LoveType quiz and have him or her wear a LoveType sticker with his or her LoveType on it (such as *ENFP—Social Philosopher*, for example) during each meeting.

Step Four: Spread the word. Let everyone know about your group!

Get busy promoting your club. You don't have to spend much money, or even any at all. Local radio or TV can give your club free public service announcements. You can also send out press releases about your LoveType singles group to local newspapers. Based on the information you send, the newspaper can insert a free listing announcing your club meetings, or the editor can decide to run a feature story on your group. Either option should attract potential members to your meetings.

Other promotion tactics include the following: placing ads or announcements in singles publications or on the Internet, passing out inexpensive flyers for club events and parties, calling local singles and business organizations to recruit new members, and holding fund-raising events such as bachelor or bachelorette auctions.

Make sure you stress the benefits of joining a Love-Type singles group in all your promotional materials. After all, the main benefit—learning how to meet and develop a compatible relationship with an ideal love mate—speaks for itself.

Step Five: Make new members feel welcome at the meeting

This is perhaps the most crucial step for any beginning LoveType singles group. Remember that every new member who walks through your door is the lifeblood of your organization and one of your brother or sister LoveTypers.

Chances are, these new members are also bringing a certain degree of loneliness, bitterness, regret, and frustration to the club, but that's okay. Most newcomers begin at the same place: They are tired of wasting their lives in miserable, incompatible relationships, and they want to meet their soul mate—the person who will mesh with them in every way.

Although many members improve their psychological well-being by participating in a LoveType singles group, it's important to understand that the club is not designed to provide therapy to people who suffer from mental health problems. If anyone in your club has a serious psychological disorder, you should immediately refer him or her to qualified professionals.

Always remember: Your task as the founder of a Love-Type singles group is to bring a group of people together who have suffered from the same difficulties in finding lasting love. These formerly frustrated people are now in the position to support each other as they apply a powerful system for finding their soul mate—a system that will change their lives and make their world a better place.

LoveType Singles Resource Directory

Note: Since phones and addresses change, it's a good idea to check the latest listing of these organizations in the Encyclopedia of Associations, available at your local public library.

Caveat: Although the designated LoveTypes tend to predominate in these groups, you can meet almost any Love-Type in most of the organizations.

Sierra Singles: 85 2nd St., 2nd Floor, San Francisco, CA 94105; 415-977-5500.
A national organization that offers outdoor social activities for singles who care about the environment and enjoy spending time in nature.

- A fine option for meeting nature-loving Gentle Artists (ISFPs), Caretakers (ISFJs), Craftspersons (ISTPs), and Traditionalists (ESTJs), among others.

Single Booklovers: Box 117, Gradyville, PA 19039; 610-358-5049.
This organization was established in 1970 and serves

as a correspondence club for single men and women who enjoy books and who want to meet each other by mail.

- Perfect for meeting Introverts: especially Idealistic Philosophers (INFPs), Mystic Writers (INFJs), Scholars (INTPs), and Experts (INTJs)

The Single Gourmet: 133 E. 58th St., New York, NY, 10022; 212-980-8788.
This is an international social dining club with national local branches. The Single Gourmet gives single men and women the opportunity to share good food and drink while engaging in interesting and intelligent conversation.

- Excellent for meeting Dutiful Hosts (ESFJs), Social Philosophers (ENFPs), Generals (ENTJs), Scholars (INTPs), Experts (INTJs), and Growth Teachers (ENFJs).

Star Trek: The Official Fan Club and **Star Wars: The Official Fan Club:** 3720 Revere St., Denver, CO 80239; 303-574-0907.
These are clubs where you can indulge your craving for the Star Trek (or Star Wars) experience and meet your fellow Trekkies (or Star Wars fans) at the conventions.

- The ideal choice for meeting the Knowledge Seekers, especially the brainy Scholar (INTP) and Expert (INTJ).

Notes on Sources

Chapter Two
For more information on Jung's theory of psychological types, see *Psychological Types*, by Carl Jung. Princeton, NJ: Princeton University Press, 1971.

For more information on the groundbreaking work of the Myers-Briggs team, see *Gifts Differing*. Palo Alto, CA: Consulting Psychologists Press, 1980.

Chapter Three
For more information on the 1981 Sherman study and her findings on male Introvert/female Extravert pairings, see "Typology and Problems in Intimate Relationships," by Ruth Sherman. *Research in Psychological Type*. Volume 4, 1981.

Chapter Four
For more information on the 1992 Rytting and Ware study and their findings on the Focusing Dimension, see "Type and the Ideal Mate: Romantic Attraction or Type Bias?" by Marvin Rytting, Roger Ware, and Patricia Hopkins. *Journal of Psychological Type*. Volume 24, 1992.

Chapter Eight

For the finding that male Idealistic Philosophers (INFPs) have a strong tendency to marry their Idealistic Philosopher counterpart, see *The Relationship Between Couples' Satisfaction and Their Scores on the Type Differentiation Indicator*, a paper presented by Nancy Marioles, Donald Strickert, and Allen Hammer at the 10th Conference of the Association for Psychological Type, Newport Beach (July 10, 1993).

Chapter Nine

For more information on compatible pairings between Mystic Writers (INFJs) and Wheeler-Dealers (ESTPs), see David Keirsey and Marilyn Bates's book, *Please Understand Me: Character and Temperament Types.* Del Mar, CA: Prometheus Nemesis Book Company, 1978.

For the finding that Mystic Writers (INFJs) have the longest marriages among the Meaning Seekers (NFs), see *Type and Couples: Part 2,* a paper presented by Nancy Marioles, Donald Strickert, and Allen Hammer at the 11th Meeting of the Association for Psychological Type, Kansas City (July 1995).

Chapter Ten

For the finding that men consider female Social Philosophers (ENFPs) to be among the top two (sharing equal billing with the Dutiful Hosts—ESFJs) ideal mates, see "Type and the Ideal Mate: Romantic Attraction or Type Bias?" by Marvin Rytting, Roger Ware, and Patricia Hopkins. *Journal of Psychological Type.* Volume 24, 1992.

Chapter Eleven

For more information on the compatibility of the exact opposites—Growth Teachers (ENFJs) and Craftspersons (ISTPs)—see David Keirsey and Marilyn Bates's book, *Please Understand Me: Character and Temperament Types.* Del Mar, CA: Prometheus Nemesis Book Company, 1978.

Chapter Twelve

For the finding that Scholars (INTPs) have a strong tendency to marry each other, see Margaret Hartzler and Gary Hartzler's manual, *Using Type With Couples*, Gaithersburg, MD: Type Resources, Inc., 1988.

For the finding that male Scholars (INTPs) scored the highest on the obliviousness index in the Marioles et al. study, see *The Relationship Between Couples' Satisfaction and Their Scores on the Type Differentiation Indicator*, a paper presented by Nancy Marioles, Donald Strickert, and Allen Hammer at the 10th Conference of the Association for Psychological Type, Newport Beach (July 10, 1993).

For the finding that Scholars (INTPs), regardless of gender, had the shortest marriages in the Marioles et al. study, see *Type and Couples: Part 2*, a paper presented by Nancy Marioles, Donald Strickert, and Allen Hammer at the 11th Meeting of the Association for Psychological Type, Kansas City (July 1995).

Chapter Seventeen

For the finding that Administrators (ISTJs) were married the second longest, next to the Dutiful Hosts (ESFJs), in the Marioles et al. study, see *Type and Couples: Part 2*, a paper presented by Nancy Marioles, Donald Strickert, and Allen Hammer at the 11th Meeting of the Association for Psychological Type, Kansas City (July 1995).

Chapter Eighteen

For the finding that Dutiful Hosts (ESFJs) had the longest marriages in the Marioles et al. study, see *Type and Couples: Part 2*, a paper presented by Nancy Marioles, Donald Strickert, and Allen Hammer at the 11th Meeting of the Association for Psychological Type, Kansas City (July 1995).

For the finding that female Dutiful Hosts (ESFJs) are highly rated as desirable partners, see "Type and the Ideal Mate: Romantic Attraction or Type Bias?" by Marvin Rytting, Roger Ware, and Patricia Hopkins. *Journal of Psychological Type*. Volume 23, 1992.

Chapter Nineteen

For the finding that male Traditionalists (ESTJs) married the second most often (next to the wedding-happy female Craftspersons—ISTPs) in the Marioles et al. study, see *Type and Couples*: Part 2, a paper presented by Nancy Marioles, Donald Strickert, and Allen Hammer at the 11th Meeting of the Association for Psychological Type, Kansas City (July 1995).

Chapter Twenty-One

For more information on the compatible match between the exact opposites—Craftspersons (ISTPs) and Growth Teacher (ENFJs)—see David Keirsey and Marilyn Bates's book, *Please Understand Me: Character and Temperament Types*. Del Mar, CA: Prometheus Nemesis Book Company, 1978.

Chapter Twenty-Three

For more information on compatible pairings between Wheeler-Dealers (ESTPs) and Mystic Writers (INFJs), see David Keirsey and Marilyn Bates's book, *Please Understand Me: Character and Temperament Types*. Del Mar, CA: Prometheus Nemesis Book Company, 1978.

Suggested Reading

Atwood, Nina. *Be Your Own Dating Service*. New York: Henry Holt and Company, 1996.

Beakman, Claudia, and Karla Dougherty. *Playing the Personals*. New York: Pocket Books, 1996.

Bhaerman, Steve, and Don McMillan. *Friends & Lovers: How to Meet the People You Want to Meet*. Cincinnati: Writer's Digest Books, 1986.

Brownsword, Allen. *It Takes All Types*. San Anselmo, CA: Baytree Publication Company, 1987.

Fox, David. *Love Bytes*. Corte Madera, CA: Waite Group Press, 1995.

Gabor, Don. *How to Start a Conversation and Make Friends*. New York: Simon and Schuster, Inc., 1983.

Hirsh, Susan, and Jean Kummerow. *LIFETYPES*. New York: Warner Books, 1989.

Jung, Carl Gustav. *Psychological Types*. Princeton, NJ: Princeton University Press, 1971.

Keirsey, David, and Marilyn Bates. *Please Understand Me: Character and Temperament Types*. Del Mar, CA: Prometheus Nemesis Book Company, 1978.

Kroeger, Otto, and Janet Thuesen. *Type Talk*. New York: Dell Publishing, 1988.

————. *16 Ways to Love Your Lover*. New York: Delacorte Press, 1994.

Lawrence, Gordon. *People Types and Tiger Stripes*. Gainesville, FL: Center for Application of Psychological Type, Inc., 1982.

Myers, Isabel Briggs. *Gifts Differing*. Palo Alto, CA: Consulting Psychologists Press, 1980.

Sherman, Ruth. *Psychological Typology and Satifaction in Intimate Relationships*. Doctoral Dissertation. Humanistic Psychology Institute, 1981.

Tieger, Paul, and Barbara Barron-Tieger. *Do What You Are*. Toronto: Little, Brown, and Company, 1992.

Wolf, Sharyn. *Guerrilla Dating Tactics: Strategies, Tips, and Secrets for Finding Romance*. New York: Plume, 1994.

Zimbardo, Phillip. *Shyness: What It is, What to Do About It*. Reading, MA: Addison-Wesley Publishing,1977.

The Type Reporter. This publication has interesting articles about various aspects of psychological type, including relationships. Contact: Susan Scanlon, Editor, 11314 Chapel Road, Fairfax Station, VA 22039.

LOVETYPE RESEARCH QUESTIONNAIRE
FREE BONUS GIFT: SPECIAL REPORT

Dear Reader:

In the interests of ongoing LoveType research, we would be grateful if you could return the following short questionnaire. As a bonus gift for filling it out, I will send you—FREE—*Special Report Number Two: Don't Get Caught in the Focusing Dimension.*

We will keep your answers confidential and use them only for the documentation and support of LoveType recommendations.

Also, we would love to hear your success stories. Please return this form to LoveTypes International, P.O. Box 40, Alhambra, CA 91801 or e-mail answers to lovetype4u@aol.com

Circle the answer(s) that apply to you:

Name: _____

Gender: _____

LoveType: _____

Race/Ethnicity: Caucasian Hispanic Asian African-American
Native American   Other

Educational Status: Some High School   High School Graduate
Some College   College Graduate
Some Graduate School   Graduate Degree
(M.B.A., M.A., Ph.D., J.D.)

Occupation: _____ **Age:** _____

Address: _____

Phone: _____

Relationship Status: Married Separated Divorced Never Married
Widowed

In the past, your most compatible relationship was with someone who was more likely (circle the preferences they primarily exhibited):

Introvert   Extravert
Intuitive   Sensor
Thinker   Feeler
Perceiver   Judger

Comments _____

_____

Thank you very much.

Publisher not responsible for fulfillment.

FREE LOVETYPE DATING SUCCESS CATALOG

You can start enjoying dating success today by requesting your FREE LOVETYPE DATING SUCCESS CATALOG and using the following cutting-edge LoveType innovations:

- **Personal LoveType Coaching:** Consult by e-mail, phone, or in person with dating coach Dr. Alexander Avila as he helps you design a customized romantic plan that accentuates your LoveType strengths and minimizes your weaknesses.
- **LoveType Card Deck:** Put the LoveType system at your fingertips with this handy, pocket-sized LoveType card deck. With everything you need to know—the LoveType questions, an answer key, and a mini profile of each LoveType—in a convenient carrying kit, you can easily break the ice and LoveType anyone, anywhere, in a manner of minutes.
- **LoveType Dating Secrets Cassettes and Videotapes:** Learn the inside tips for attracting, romancing, and winning the love of your ideal LoveType(s) based on their LoveTemperaments. Four cassettes, videotapes available—one for each LoveTemperament.
- **LoveType Special Reports:** These special reports contain the latest LoveType research and offer valuable strategies for creating successful relationships. Topics range from *How to Avoid the Energizing Dilemma* (when one partner always wants to go out and the other always wants to stay in) to *Working Through the Organizing Dimension* (when one partner is always late and the other is always early).
- **LoveType Newsletter:** Subscribe to the only newsletter that lists available singles by their LoveType, and place as many free personal ads as you want. Expand your LoveType network, and meet your ideal LoveType by mail as you read about cutting-edge LoveType research developments, dating tactics, and success stories.

To receive your FREE LOVETYPE CATALOG, call me at 310-226-8090 or toll free 1-888-Lovtype; write to LoveTypes International, P.O. Box 40, Alhambra, CA 91801; or send e-mail to lovetype4u @aol.com. See our Website at http://www.Lovetype.com

Publisher not responsible for fulfillment.

Sunny Seki

DR. ALEXANDER AVILA holds a Ph.D. in clinical psychology and a doctorate in jurisprudence. A popular college professor, public speaker, and relationship authority, Dr. Avila has been conducting LoveType™ seminars throughout southern California since 1993, helping his students achieve successful relationships that last a lifetime.